THE EARLIEST
LATIN COMMENTARIES
ON THE
EPISTLES OF St. PAUL

OXFORD
UNIVERSITY PRESS

Great Clarendon Street, Oxford OX2 6DP

Oxford University Press is a department of the University of Oxford.
It furthers the University's objective of excellence in research, scholarship,
and education by publishing worldwide in

Oxford New York

Athens Auckland Bangkok Bogotá Buenos Aires Calcutta
Cape Town Chennai Dar es Salaam Delhi Florence Hong Kong Istanbul
Karachi Kuala Lumpur Madrid Melbourne Mexico City Mumbai
Nairobi Paris São Paulo Singapore Taipei Tokyo Toronto Warsaw

with associated companies in Berlin Ibadan

Oxford is a registered trade mark of Oxford University Press
in the UK and in certain other countries

Published in the United States
by Oxford University Press Inc., New York

© Oxford University Press 1927

British Library Cataloguing in Publication Data

Data available

ISBN 0-19-827001-1

1 3 5 7 9 10 8 6 4 2

Printed in Great Britain
on-acid free paper by
Bookcraft (Bath) Ltd.,
Midsomer Norton

THE EARLIEST
LATIN COMMENTARIES
ON THE
EPISTLES OF ST. PAUL

A STUDY

BY

ALEXANDER SOUTER
M.A., Magdalen College

OXFORD
AT THE CLARENDON PRESS

TO ALL
MY NUMEROUS
AMERICAN FRIENDS
WITH MUCH GRATITUDE

PREFACE

IT is now twenty-eight years since I began to take an active interest in the subject of the present work. In the Michaelmas Term of 1910-11 I had the honour to give a course of lectures on it before the University of Oxford, having been appointed by the Delegates of the Common University Fund to do so. These lectures were revised, and in fact altered almost out of recognition, to form the basis of a course which I delivered, at the kind invitation of the authorities, in Princeton Theological Seminary, New Jersey, U.S.A., under the L. P. Stone Foundation, early in December 1924. Only the more readable portion of the present work was actually delivered, but I have ventured after some hesitation to publish the whole material, without being over-careful to destroy all traces of the lecture form; and I am deeply indebted to the Delegates of the Clarendon Press for undertaking the publication of the work.

Important studies of the language of St. Augustine have appeared recently in the 'Patristic Studies' of the Catholic University of America (see page 200 below). Since this book was written the text of Pelagius' *Expositions* (see page 205) has been published by the Cambridge University Press. I should like also to call attention to an entirely independent treatment of the authorities for the text of the Epistles of St. Paul in Latin, by Dr. Ernst Diehl of Innsbruck, entitled 'Zur Textgeschichte des lateinischen Paulus', in the *Zeitschrift für die neutesta-mentliche Wissenschaft*, Bd. xx (1921), pp. 97–132, and to

Dr. Hans von Soden's just published article, 'Der lateinische Paulustext bei Marcion und Tertullian', in the *Festgabe für Adolf Jülicher* (Tübingen, 1927), pp. 229–81. Lastly, another MS. of Sedulius Scottus (see p. 212), unknown to Traube and Hellmann, has turned up at Basle, Univ.-Bibl. ii. 5 (saec. x–xi, of the St. Gall school), and is described in Dom Morin's as yet unprinted catalogue.

ABERDEEN, SCOTLAND,
28 *Feb.* 1927.

CONTENTS

INTRODUCTION

THE various writings which at an early date came to be called the New Testament were composed, roughly speaking, within the period A. D. 50 to 150. The fourfold Gospel must already have attained authority among Christians before the middle of the second century, and a collection of Pauline Epistles, foreshadowed in Polycarp, is a reality in the time of the author of the Second Epistle of St. Peter; and *he* may have been contemporary with Marcion, whose collection is the earliest of which we know anything definite.

As in the case of the Old Testament, the Homeric poems, and other great works, authority is a necessary antecedent of commentary. People do not trouble to write, and people certainly do not trouble to read, commentaries on works which have no authority. It is therefore no surprise to find that the earliest commentaries on a part of the New Testament, of which history tells, are posterior in date to the period at which their authority had become established. About the middle of the second century commentaries on the New Testament books began to be written, at first it is true in the interests of particular sects, but later for the great body of Christians. About the end of the second century commentaries began to be written in catholic circles, of course in Greek, which was even at that time the language of the greater number of Christians. And just after that period comes Origen, whose figure dominates subsequent efforts for centuries, to a degree which may perhaps be imagined, but can never be adequately estimated thanks to the irreparable loss of the greater part of his exegetical writings.

Revolving time brought about a gradual cleavage and the final division between the two parts of the Roman

B

Empire. About the beginning of the fourth century there were already many Christians in the West who could not read Greek, and at the end of that century it was the exception to find persons in that part of the Empire who could. It is in this period, then, that Latin commentaries begin. The oldest extant is that of the martyr Victorinus of Poetouio (Pettau) on the Apocalypse, written about the year A.D. 300. Then come the works of Hilary of Poitiers about the middle of the fourth century. His later contemporary, Victorinus Afer, comes next, in the decade A.D. 355 to A.D. 365. He is followed by the so-called 'Ambrosiaster', A.D. 370–85. Then come Jerome, Augustine, and Pelagius. Of these Ambrosiaster and Pelagius commented on all thirteen Epistles. Of Victorinus Afer we possess commentaries on three Epistles only; Jerome wrote commentaries on four only, and Augustine on two.

It will perhaps be of some service to our study if I explain my point of view on certain subjects. I approach the investigation that is to follow as a Christian believer, yielding to none in his sense of the value of Scripture study for all. If I select the Epistles of St. Paul as that part of Scripture to which our attention is exclusively to be directed, it is because I believe these Epistles to be of all parts of Scripture the most important for the Christian faith and life of those who, like most people in Europe and the United States, are non-Jews and at the same time inheritors of the Graeco-Roman civilization. And I arrive at my belief by a process of what seems to me inexorable logic. However we explain the miracle wrought on the way to Damascus, there can be no doubt that Saul of Tarsus was directly and specially commissioned by the risen Christ, who is identical with Jesus of Nazareth, to make known His Gospel to non-Jews in the Roman Empire. The studies of my honoured teacher and predecessor in Aberdeen, Sir W. M. Ramsay, have made clear

to us the unique fitness of St. Paul for this task. He was
the inheritor of the purest form of Judaism ; he had been
thoroughly trained in the most morally elevating of all
the Greek philosophies, the Stoic ; and as a Roman citizen
he knew and appreciated the significance of the Roman
Empire.

To the peoples he evangelized his voice was as the voice
of Jesus Himself. Probably he had known Jesus in the
flesh, but whether or no, he was an absolute master of
Jesus' message, and was the one man who could be
trusted to deliver it, in pure form, to the Gentile peoples.
This he did, principally by preaching. But the preaching
was supplemented by letters, as difficulties arose in his
absence. These letters, while they were each written to
suit a particular occasion or particular circumstances, were
in great part preserved, as of superlative value not only for
their original recipients, but for all who should come after.
I do not hesitate to say that in my opinion they are the
most valuable writings in the world.

But you may say, they were written for special contemporary circumstances, and we have outgrown them.
Have we? I would ask you to consider carefully what
this attitude means. A careful reading of the letters themselves shows that there are portions in them where Paul
speaks explicitly κατὰ ἄνθρωπον 'as a mere human being '.
What does this imply? It implies that all the rest of the
Epistles are to be regarded as the words of Christ. In
the first instance, no doubt, as the words of Christ to the
particular groups of persons addressed. Admitting for
the moment the possibility that some of the teaching is
applicable only to these recipients, it is a most hazardous
proceeding to seek to separate that element, and we have
not yet, I think, arrived at the state of knowledge which
would permit us to do so. In particular I would impress
on all the importance of far more extensive archaeological

work than has yet been undertaken. Every site which St. Paul visited should be thoroughly excavated, no matter the cost. Every relic, in particular every inscription, in Tarsus and elsewhere, should be preserved, copied, and studied. When this has been done, and not till then, can we say that it will be possible to detach the temporary and accidental from the permanent and essential. And it will require generations of reverent work to achieve this end.

But, you may say, are the letters authentic productions of St. Paul ? To prove that I am no obscurantist, let me state the opinions at which I have arrived. I see no reason whatever to reject any of the Epistles addressed to churches, or the Epistle to Philemon. I am still as certain as I was in 1911 that the so-called Epistle to the Ephe-sians is not a secondary production, based mainly on the Epistle to the Colossians, as some hold. The true text of i. 15, which is the shorter form, in itself proves that Ephe-sians cannot depend on Colossians. That verse should be translated : ' having heard of the faith in the Lord Jesus that is among you, and that is in all the saints ', as it was rendered by the Bohairic translator many centuries ago. I am equally certain that the fifteenth and sixteenth chapters of Romans could not have been addressed to any other community than the Roman community, and that they are an authentic part of at least one form of the Epistle to the Romans. But I cannot accept the so-called pastoral Epistles, namely the Epistles to Timothy and Titus, in their present form, as productions of St. Paul, holding rather with Dr. Harrison and others that they were compiled by a later person, a Paulinist, who incor-porated genuine fragments of St. Paul in them. Such is my position with regard to the critical questions involved.

But, admitting the importance of the Epistles of St. Paul as you define it, I may be asked, why do you discuss Latin commentaries instead of Greek commentaries ?

Surely, I shall be told, Greek commentators, writing in the same language as that in which the Epistles are themselves written, are likely to be more valuable than Latin. I concede this point at once, and will proceed to explain why I choose the Latin. There are two reasons. As a young student of classics I devoted myself perhaps more eagerly to Greek than to Latin study. It is the way with young students of classics in England (I might say Great Britain); whether it is so in the United States, I do not know. But early in my twenty-first year I came into personal contact with one of the greatest Latin scholars of all time ; I refer to Professor John E. B. Mayor, of Cambridge, whose edition of Juvenal must be as well known in the United States as it is in Great Britain. Mayor revealed to me as in a flash the vast store of unrecorded wealth in the later Latin literature, say from A. D. 150 to 750. I saw the men round me devoting themselves intensely to Greek. I saw that they were able to get the highest honours in classics by study that was almost exclusively Greek. I began to feel that their success in examinations must be due to the fact that their elders were doing the same, that in fact the same standard of difficulty was not generally aimed at in the study of both languages. I felt also that the result of this one-sidedness would be the loss of that knowledge of Latin, both comprehensive and minute, which the greatest scholars of previous generations had laboured to acquire. I there and then decided to devote such leisure from public duty as might be afforded me to the exploration of the Latin of these six centuries, in order that I might have a share, however small, in handing on the torch of Latin learning.

The literature of that period is vast, and those who know something of it will want to know why the Latin commentators on St. Paul's Epistles have come to claim my special attention. That also I can explain. I had been reading freely in St. Augustine, recording his vocabulary and idiom, when at the end of 1898 the promoters of the great *Thesaurus Linguae Latinae* accepted my offer to excerpt for that work the greater part of the writings contained in the fourth and last volume of the works of St. Ambrose of Milan, the seventeenth of Migne's *Patrologia Latina*, which is entirely taken up with works falsely attributed to St. Ambrose. Among these is the Ambrosiaster commentary on St. Paul. A few years later I was appointed Yates Professor of New Testament Greek and Exegesis at Mansfield College, Oxford, and was privileged to devote eight years of my life to special study of the Greek New Testament. I learned something of textual criticism in those years, and began to see that the field in which I was called to labour was the field where my two greatest interests, St. Paul and Latin, converged, the earliest Latin commentaries on the Epistles of St. Paul.

There is a defect of which I am deeply conscious, and that is the want of a specifically theological training. I mention this, though indeed it will be apparent enough from the treatment that is to follow. The treatment is that of a Latin scholar passionately devoted to St. Paul.

A writer who attempts to treat this subject has some right to consideration from his readers, on the ground that the field has been so little worked. In a sense everything has yet to be done. Nothing equal in importance to the work of Richard Simon has appeared since his day, that is, over two centuries ago. Victorinus, also, was inaccessible to him, his commentary having remained unprinted until its discovery (or rather rediscovery) by the indefatigable Mai in the early decades of the nineteenth century. It is true that as a guide to the theology of Victorinus we have the masterly article of Bishop Gore in the *Dictionary of Christian Biography* and other studies, but of his place in the history of exegesis I know no treatment.

Nor have we any such up-to-date and reliable guide to
the history of Latin exegesis as Professor Turner has provided for that of Greek exegesis. There is doubtless
a disposition in some quarters to assume that there is
nothing original in Latin exegesis, that it is entirely dependent on Greek exegesis, and that it may therefore be
safely neglected. I cannot call it anything else but unfair,
for example, when I read in the excellent commentary of
Von Dobschütz on the Thessalonian Epistles,[1] 'The
Latins have hardly any value except in so far as they com-
municate to us the exegetical tradition of the Greeks', and
I can only forgive the remark on account of his admission
that Ambrosiaster and Pelagius have independent value.
In the absence of such comprehensive treatment it is
a pleasure to turn to the more modern commentators who
have troubled to look into these Latin authors. It is
hardly to the credit of non-episcopal communions that they
have left this interest almost entirely to the Roman and
Anglican communions. In the commentary of Cornelius
à Lapide and other Roman Catholics on the one hand,
and in such nineteenth-century commentaries as those of
Lightfoot, Westcott, Sanday, Swete, Robinson, Bornemann,
and Von Dobschütz on the other, we find welcome evidence
of interest in the old commentaries and use of them. This
present age is one that shows signs of squandering the
heritage of the past, much more by neglect than by misuse,
and it can never cease to be of moment to the real lover of
Scripture what was thought of its meaning by any patient
investigator in any country or in any age. It is the more
to be regretted that an illustrious Bampton Lecturer on
the History of Interpretation should have ignored the
oldest Latin commentators entirely. How his hearers or
contemporary readers took this I have not had leisure to
inquire.

[1] p. 51.

I

MARIUS VICTORINUS

GAIUS MARIUS VICTORINUS,[1] as the further surname
'Afer' indicates, was a native of the province of Africa.
At what age he removed to Italy is uncertain, but we know
from Jerome and Augustine that in Rome he gained the
highest distinction as a professor of rhetoric and a Neo-
platonist philosopher. Some time before A. D. 357 he
became a public convert to Christianity, and during the few
years which remained to him after he took that step, he was
busy writing in support of his new faith, while retaining his
public position till the decree of Julian in A. D. 362 compelled
him to lay it down. As a successor of Plotinus and Por-
phyry he made a translation of the latter, perhaps also
of the former; certain works of Aristotle also were rendered by him into Latin. But these versions are all lost.
The works he wrote in connexion with his profession have
been more fortunate in surviving the ravages of time; we
have from his pen an *Ars Grammatica*, a commentary on
Cicero's *De Inventione*, and a *De Definitionibus*. His
Christian works must have been very numerous, as we
see from the abundant references he makes to them in the
course of the few now extant. He came forward as
a champion of Nicene orthodoxy, with his *De Generatione
Verbi Divini* against the Arian Candidus, and his four
books against Arius. His polemic is directed specifically

---

[1] See M. Schanz, *Geschichte der römischen Litteratur*, iv. Teil,
1. Hälfte (München, 1904), §§ 828 ff. (= pp. 137 ff.); W. S. Teuffel,
*Geschichte der römischen Literatur*⁶, 3. Bd. (Leipzig-Berlin, 1913), § 408,
pp. 231 ff.; O. Bardenhewer, *Geschichte der altkirchlichen Lit.*, Bd. iii,
pp. 460 ff.; on his pagan period and conversion, see the brilliant pages
of P. Monceaux, *Les Africains* (Paris, 1894), pp. 402-7 = *Hist. litt. de
l'Afrique chrét.*, t. iii (Paris, 1905), pp. 373 ff.

against the Homoeousians and particularly the second creed
of Firmum in A.D. 357. We cannot enter here into the
question of the authenticity of other works attributed to
him, but must confine our attention to the commentaries on
the Epistles to the Galatians, Philippians, and Ephesians,
composed after 360,[1] and published for the first time by
Cardinal Mai in 1828.[2]

Mai tells us he used three MSS. in the Vatican library,
the Ottobonian MS. 3288 A, of the fourteenth (according to
Haussleiter, the fifteenth) century; 3288 B in the same
collection, of the sixteenth century, a copy of the preceding;
and Vatican MS. 3546, also of the sixteenth century, a copy
of one or other of the preceding.[3] There is thus practically no variation in the texts of the MSS. They all
show the same lacunae, the same corruption or ambiguity,
and the same obscurity: the only real difference is that the
orthography of the oldest is of a more ancient character.
The contents of the MSS. are interesting. First comes
Victorinus (of Pettau, of course) on the Apocalypse, with
Jerome's prefatory letter, and then our Victorinus on
Galatians and Philippians. These are followed by two
tiny works, one on the words of Genesis, 'factum est
uespere et mane dies unus', and another, 'Contra Duo
Principia Manicheorum'. The MSS. next contain the
commentary on the Epistle to the Ephesians, and
lastly a little work entitled 'De Physicis' (without an
author's name).

These appear to be the only MSS. now existing, but in
the time of the great patristic scholar, the Jesuit Jacques
Sirmond, yet another existed, 'Herivallensis', i. e. in the
monastery of Herenthals in Belgium, about twenty miles

---

[1] Dated by Monceaux, *Hist.*, t. iii, p. 403.

[2] *Scriptorum Veterum Nova Collectio e Vaticanis codicibus edita*, tom. iii
(pars ii), (Romae, 1828).

[3] p. 147.

east of Antwerp.[1] From this MS. Sirmond printed the
short works to which I have just alluded, and also mentions
that it contained some of Victorinus' commentaries on the
Epistles. We can express regret that Sirmond did not
edit these also, but his life was crowded with the publication of one ἀνέκδοτον after another, his indefatigable
search having been rewarded by a succession tumbling
into his hands. It may be that this Herenthals MS. was
the parent of the elder Ottobonian, and that we ought to
look for the parent of the Herenthals MS. itself in some
insular MS. descended from the books which the Irish
Church acquired in the first half of the fifth century. But
on this matter we can only speculate. As causes for this
meagre manuscript tradition we may suggest the fact that
the commentaries were superseded by the handier and
more interesting works of Ambrosiaster and Pelagius,
which fall to be considered later. The commentaries of
Victorinus seem to have exercised little influence on
succeeding works, and indeed Jerome alone mentions their
existence.

The archetype from which our manuscripts derive must
have been itself defective, for text and commentary alike
are lacking for Gal. iii. 10^b-19, v. 17^b-vi. 1^a, Phil. i. 1–14,
Eph. vi. 1–12. The Migne text is a fairly accurate reprint
of the *editio princeps*, and errors such as we note in the
later edition are generally found to have been taken over
from the earlier. The text itself may be said to be in
a fairly good state, especially if we consider the date of the
manuscript. One thing that inspires confidence is the fact
that the Biblical text of Victorinus shows very few, if any,
signs of having been contaminated with later MSS. of the
Vulgate. It may have incurred this contamination in

---

[1] *Jacobi Sirmondi . . . Opera Varia*, tom. i (Venet. 1728), p. 200.
From another MS. of the same monastery he published Leporius and
Capreolus (*ibid.*).

the following places: Gal. i. 14 (*meos*), 15 (*ex*), ii. 18 (*iterum haec*), v. 13 (*spiritus*); Phil. i. 23 (*esse cum Christo*), 24 (*est* omitted), ii. 1 (*siqua* tert.), 9 (*exaltauit illum* [1]). iii. 10 (*cognoscendum*), 12 (*quomodo*); Eph. i. 1 (*Jesu Christi*), 10 (*dispensatione*), 21–22 (remarkable here), ii. 5 (*in*), 15 (*ipso*), iii. 7 (*operationem* in one of two quotations), v. 33 (*uxorem suam*): a very brief list, especially when we consider the character of the tradition, and the fact that these may be after all genuine Old-Latin readings which crept into later Vulgate MSS. I venture to think that this situation will compare favourably with that in any other author.

If we apply another test, that of agreement between the text cited and the text which lies behind the commentary, we shall find the result no less reassuring. It is altogether the exception to find any disagreement between the two. The following is probably a full list of instances where variation occurs, and where the commentary enables us to correct the text:—

Gal. i. 12 text *excepi*: comm. repeatedly suggests *accepi*.
 iv. 14 text omits *dei*: comm. twice shows that it ought to be read.
 iv. 29 comm. shows that *is qui secundum carnem natus fuerat persequebatur eum* is omitted from the text by homoeoarcton.
 iv. 31 text *simus*: comm. shows he really read *sumus*.
 v. 8 *nos* of text should be altered to *uos*, as comm. shows.
Phil. i. 25 *gloriam* of text should be *gratiam*, as comm. proves. This confusion might occur as far back as an insular MS. of the eighth century, in which the symbol $\overline{gram}$ was misread as $\overline{glam}$.
 ii. 9 *quod est super omne nomen* (or such like) omitted by homoeoteleuton in text, as comm. shows.
 iii. 12 *comprehendar* should be, as the comm. repeatedly shows, *comprehendam*.
 iv. 1 comm. shows that *carissimi et* is wrongly omitted from the text.

[1] Especially as the order *illum exaltauit* occurs below.

Eph. i. 4 (1241 c) *mundi* accidentally omitted before or after *constitutionem*, as comments show.

ii. 7 (1255 c) comm. repeatedly shows that *gloriae* of text is an error for *gratiae* (cf. Phil. i. 25, above).

iii. 2 (second citation) *dispensationem* shown by comment as well as by previous citation to be an error for *dispositionem*.

iv. 31 *et ira* omitted accidentally from text, as comment shows.

vi. 18 *rationem et obseruationem* of text may be safely emended to *orationem et obsecrationem* from the repeated statements of the commentary.

Again a small list, which inspires confidence.

Yet the text is by no means in an immaculate state. Victorinus is not an easy author, and I may have been wrong in adding a mark of corruption to my copy of the text in something like ninety passages, and in suggesting corrections, most of them probably wrong, in a number of others. But there can be little doubt, I think, that we ought to make the following alterations :—

Gal. i. 13–14 (Migne, viii. 1152 c) *uidit* for *uidi*.

ii. 4–5 (p. 1159 B) *adire* for *addere*.

ii. 4–5 (p. 1159 c) *fiduciae* for *fiducia*.

ii. 11 (1162 A) *beneficum* for *bene officium*.

iii. 3 (1167 c and D) *consummemini* for *consumemini* and *consummetis* for *consumetis*. It is strange that Mai should not have made this correction ; the confusion is one of the commonest in MSS.

iii. 23 (1172 B) surely *autem* for *ante*.

iv. 4 (1177 A) *perfecti simus* for *perfectissimus*.

iv. 27 (1186 B) *magis quam* for *magis quae*.

v. 10 (1191 A) *poenae* for *paene*.

v. 15 (1192 A) *concordiae* for *ad concordiam* of Mai (MSS. *concordia* simply).

v. 15 (1192 B) alter punctuation; end sentence at *ceterisque rebus*, and begin next with *Pertinenter ergo* . . .

vi. 3 (1193 B) *aestimat* or *existimat* for the vox nihili (common as it is in MSS.) *extimat*.

Gal. vi. 7 (1194 c) *malum seminauit quicumque* . . . for *m. seminat quicumque.*

vi. 8 (1195 A) remodel last sentence by removing the comma after *spiritu*, *hic* being the adverb, and insert a *sed* before *seminat.*

vi. 14 (1196 D) read *adfixus* for *adfectus.*

Phil. i. 27 (1202 B, l. 22 of page) *una* should probably be *una anima* as twice above (*aia* could be easily omitted).

i. 29–30 (1202 D) *exhortationi* for *exhortatione.*

ii. 6–8 (1207 A) (l. 11 of page) add *ut* after *aliud.*

ii. 6–8 (1207 B) read *plenius* for *plenus* (as in Mai).

ii. 9–11 (1210 c) *uicta* for *uita* (and again 1211 B).

ii. 12–13 (1212 A) Professor W. B. Anderson of Manchester is right, I think, in inserting *nobis* before *consulentes.*

ii. 20–21 (1214 c) om. *ad.*

ii. 28 (1216 c) for *tristis* read *tristior* (MS. *tristius*).

iii. 1–3 (1217 c) om. the second *non* (before *scribere*).

iii. 21 (1226 c) for *in continuum* read *incontinuum* (one word) and perhaps also *inconiunctum* for *non coniunctum.*

iv. 3 (1228 A) perhaps add *se* to *promisisse.*

Also there is an inconsistency between *laborauerunt* (of text) and *laborant* (twice) in commentary, which ought probably to be remedied by putting the non-Vulgate reading in the text.

iv. 18 (1234 A) read *odor*, of course, for *ordo.*

Eph. i. 4 (1239 c) read *et* (or *aut*) *excludat* for *ut excludat.*

i. 4 (1240 A) read *qui sint sensus* for *qui sunt sensus.*

i. 4 (1240 B) similarly *sint aeterna* for *sunt aeterna.*

i. 4 (1240 c) for *etsi* (one word) read *et, si* (two words).

i. 8 (1244 B) *praestant* for *praestat.*

i. 8 (1244 D) *ratione qua* should be read for *ratione quia.*

ii. 12 (1257 D) *alienus* should surely be read for *alius.*

iii. 1–2 (1262 B) prob. read *habendi* for *habiti* (MS. *habenti*).

iii. 13 (1267 c) read *Sic* for *Sit* (probably).

iii. 13 (1267 D) surely *mea ; uestra, inquit* not *uestra ; mea, inquit.*

iii. 18–19 (1270 A) *quae altitudo* is omitted after *quae latitudo* by homoeoteleuton.

Eph. iv. 20–21 (1278 c) *docuit* (with Mai) for *docui*.
    v. 2 (1283 A, B) three times read *fragrantiae* or *fra-glantiae* for *flagrantiae* (a very common confusion).

There is still room no doubt for further emendation: I cannot find that any one has published anything on the text. As an illustration of the ancient relics that remain in it, let me cite the genitive *fili* (Phil. ii. 11, p. 1211 A, &c.), the spelling *adque* (Eph. i. 4, p. 1241 B), and the regularity of such forms as *aliqui*, &c. (Eph. iii. 18–19, p. 1269 C, &c.) for the usual *aliquis*, &c. The Migne edition some-times fails to print parts of the text in italics (e. g. p. 1250 A, &c.), and there are some other defects of printing which need not be specified. We can now proceed to consider the two main divisions of our subject, the text and the commentary.

The Biblical Text.[1]

As has been indicated, the text of the three Epistles commented on is given complete, except in the places already named, where text and commentary alike have perished. I cannot find that any scholar has published an exhaustive treatment of it, and one must consult the works of Ziegler, Corssen, and F. Zimmer for any help there is to be had. As far as Galatians is concerned, Zimmer's *Der Galaterbrief im altlateinischen Text, als Grundlage für einen textkritischen Apparat der Vetus Latina* (Königsberg, 1887) provides an interesting conspectus of types of Latin text current in the early centuries. He distinguishes four different types: (1) that of Tertullian and Cyprian; (2) that of d, g, Victorinus and Ambrosiaster, which he identifies with that which Jerome calls 'vulgata'; (3) r, z (= r₃), Augustine, &c.; (4) the Vulgate. As Victorinus did not

---

[1] On Victorinus' Biblical text in general see P. Monceaux, *Hist. Litt. de l'Afrique chrét.*, t. i (Paris, 1901), pp. 132–4; on his Matthaean text, *Old-Latin Biblical Texts*, vol. ii (Oxford, 1886), p. lxxxv f.

become a Christian till late in life, we do not expect to find
him using an 'African', even a late 'African' Biblical text.
He had been so long resident in Rome that we should
expect him to have used an European (or as some would
prefer to say, an Italian) type of text. And this is really
what we find. It is particularly instructive that we observe
a close agreement in many places with the text of Ambrosiaster, and this agreement is not always shared with the
Vulgate. It sometimes is, not infrequently is, but in
the following readings in Galatians they agree against the
Vulgate. Where there is other support for the reading,
I give it also :—

     Gal. i. 23 audiebant (Pel.).
        ii. 2 exposui (g).
        ii. 4 subinductos.
        ii. 4 subintrauerunt (Pel.).
        ii. 13 consentiret simulationi eorum.
        ii. 16 Christi (*alt.*) *om.* (g Pel.).
        ii. 16 quoniam (g Pel.) *for* propter quod (vg.).
        ii. 16 iustificatur (Hier. gal *codd.*).
        ii. 20 sed. *for* uero vg.
        ii. 21 sum ingratus gratiae.
       iv. 20 nunc (Pel.).
       iv. 24 nam (Sedul.).
       iv. 24 quod.
        v. 8 uestra (Hier. Pel. Sedul.).
        v. 10 fuerit.
        v. 14 uniuersa.
       vi. 18 amen *om.* (g Pel.).

All of these, with the exception of Gal. ii. 4 (*bis*), 13, 16
(*bis*), 20, 21, v. 14 and vi. 18, are also attested by the
Augustine group. That is, exactly half are attested by
the Augustine group. There can be no doubt that
Augustine in the Epistles used a text very much the same
as his contemporaries in Italy.[1] In other words d and r

---

[1] See *Les Fragments de Freising*, éd. par Donatien De Bruyne (Coll.
Bibl. Lat. v), (Rome, 1921).

are sisters, we might say twin sisters. There are no facilities known to me for a similar comparison in the case of the text of Ephesians and Philippians, but there can be little doubt that we should find the situation the same. A codex of the Apostle was one volume, and generally homogeneous in textual character. Victorinus, then, employed, as we should expect, an up-to-date text of his own period, that of the generation preceding the Vulgate, a text in character closely related to the Vulgate. Let us now note certain characteristics of this text in the matter of rendering, and then point out some anomalies in it.

Of characteristic renderings the following may be noted:

NAM as a rendering of γάρ in preference to *enim* in the following places:—

Gal. ii. 21; iii. 27; iv. 24; v. 6 (= vg.); 17; vi. 3 (= vg.), 5; 9.

Phil. ii. 2 (= vg.); iii. 3.

Eph. ii. 8; v. 9; 12.

Of course *enim* is commoner even here, and sometimes γάρ of the Greek is left untranslated, but there is a decided tendency to use *nam*, where the Vulgate goes the opposite way, and there are only one or two examples (e.g. Eph. iv. 31) where Victorinus has *enim* and the Vulgate either nothing or *nam*.

UNIUERSUS as a rendering of πᾶς, ὅλος in preference to *omnis* or *totus*:

Gal. v. 3 (= vg.); 9; 14.

Phil. iii. 8; 21; iv. 22.

Eph. i. 11; iii. 9.

Occasionally there is no equivalent (e.g. Eph. i. 15 $\frac{2}{3}$; vi. 21, 24).

QUEM AD MODUM as a rendering of καθώς, ὡς, instead of *sicut*:

Phil. i. 20; ii. 12; iii. 17.

ERGO, either as a rendering of οὖν, &c. (against *igitur, itaque*, &c.), or added to the Greek:

Gal. ii. 17; (iv. 15 = vg.; 16 = vg.); iv. 31; v. 1, &c.

Phil. ii. 29.

Eph. iv. 17; v. 15.

Yet *itaque* (Phil. ii. 28; iii. 15) where vg. *ergo*.

MYSTERIUM (as against *sacramentum*) to render μυστήριον (only in Eph. of our Epistles):

Eph. i. 9; iii. 3; 9; v. 32; (vi. 19 = vg.).

QUONIAM as a rendering of ὅτι (against *quod, quia, propter quod*):

Gal. ii. 7; 14; 16; (iv. 6 = vg.); iv. 12; 15; 27; (v. 2 = vg.).
Phil. i. 19; 20; 25; 27; 29; iv. 15.
Eph. ii. 12; (18 = vg.); v. 30.

But *quia* (Gal. ii. 6) where vg. *quod, quod* (Gal. iv. 22) where vg. *quoniam*, and *quod* (Phil. ii. 11) where vg. *quia*.

ILLE: the translator seems to have preferred this word to *is, ipse*:

Gal. i. 1; ii. 13; iii. 23 (altero loco).

Eph. i. 9; 20 (where vg. omits); 23; iv. 21; v. 25; 29.

GRATULOR in the sense of *gaudeo* (χαίρω):

Phil. ii. 17 (cf. vg. *congr-*); 28; (*gratulatio*) 29; iii. 1; iv. 10.

IPSE: there are signs of a partiality for *ipse* in Eph. where it is appropriate:

Eph. i. 4; 7 (10 = vg.); 12; iii. 12; (iv. 10 = vg.); iv. 15, v. 30.

(*plur.*) Eph. iv. 18.

SED in preference to *autem, uero, uerum*: Gal. i. 15; ii. 20; iv. 6; Phil. ii. 22; 27.

I fear these data do not prove much. Probably μυστήριον is the only word that is consistently rendered throughout. One must not expect to find in a text like this the remarkable results that were obtained from that of k (codex Bobiensis) in the Gospels. But a study of k's Latinity will show that we have travelled far to reach a text like that of Victorinus. In k *totus, quomodo, igitur* (*sacramentum* in the only place where μυστήριον occurs) are the favourites. In fact the two texts show no analogy but in the vulgarism *quoniam*, of which both are rather fond. A similar result is got by comparing Cyprian's text with that of Victorinus: *enim* is characteristic of Cyprian; *uniuersus* is very rare in

him, as also *quemadmodum, ergo* (never ?), *mysterium* never
—it is a European word,—*gratulari* never—again European.
We have a strong argument for the European character of
Victorinus' text, and this is strengthened if we follow
another line of evidence, and compare all the verses
Cyprian cites from the three Epistles with which we are
concerned. In all Cyprian quotes 79 verses from these
Epistles, and of these 79 we find 65 in Victorinus. If we
first note all the differences between Victorinus' form of
these verses and that of the Vulgate, and then compare all
the places where Victorinus differs from the Vulgate with
the Cyprianic form, we shall find that there is very little
resemblance indeed between the two. The following is
a complete list of their agreements:

Gal. i.   6   a matter of underlying reading : *om.* Christi (so Lucif.
         Ambst.).
     v.   15   order of words (so m).
    vi.   7   deridetur (so g Tert. Ambst. Pelag. vg^tol. D).
Phil. ii.   6   constitutus (so d).
     ii.   7   similitudine (so d Nouatian).
     ii.   9   order of words (cf. Ambst. Ambr. Nouatian).
    iii.   19   est interitus (so d Ambst.).
    iv.   18   sacrificium acceptum.
Eph. ii.   17   nothing after *longe* (so d Ambst. Pel.).
    iv.   29   de (so Ambst. Pel.).
    iv.   31   auferatur (so Ambst. Pel.) (Cypr. auferantur).
     v.   26   eam (so Ambst. Aug. Pel.).
     v.   31   matrem (without *suam*) (so Ambst. Pel.).
    vi.   13   hoc.
    vi.   17   no word after *salutis* (*saluationis*) (so d m Lucif.
         Ambst. *codd.*).

There are only two places where Cyprian and Victorinus
stand alone, or appear to stand alone, against all other
authorities: Phil. iv. 18 and Eph. vi. 13 ; even there it may
be only lack of evidence which leaves them alone. It is
quite clear, therefore, that there is no near connexion

between the texts used by Cyprian and Victorinus : Phil. iii 21 will very easily show how wide apart they are :

Cypr. qui transFORMAuit (*sic codd. Test. ad Quir.*) corpus humilitatis nostrae CONFORMATUM CORPORI CLARITATIS SUAE.

Victorin. qui transFIGURAuit corpus humilitatis nostrae UT SIT AEQUIFORME CUM CORPORE GLORIAE IPSIUS.

We may fitly conclude our short examination of this out-and-out European text of the fourth century by citing some curiosities of it, especially one or two instances of punctuation :

Gal. i. 14. *abundantius* he takes with what precedes, and evidently punctuates after it (p. 1154 B).

Gal. ii. 5. He knows both the positive and the negative readings, and uses the text with the positive, and approves it.

The break into two books in the commentary on Galatians coincides with the beginning of capitulum 15 of Vulgate MSS. (chap. iii, v. 20).

Phil. ii. 23. He stops at *mox*, which is interesting as showing the point of view of a trained grammarian and rhetorician with regard to such expressions as *mox ut* and *statim ut*: apparently it is our duty to punctuate before the *ut*, not before the *mox* or *statim*.

Phil. iii. 1. He gives as Latin text *manifestum*, but prefers the Greek *firmum et tutum* (ἀσφαλές) (vg. *necessarium*).

Phil. iii. 7-8. There would appear to be some confusion about the text at this point, but the matter is hardly worth dwelling on.

Phil. iii. 8. His Latin has *eminentiam* only : he notes that the Greek has *cognitionis* after it (vg. *eminentem scientiam*).

Phil. iv. 7. Perhaps the most interesting case of all,

and there is no doubt that the reading is that of Victorinus'
copy, as it is abundantly confirmed by the commentary:
Et pax dei quae HABET *omnem intellectum.* This gives
practically the opposite meaning of that intended by the
Apostle, and I can only suggest that his copy was in
error, and that the word *dehabet* may have been what this
form of version really read: it of course = *non habet.*

Phil. iv. 12–13. The translator of the text adopted by
Victorinus made or found between these two verses a
punctuation different from the usual, namely: *et abundare
et egere in omnibus possum* (stop): (then) *per eum qui me
confortat.*

Phil. iv. 17. V. undoubtedly had *oratione* (and not
ratione) in his text, as is clearly shown by the comment;
similarly Vg. ᵃᵐ* and certain Pelagian manuscripts have
orationem. The mistake is perhaps excusable, as the
Greek is λόγον, and not every translator would at once
catch the commercial sense of the word.

Eph. iii, between verses 2 and 3, again an interesting
punctuation: *quoniam* is absent altogether, and *secundum
reuelationem* is taken closely with *quae data est mihi in
uos,* a new clause being begun with *Notum mihi factum est,*
&c. It is the 'grace of God that is given me to you-
ward according to revelation'.

The division of Ephesians into two books has no relation with the capitula regularly found in Vulgate MSS.,
for it takes place shortly after the beginning of capitulum 15 (iv. 9).

Eph. v. 19–20. Another interesting punctuation, by
which he unconsciously offers a solution of a difficulty of
interpretation. He puts the stop at *psallentes,* and takes
in cordibus uestris domino gratias agentes together.

With this must end our short discussion on the Biblical
text, and we must now come to the Commentary.

The Commentary.

Any connected study of the commentary must come from the theologian. I can only attempt to indicate very briefly certain interesting points with regard to it, and will try to take the points in something like a rational order.

Of the Victorinian commentaries which survive it would appear that Ephesians is earlier than Philippians. In Phil. ii. 6–8, the great passage about the Kenosis, he remarks after some sentences, 'plene de hoc et hic tetigi ⟨et⟩ ad Ephesios', &c.: the commentary on Ephesians therefore preceded that on Philippians. But that Ephesians was not the first of his Pauline commentaries is proved by a statement (i. 4) that he has treated a certain subject 'et in aliis epistulis'. On Gal. vi. 14, the reference 'omnis qui gloriatur, in deo glorietur', *de quo supra tractauimus*, proves that there was a commentary on Second Corinthians, for this quotation comes from 2 Cor. x. 17. It seems probable that he wrote on most, if not on all of the Pauline Epistles.

Length of these commentaries. If we compare the size of the Victorinus commentaries with Ambrosiaster and Pelagius, we get roughly the following result; the numbers are columns of Migne:

	Victorin.	Ambst.	Pelag.
Gal.	51	36+	19
Phil.	37	18½	13
Eph.	60	32	19

He is thus much the longest of the three, and perhaps we may put this fact down to the rhetorician's love of prolixity. It must be remembered of course that he was the first Latin commentator on the Epistles, and had therefore the task of setting a standard. Leaving Jerome out of account, as he is altogether a special case, we can see that the tendency at this period was for commentaries to become briefer and briefer.

Character and Method. After quoting a clause or two of the sacred text, amounting to about one or two of our modern verses, he gives his comment, which is perhaps on an average about five times as long as the text commented on. He frequently begins by repeating the text almost in its exact words, introducing this paraphrase by *inquit*; for example, on Gal. i. 12, the paraphrase of *sed per reuelationem Iesu Christi*, in this case deferred somewhat, is *sed reuelatum est mihi*, inquit, *a Christo Iesu*. Until this 'inquit' is understood, the reader is apt to treat the paraphrase as a real form of the text, but numerous instances show that it is not so. In fact we may go almost so far as to say that he uses 'inquit' as the sign of a paraphrase; and a great part of the commentary consists, like the sermons of young and inexperienced preachers in our own day, of a repetition of the text. The actual comments are generally such as good sense would dictate, those of a man of the world, of real human feeling, whose heart Christ has touched, but not those of a trained theologian. What especially distinguishes them from other (later) commentaries, is that scripture is rarely quoted in illustration of scripture. In this connexion one naturally recalls Jerome's criticism of Victorinus, none too harsh, it would seem, '*occupatus ille eruditione saecularium litterarum, scripturas omnino sanctas ignorauit*' (*Comm. in Ep. Gal. praef.*). When he does quote, it is generally from the context, and rarely even from any other part of the epistle. The quotations from other parts of the Bible are a mere handful, and are quite ordinary. We can learn, therefore, practically nothing of his Gospel text from these commentaries on the Epistles. Examples are Ioh. i. 3 (on Gal. i. 11), Mt. xvi. 18 (on Gal. i. 18), Rom. vii. 2 (or perhaps rather 1 Cor. vii. 39) (on Gal. iv. 4), Ps. l. 14 (on

Gal. iv. 9), Rom. viii. 30 (on Gal. v. 8), 1 Cor. viii. 1 (on
Gal. vi. 10), 2 Cor. x. 17 (on Gal. vi. 14). These are all
I have noted in the commentary on Galatians. Practically
all are allusions, not citations, and not one is referred to
its source by Mai or Migne. The situation in Ambrose
is somewhat analogous. He also started the study of
scripture late in life ; he also is careless in his quotations,
but he is much more abundant. But if Victorinus is
meagre in his references to the sacred text, there is
perhaps no other ancient writer who refers so often to
utterances of his own, past, present, or future. In all
I have counted some eighty such references in these three
commentaries. They are nearly always couched in the
first person plural, and, as I have said, can sometimes be
traced to passages in the commentaries themselves, but
more often perhaps allude to works of the author which
are now lost. Examples of these phrases are : *in multis
locis probauimus* (1148 A), *sicuti multis ostendimus* (ibid.),
saepe exposuimus; *saepe, cum occasio erit, dicemus* (1148 B),
quod supra exposuimus (1150 A), *uti dixi* (1152 B), *ut post
docebimus* (1153 A), *quod loco suo quid sit docebimus* (1153 B) ;
these are all from six successive columns of Migne. The
good side to this is that it shows he felt an inner connexion to subsist among his various expositions of
Christian truth, and indeed it is also characteristic of his
work that he remembers the different parts of an Epistle,
and does not comment on each section as something quite
separate from the rest. His references to Greek, too, are
not infrequent, and this is a characteristic shown by no
other Latin commentator except Jerome. Sometimes it is
to the Greek of the scripture text, or something illustrative
of that Greek ; we have seen a case or two of this already :
others are Gal. i. 10 (the clause ἀνθρώπους . . . θεόν); vi. 6
(κατηχίζειν) ; Phil. ii. 7 (σχῆμα), 8 (ὑπήκοος γενόμενος), 15
(Gk. = 'sine culpatione ') and ἄμωμα τέκνα, 22 translated

more accurately, iii. 8 (the second ἡγοῦμαι [1]) ; Eph. ii. 20
(φραγμός and ἀκρογωνιαῖος), iii. 19 (πλήρωμα). The original
language is quoted, not from ostentation, but to get
more accurately at the meaning of St. Paul than his
Latin version allows. At other times he has occasion to
refer to Greek ideas, and uses the Greek word, for
example λόγος (1208 C, 1209 D *quinquiens*, 1210 B *ter*, C
quinquiens, 1236 B, &c.), ὕλη (1210 A *bis*, 1240 A), ὤν (1251 C
quater), νοῦς (1288 C, D).

Occasionally he is in doubt as to the correct interpretation, but this rarely occurs. Instances are to be found on
Phil. iv. 21, where he asks whether *in Christo Iesu* goes
with *sanctos* or *salutate* ; and on Eph. iv. 2, where he says
that *inuicem in caritate* may be taken either with *portantes*
or with *sufferentes*.

Some interesting examples of his exegesis may now be
given. On Gal. i. 1, he suggests that the words ' not from
men ' hint at Matthias (the apostle elected to take the
place of Judas), who did learn from men. On ii. 3, he
takes neither side on the question whether Titus was
actually circumcised or not.[2] On iii. 1, he has a curious
view as to the meaning of *proscriptus est*: ' Christ, therefore, was *proscriptus*, i. e. his property was parted into lots
and sold, the property of course which he had in us, and
which was advertised, sold, and destroyed by the per-
suasive influence of Judaism.' In iv. 4, having the reading *editum ex femina*, he instances the variant *muliere*
(which happens to have been adopted by the Vulgate).
He says *femina* is the equivalent of γυνή, and defines
every *femina* that gives birth to a child as a *mulier*; he
then goes on to say: ' all things that are perfect (complete)
are called " a man " (*vir*), and all things which are imperfect
are called " a woman " (*femina*),' and winds up by saying

---

[1] The MSS. of Vict. have ἡγούμενον.
[2] Ambrosiaster takes the view that Titus was *not* circumcised.

that when the world, or we in the world, are not perfect,
we are spending our life like *feminae* and *mulieres*; an
exegesis truly quaint, and without much bearing on the
text concerned! On vi. 11, he contrives, like his suc-
cessors, to avoid all reference to the *size* of the letters
which St. Paul wrote to the Galatians, though he has
quantis in the text. Theological students may be invited
to read his view of the famous ' Kenosis' passage (Phil. ii.
6-8). As it stands it is excessively difficult to make out,
and a very good exercise : '*forma*', for instance, he says
is ' non figura, non uultus, sed imago et potentia' (with
regard to this word something must be said later); ' God
is *existentia*, and even more that which is above *existentia* :
the *forma* of *existentia* is to move, understand, live ' ; ' Christ
is life and knowing and understanding'. Other pas-
sages of his works are in the same vein.[1] Phil. ii. 9 has
this interesting comment among others: ' That power
(*uirtus*) which is called the Father is above that power
which is called the Son : nevertheless the names Son and
Father are equal the one to the other.' In Phil. iii. 21,
in common with several other Latin authorities, he reads
and interprets the perfect *transfigurauit* as well as the
future *transfigurabit*: ' by the mystery of his advent,
crucifixion, and resurrection he transformed the humility
or form of our body, or rather the body of our humility.'
. . . The γνήσιε σύνζυγε (*germane uniiuge*) of iv. 3 is interpreted as Epaphroditus! On iv. 19-20, if the text is
right,—and similar passages seem to confirm it,—he
interprets *Deo nostro* as ' scilicet Iesu Christo patri nostro '.
On Eph. i. 4, he twice gives expression to the view that
(our) souls existed before the universe; again, they are
not to be identified with *spiritus*, but they are such as can
receive (*recipere*) *spiritus* (singular : ' spirit ', or ' the Spirit ').

[1] See *Marius Victorinus Rhetor und seine Beziehungen zu Augustin*
(Inaug. Diss.), by Reinhold Schmid (Kiel, 1895), pp. 24 ff.

On i. 11, he is emphatic enough: 'nihil enim est quod fit, quod non a deo praedestinatum sit, et ante quodam modo factum. nunc *sensibiliter* fiunt quae *spiritaliter* a deo sunt constituta.' On i. 21-3, he gives an interesting explanation of the phrase 'on his right hand': 'Christ is the movement of God: movement shows itself in work ; the working which belongs to movement is always in the right hand: therefore Christ is set on the right hand of God.' On ii. 12, God and Christ are declared to be absolutely identical: 'ecce et hic deum "Christum" appellauit', where 'Christum' is in the predicate. One of the commonest expressions throughout is *Christi mysterium* (cf. Eph. iii. 4), by which appears to be meant 'the incarnation' (1169 A, &c.).

Sources. The chief source of the commentary is no doubt the intelligence of the author himself, trained in the study of language and philosophy. Students of the history of philosophy can trace in him the influence of the school to which he had belonged, and students of Scripture can see how little he owed to the sacred books for the material of his commentary. In connexion with his study of Scripture it is interesting to note what would appear to be, if we could trust the reference, a knowledge of the Psalms in Hebrew. On Phil. iii. 1-3, Psalm lxvii. 24 is cited by its Hebrew number, lxviii. This must, however, be an accident, an error in transcription, and in fact we find that on Eph. iv. 8 he cites Psalm lxvii. 19 by the usual Septuagint number. Any theory, therefore, that this African author passed from the knowledge of Punic to that of the cognate Hebrew must be dismissed at once. There can be little doubt that our author derived his theology, in part at least, from Athanasius. He could hardly have adopted the role of a champion of orthodoxy without depending on him, and on the whole it is probable that he depended directly on him rather than on Hilary, his greatest Latin interpreter. The question

whether Victorinus used Origen for his commentary on
Ephesians[1] is to be answered in the negative, as no
certain case of borrowing can be produced. There is
clear evidence that he knew the Marcionite prologues to
the Epistles. These prologues, found in many Vulgate
MSS., have been proved by Dom De Bruyne[2] and
Dr. Corssen[3] to be of Marcionite origin, and at the end
of the commentary on Philippians and the beginning of
that on Ephesians there are distinct traces of them. The
mention of 'pseudoapostoli' on Phil. iv. 23, and again in
Victorinus' prologue to Ephesians, are best explained by
the theory that our author is here under the influence of
these prologues : I rather fancy that their influence can
be traced in Victorinus' prologue to Galatians also. Of
heretics only the Symmachiani, I think, are mentioned by
name, and they occur twice (1155 B, 1162 D) in connexion
with the Apostle James. The creed of Nicaea is alluded
to on p. 1265 c (in Eph. iii. 9), 'Christus qui est lumen ex
lumine et deus ex deo'.[4] On p. 1274 A 'in infernum
descendit' reminds one of the Aquileian form of the
Roman Creed.[5] Victorinus has sedulously kept his
classics out of the way: a couplet from Virgil (*Aen*. i.
58-9) on Eph. ii. 2, and a more general reference to the
poets and Mercury, messenger of the Father of Light (in
Phil. ii. 6-8) seem to be the sole recollections of his earlier
studies he has allowed to creep in.

[1] Ed. J. A. F. Gregg in *Journal of Theological Studies*, vol. iii
(1901-2), pp. 233 ff., 398 ff., 554 ff.

[2] *Revue Bénédictine*, xxiv (1907), pp. 1-16.

[3] *Zeitschrift N. T. Wiss.* x (1909), pp. 37-9.

[4] Note *ex*, the normal form, and not *de* (*de* is the form, e.g., prefixed
to the anathemas of pope Damasus, about A. D. 378-80, cf. C. H. Turner,
The History and Use of Creeds, &c. (London, S.P.C.K. 1906), p. 99, or
Eccl. Occ. Monum., tom. i (Oxonii, 1899-1913), p. 283; statistics of *ex*
and *de* on p. 321, cf. p. 327): *ex* is used also by Gregory of Elvira
(*Origenis Tractatus*, ed. Batiffol and Wilmart (Paris, 1900), p. 67, l. 22).

[5] Where it first appears : J. Pearson, *Exposition of the Creed*, Art. V.

Style and Language.

The style of these commentaries was rightly characterized long ago by the great master Sirmond, who said: 'obscuritatem hanc Victorinus in dogmaticis praecipue libris sectatus uidetur. In Commentariis enim aliquot epistolarum S. Pauli . . . stylus planior et apertior.'[1] It is well known that his usual style is obscure, 'only to be understood by learned men' as Jerome[2] puts it, but here he has clearly made an effort to write more plainly, more down to the level of the ordinary educated Christian. This has been observed by one of the best modern students of his works, Koffmane. The strange thing, of course, is that one of the first rhetoricians of his age should write obscurely at all. But such is the fact. The style he here employs is what the rhetoricians themselves called the ἰσχνόν, *tenue*, the plain, unvarnished, unadorned style. He himself speaks of his work in one place as *commentatio simplex* (1273 c). There is therefore not very much to say about his style. He does not altogether escape obscurity: p. 1207, ll. 25 ff. and 34 ff. are good examples of the difficulty occasionally to be experienced in following him, but on the whole what want of clearness there is may be charged to the MS. tradition. Some of the mannerisms of his style and vocabulary may fitly conclude our sketchy treatment of Victorinus. The rhetorician comes out occasionally in the repetition of synonyms. The coupling of synonymous words is frequent in him as in other writers,[3] e. g. *utilis et commoda* (1153 c), *hortatur et monet* (1211 c, cf. 1239 a), *admonet et hortatur* (1261 d), *mentitur ac decipit* (1239 d), *fallit ac decipit* (1193 c), *plena et perfecta* (1239 d), *perfecta atque plena* (1221 a), *calcatis et con-*

---

[1] *Opera* (1728), tom. i, p. 200.
[2] *Vir. Inl.* 101.
[3] Cf. A. Souter, *A Study of Ambrosiaster* (Cambridge, 1905), pp. 65 ff.

tritis (1241 B), *comprimit et extinguit* (1291 D), *curam et sollicitudinem* (1161 C, 1294 C), *precatur et optat* (1294 C), *imploret et roget* (1249 A), *precatur et rogat* (1269 B), *roget atque obsecret* (1228 A), *arguit et accusat* (1162 A), *distracta et uendita* (1167 A), *carissimos et dilectissimos* (1211 C), *caritas et dilectio* (1227 B), *reprehendit et monet* (1167 D), *admurmuratio et querella* (1213 A), *adnuntiare et euangelizare* (1201 A), *euangelizat et praedicat* (1267 C), *exponit et explicat* (1206 C), *aperte et plene* (1209 A), *caelestia et diuina* (1229 C, cf. 1234 B), *donauerit atque concesserit* (1209 C), *largitur et dat* (1234 B), *reditu atque reuersione* (1210 A), and many more.

Specially characteristic of the author is what has been called the 'triple beat': *agnoscant, custodiant, seruent* (1228 B); *adnuntient, asserant, euangelizent* (1228 B); *plene, certe, proprie* (1243 A); *ignaua sunt, uitiosa, pigra* (1246 A); *exposui, tradidi, docui* (1290 A); *eundum, properandum, festinandum* (1291 B); *duo iungit et copulat et unum reddit* (1261 C); *rector et dominus et princeps* (1260 C). There is actually an instance of four such words: *corrumpatur, putrescat, pereat, intereat* (1194 D), where there are two pairs, the second member of each pair being stronger than the first.

If we turn from style to vocabulary, there is something more definite to be said. It is an interesting situation to find a highly trained pagan rhetorician face to face with the necessity for expressing Christian ideas. For this task, of course, he had been prepared by his parallel study of philosophy. Of his Christian terminology the most interesting feature is his use of *liberatio* in the sense 'salvation': he has *saluatio* also (1161 C, 1171 A, 1188 B, C, 1197 B, 1201 A, 1216 B, 1220 A, 1237 B *bis*, 1239 A, &c.), which is by no means common in the early days: in fact the dictionaries give no example earlier than Jerome.[1] As for

---

[1] But see Sanday-Turner, &c., *Novum Testamentum S. Irenaei* (Oxford, 1923), p. xc.

liberatio, which occurs 1176 A, 1178 A, 1188 B, 1236 A, 1239 A, 1245 A, B, 1267 A, B, &c., I cannot find that it is used else-where to any extent: I note one instance in Ambst., and one or two in Aug. It would appear to be a coinage of the author's, as is perhaps *saluatio* also.[1] *Potentia* is a favourite word of Victorinus in the sense of *persona*, according to Mai. Whether Mai was exactly right in defining the word thus, it must be left for theologians to decide. In any case it is a characteristic word, and it means something like *persona*. Another interesting use is that of *tractatus*, not in its regular Christian sense of 'homily', but in the sense of 'subject', or 'treatment of a subject'. As the word in the sense of 'homily' has been the subject of rather a long article by Dr. Zahn, it may be of some interest to gather together the references to the passages where Victorinus uses it in the sense mentioned. They are: 1180 B, 1186 B, 1192 A, B, 1193 A, 1205 A, 1209 D, 1217 C, 1238 B, 1248 B, 1273 B, C *bis*. We may now follow this slight treatment with a list of in-teresting words used by our author, giving them in alpha-betical order, and end with the mention of some ordinary words, the use of which he affects. This is by no means a complete study even of the rare words, but adequate evidence will be provided in support of my view that Victorinus' latinity deserves a monograph, after the fashion in which Tertullian, Cyprian, Hilary, Jerome, and others have already been studied.

Where Victorinus is cited for a word in the new *Thesau-rus Linguae Latinae*, which is published from A—Do and F—Funus, I propose to mention the fact always. The editors were not in possession of any collection on the latinity of Victorinus' commentaries when they commenced

---

[1] This view is supported by the fact that he sometimes combines the two expressions *liberatio* and *saluatio* (1188 B, 1239 A), as if he were feeling his way to adequate expression of the idea 'salvation'.

their task of compilation, and I cannot find any definite
mention of such a collection even in volumes 3 and 5: but
there is evidence in the body of the work that they have
something at hand on the subject.

abscisio, which few editors before the nineteenth century were
able to distinguish from *abscissio*, 1191 c. It is doubtful, in
fact, if *abscissio* existed in ancient times.

accepto 1160 A.

admixtio 1186 c, Vict. (not comm.) cited.

admurmuratio 1213 A. Cited from Cicero only (five times)!

adnuntiatio 1261 B : occurs from Tert. onwards.

adoptatio 1243 B.

adsocio 1239 A, 1252 c, 1262 A : Vict. (not comm.) cited.

adsono 1194 A *ter*: cited only from Pomponius, Ovid, Persius,
Apuleius, Cassiodorus.

aduento 1229 A, 1249 A.

aeternus: the adverbial phrase *ex aeternis* 1254 c, 1255 B, cited
from nowhere ; *ex aeterno* from Damasus and Aug.

apostrofo 1173 B : cited only once from a gloss, and once from
a grammarian.

Christianismus 1159 B, 1166 c, 1180 A, 1187 c ; Tert. Victorin.
Hil. Ambst. (5 times), Hier. Aug. According to Koffmane,
Geschichte des Kirchenlateins, i (Breslau, 1879), p. 20, it is
the earlier word, and it is natural that it should be so, being
an easy transliteration from Greek. See also *Thes. Ling. Lat.*

Christianitas 1169 D, 1205 A, 1269 c, 1283 A, &c. Ps.-Cypr. Ambst.
(4 times) Filast. Zeno Ambr. Petil. Aug. Cod. Theod.
Pelag., &c. See *Thes. Ling. Lat.*

circumformo 1207 c : only ex. in *Thes.*

circumseco 1191 c : *Thes.* has this ex.

coacesco 1190 c. *Thes.* has this ex.

coaedificatio 1262 A : this and two examples from Aug. in *Thes.*

cognitor 1179 A–B several times, in the sense 'one who knows':
Fronto Apul. Tert. Cypr. Hil. Ambr. Aug., &c. : lexx. before
Thes. took no account of this use.

cognoscentia 1178 c *bis*, 1207 c *bis*: possibly in Victorinus alone.
It belongs to the same type of word as *existentia* ; cf. Graden-
witz, *Laterculi Vocum Latinarum*, p. 290 f. for words of this
class. See also *Thes.*

conciliator 1222 c : *Thes.* has this ex.

conseruio 1198 a : *Thes.* has this (solitary) ex. from Latin.

constitutus 1253 a, perhaps elsewhere also : an equivalent for ὤν, very common of course in late Latin : no ex. in *Thes.* from Victorinus. *Positus* is commoner here, as we should expect in an European writer, 1226 a, 1236 c, 1239 b, 1243 a : cf. Ambst. (*Study of Ambst.*, p. 93), where the situation is the same.

copulatio 1259 a : *Thes.* has three exx. from Victorin., but not this.

corroboro 1159 b : *Thes.* has one ex. from Victorin., but not this. The word is not at all rare in Latin.

credulitas (= the Christian's *faith*) 1165 b (in *Thes.*). Arnob. seems to be the earliest writer to use the word in this sense.

(*crucifigo*), or rather the separation *fixus* sit *cruci*, 1166 a : not excessively rare. The earliest uses were *cruci figere*, *adfigere*, and the words were then separate. It was only later that they became inseparable in the order *crucifigo*, like *terrae motus* (Ital. *terremoto*).[1] Exx. of the separated older form are in *k* and other Old-Latin MSS., also in Iren.-lat. Ambst., &c., and as early as Phaedrus. *Thes.* gives a fairly good account, but not our ex. The combined word *crucifigo* probably came into existence in the fourth century : this we infer from the fact that there is no sign of *crucifixio* and *crucifixor* till about the end of that century (the former first in Hier., the latter first in Aug. or Paul.-Nol.). These forms presuppose *crucifigo* as one word.

decalogus 1190 a, 1191 d : *Thes.* has the former example, but they have not incorporated all they had at their disposal. They give Tert. and others, but not Iren.-lat.

deceptor 1239 d, 1242 a : *Thes.* has both.

deificus : this 'unliterary word' (Watson, *Style and Language of St. Cyprian*, p. 228), 1273 a. The following writers have it : Sacra Scriptura, Tert. Cypr. Ps.-Cyprianic writings (a few times), Greg.-Illib. Iren.-lat. Ambst. (*bis*) Ambr. Optat. Cael.-Aurel. Aug. *Anon-Hiob* Innoc.-pap. Bened. *reg.* Caesar. Inscr. of

---

[1] In Tacitus' time the reverse order *motus terrae* was still possible, at least to him.

Capua (Dessau 7805) Gildas *gloss.*, &c. Lact. Lucif. are without it.[1]

deitas 1178 B, 1207 C, 1259 B, 1262 D, 1288 C *bis*. This word is illustrated by an interesting remark of Augustine, who apologizes for the use of it. In his *De Ciuitate Dei*, vii. 1 (written about 415–16) he says: 'hanc diuinitatem uel, ut sic dixerim, deitatem (nam et hoc uerbo uti iam nostros non piget, ut de Graeco expressius transferant quod illi θεότητα appellant'; cf. x. 1: 'diuinitati uel, si expressius dicendum est, deitati.' This a century after Arnobius (perhaps the earliest writer that uses the word) had already apologized for it (i. 28): 'ipsam deitatem, ut ita dicam.' The Europeans were less squeamish about its use. It occurs in the following writings: Ps.-Cyprian *De Aleatoribus*, Hil. Ambst. (*Quaest.* 8 times) Hier. Rufin. Prud. *Anon.-Hiob* Iulian.-Aecl. Arnob.-iun. *al. Thes.*[2]

distinctius comp. adv. 1252 C: Cic. Plin. h. n. Plin. epist. Suet. Gell. Aug.

effatio 1252 A: Paucker (*Supplementum Lexicorum Latinorum* (Berol. 1885), p. 228) has this ex. and adds Seru. Cassiod. *al.*

elumbis 1290 C: Tac. Paul. *ex.* Fest. Prud. in lexx.: add Aug.

empyrius 1180 B: Aug. (once).

eneruis 1290 C: Sen.-pat. Val.-Max. Sen.-fil. Petron., &c.: add Aug. to lexx.

enhydrus 1180 B: Amm. (as *substantive* already in Plin., &c.).

essentia 1227 C: Cic. invented it, hesitatingly: Sen. Quint. Tert. Arn. Ambst. Hier. Aug. Macr. Sidon.

etenim (1°) 1171 C, 1177 B, 1186 D, 1193 B, 1194 D, 1195 A, C *bis*, 1197 B, &c.

  (2°) 1186 D, 1256 A.

  Victorinus is therefore very much of a purist: the proportion of instances is exactly opposite in the contemporary Ambst. (cf. *Study*, 73 ff., for a full account of this use).

exaedifico 1261 A: classical; lexx. have no exx. later than Curtius Rufus.

exhortatiuus 1236 A: a grammatical word; Quintil. Macr. Isid. Others prefer *exhortatorius*.

---

[1] See Sanday-Turner, &c., *Novum Testamentum S. Irenaei* (Oxford, 1923), p. lxxviii.

[2] See *N. T. S. Irenaei*, loc. cit.

ex(s)istentia 1207 B *bis*, c *bis*, 1208 A *bis*, 1242 B *quater* : Paucker
gives five other exx. from him : it is also in Chalcid. Candid.-
Arr. Iulian-Aecl. Aug. Claudian-Mam. Ferrand. Cassiod.

explicatio 1238 B : classical; lexx. give nothing after Quintil.

expressio 1251 c : Vitr. Acron Cass.-Fel. Pallad. Hier. Ambr.
Aug. Ps.-Aug.

expugnator 1157 B : classical; add Ps.-Aug.

figmentum 1256 c : Gell.Apul.Tert., and later; add Aug.(freq.) *Thes.*

gentilitas (= paganism, pagan world) 1188 B : SS. vg. Lact.
Ambst. Hier. Rufin. Prud. Oros.

genus (=modus): *omni genere* only, 1190B, 1191A, 1221A, 1284 c :
therefore much more restricted use than in Ambst. (who has
this three times) (*Study*, 107 f.).

germanitas 1210 D : classical.

(*h*)*umectus* 1253 D : classical; add Aug.

hyle (for which he also has the Latin equivalent *materia* ad loc.)
1253 c : graecum ap. Suet. Macr.

**hylicus* 1259 D : in no dictionary, but in Iren.-lat. (7 times),
Ambst. (4 times). Like the former, Vict. has also *materialis*
(see below).

ideo ergo 1208 D, 1252 c : this pleonasm also in Tert. *Apol.* 29 ;
Ambst. (12 times) ; [Ambr.] *De Sacramentis*, i. 1, 2, *Expos.
in Ps. cxviii* (5 times); Augustine, *Epist.* 148, 1 ; 166, 21 ;
Op. Impf. in Matth., hom. i, § 24 *passim* ; Cassiod. *in Rom.*
iv. 14 ; MS. Paris B. N. lat. 653 *in 2 Cor.* xi. 12 ; Sedulius
Scottus (Migne, *P. L.* ciii. 183 B) : possibly under the influence
of the Greek ἄρα οὖν.

idolothytus 1159 c ; SS. Tert. Ps.-Cypr. Pacian. Hier. Iren.-lat.
Aug.

imaginarius 1179 c : classical; add also Tert. Aug. Ps.-Aug. to
lexx. (Never *imaginalis*, like Greg. Illib. Iren.-lat.)

inconiunctus 1226 c, if right : Ps.-Hier. Boet.

incontinuus 1226 c : Boet.

increpatio 1283 D : lexx. SS. Clem. and later; see also Paucker,
Suppl. Lex. Lat. s.v., and add exx. from *N. T. S. Irenaei*
(Oxford, 1923), pp. lxxxii f.

inculpabilis 1212 c : Solinus and later; add Aug. Ps.-Aug.

**inmaculatio* 1242 B : not in any dictionary.

insectator 1222 B : classical; see Benoist-Goelzer (after Paucker),
and add Ps.-Aug.

intepesco 1291 D : classical.

interpretator 1226 C : Tert. Hil. Charis. Iren.-lat. Aug. Salu. Orig.-lat.

iunctio 1261 B : Cic. (?) Arnob.-cod. Venant. (Paucker), to which add Aug.

magnalia 1292 D : SS. Tert. Cypr. Ambst. Hier. Aug. Max.-Taur. Greg.-Tur. *Inscr.*

materialis (rendering of ὑλικός) 1240 C, 1241 A *bis* : Tert. Chalc. Ambr. Hier. Iren.-lat. Macr. Rufin. Aug. Cassian. Ps.-Aug. Boet. Dion.-Exig. (see *hylicus*).

materialiter 1253 C : Sidon. Greg.-Magn.

messor 1194 C : classical ; add Aug.

monitio 1213 C, 1215 A : classical ; add Aug.

monitor 1231 A : classical.

mortificatio 1255 B : SS. Tert. Hier. Iren.-lat. Ambr. Aug. Paul.-Nol. Cassian. Ps.-Aug. *gloss.*

obauditor 1209 B *bis* : no other ex. of this spelling cited, but *oboeditor* Aug.

optabilis 1242 D : classical ; add to lexx. (which contain no citation later than Ovid) Aug. Ps.-Aug.

paganismus 1180 B : lexx. Aug. (once). Commoner is *paganitas* (Ambst. twice, Filast. seven times, *Cod.-Theod.* ; *Comm. in Symb.* (ed. C. H. Turner, *Monumenta*, vol. i, p. 357) ii. 97, Cassiod. three times).

paganus 1158 C, 1175 A, 1180 A *bis*, B *ter*. Victorinus, who has other examples in his other works, appears to be one of the first writers to use this word in the sense 'pagan'. He gives *paganus* as an explanation of the word 'Graecus' in Gal. ii. 3 (for which Vg. has 'gentilis'). Similarly, in the note Gal. iv. 3 we find 'apud Graecos, id est apud paganos'. In the other passages it is used quite naturally. Ambrosiaster next uses it, also abundantly. His contemporary Optatus has it 11 (12) times, Filaster 33 times, 'Comm. in Tom. Damas.',[1] Augustine, Pelagius, &c. Ambrose, Sulp. Sev. and Jerome appear to be without it. It seems to be a plebeian or slang expression in origin. A law of Valentinian of date 368 is the first document containing it, but a Sicilian epitaph of date between 300 and 330 is cited for it. See the index

---

[1] Cf. also C. H. Turner's *Eccl. Occ. Mon.* i, p. 293, l. 153.

to A. Souter, *Pseudo-Augustini Quaestiones*, Vindob. 1908,
p. 525, for many examples and references to literature on the
subject of this word.

pertinenter 1192 B : lexx. Tert. only.

peruro 1291 D : classical ; lexx. no ex. after Martial.

porro autem 1149 D *bis*, 1166 D, 1179 C, 1183 D, 1184 A, 1185 B,
1205 C, 1208 D, 1244 A, 1251 B, 1292 B : this collocation is also
found in the classical period, beginning with Terence, but
the *Thes.* (ii. 1593, 43 ff.) is woefully incomplete for Christian
authors, giving only 3 exx. from Vg., 2 from Aug., and 3 from
Sidon. The expression is common in Cyprian's latest
writings, and in some of his epistles. I have also 3 exx.
from Hilary (to which add Feder's, *C. S. E. L.* lxv, index),
17 from Ambst., very many from Aug., and 1 from Boet.

praeceptio 1205 C, 1237 A : classical ; add also Aug. to lexx.

procreatio 1244 B : lexx. give Cic. Vitr. Arn. Firm. Hier. Aug. ;
add also Ambst. Ps.-Aug.

progressio 1252 A : classical ; add to lexx. also Aug.

properatio 1229 A : classical ; add also Aug. Ps.-Aug. to lexx.

propitiator 1222 C : lexx. give Ambr. Hier. Oros. I doubt if
Aug. ever has it.

quare (as a substantive) 1168 C : this is very doubtful, and I can
find no trace of the medieval substantive *quare*, to which Mai
appeals in a note. Text here is probably corrupt.

quippe cum (already in Cicero) 1151 C, 1152 C, 1153 C, 1156 A,
1166 D, 1188 C, 1205 B, D, 1220 C, 1221 C, 1228 D, 1229 B, 1241 D,
1242 D, 1251 D, 1255 C, 1256 C, 1257 B, C, 1281 B, 1284 A (i. e. 21
exx.). Novatian has 3 exx., Ambst. a very large number
(about 80). Jerome I think also uses it.

quod is (after the accusative and infinitive) his favourite use
after verbs of saying and thinking, to introduce a fact stated
or thought. Victorinus shows himself a purist, because this
is a native Latin construction, occurring at least as early as
the *Spanish War* attributed to Caesar : instances in V. are
1176 B, 1182 A, 1185 B, 1187 B, 1191 A *ter*, 1221 A, 1235 C, &c.
Tert. Novatian Lact. Firmicus Aug. are similarly purist. But
V. once or twice uses *quoniam*, if we may trust the MSS., e.g.
1187 C. *Quia*, I think, is absent. (See the fullest collection
of statistics in Souter's article in *Nov. Test. S. Irenaei* (Oxford,
1923), pp. cix ff.)

recreatio 1204 D : lexx. Plin. Chalcid. ; add also Aug. (thrice).

reditio 1174 C : classical (but rare).

relaxatio 1189 C : classical ; but lexx. give exx. from late authors also ; add others from Aug. and Ps.-Aug.

renouatio 1245 C : classical ; but lexx. give exx. from late authors also ; add Aug. (freq.), and Ps.-Aug.

renuntiatio 1229 A : classical ; but also late (I have a number of examples from Aug. especially in our sense, unknown to L-S, ' rejection ').

resuscitatio 1250 C : lexx. Tert. Aug. Paulin.-diac.

sensibiliter 1245 C : lexx. Arn. Hier. Aug. Cassiod.

sensualis 1240 B : lexx. have Tert. Cael.-Aurel. Seru. Prud. Aug. Cl.-Mam. Dion.-Exig. ; cf. the *sensuabilitas* and *sensuabiliter* of Iren.-lat. (not in lexx.).

significantia 1253 B : Quint. Tert. and then fourth-century authors ; add Nouat. (third cent.).

stultiloquium 1283 C : lexx. Plaut. SS. Hier. ; add Iren.-lat. Cassian Aug.

substantialiter 1239 B, 1242 B *bis*, 1251 B : lexx. Tert. Hier. Rufin. ; add Ambst. (4 times) Aug. Ps.-Aug.

succutio 1253 D : lexx. classical and Apuleius ; add also Aug.

theologia 1235 A, B : lexx. Varro Aug.

tolerantia 1271 B : lexx. Cic. and other classical writers, and Vg. ; but add Gellius, Tert. Cypr. Aug. (very freq.) Pelag. Ps.-Aug.

trinitas 1178 C : Tert. Cypr. Ps.-Cypr. Hil. Opt. Priscill. Greg.-Illib. Filast. Ambst. Hier. Rufin. Aug. Paul.-Nol. Nicet. Prisc. *Auell. Cod.-Iust.* (gloss.).

turpiloquium 1280 B : Tert. Hier. Ambr. Ps.-Aug.

unanimitas (or *unian-*) 1203 C : classical ; then Hier. Hil. (lexx.) ; add Aug. Ps.-Aug.

unde in the sense ' concerning which thing ' 1184 C (Aug. Salu. cited by Mayor, *Journal of Classical and Sacred Philology*, vol. i (Cambr. 1854), pp. 392 ff.).

unitio 1272 C : older ex. (by half cent.) than any in lexx. Iren.-lat. Iul.-Aecl. Leo.-Magn. Petr.-diac. Boet.

uniuersalis 1236 C, 1252 A : Plin. Quint. Boet. in lexx. ; add. Aug. Ps.-Aug., both frequently.

usitatio 1181 A : older than Zeno and Cassiod. of lexx.

ut in sense ' why ' (indir.) in the phrase ' quid est causae ut '

(1239 B). This phrase occurs also in Ambst., generally without *causae*, Hier. Aug. (*cons. euang.* i. 25, 38, &c. though denied to be Latin by an old editor of the Pseudo-Augustinian *Quaestiones Veteris et Noui Testamenti*, who argued that the work could not be by Aug. because of the presence of this phrase.

zizania (fem. sing.) 1194 c : cited later from Aug. Cassian.

Among ordinary words which the writer very much affects, may be mentioned :

adiungo 1149 c, 1178 B, *et passim* (rather than other compounds ; but simple *iungo*, e.g. 1147 A, B, *subiungo* 1182 c).

circa is a favourite preposition.

magnificus (and *magnificentia* 1252 c), much as some English speakers affect 'magnificent' : 1157 c, 1226 A, 1237 c, 1244 B, 1249 B, 1250 A, B, 1269 A.

Like the Latin Irenaeus, Lucifer, Rufinus, Augustine, and others he affects *posteaquam*, rather than *postquam*, e. g. 1152 B, C, 1153 B, 1154 C, 1165 C, 1174 A, 1180 A, 1210 A, C, 1215 A, 1249 D.

He is extremely fond of *quemadmodum* (where he might have used *quomodo, sicut, uelut, tamquam,* or *ut*) ; exx. are 1231 A, B, C *bis*, 1242 B, 1248 B, 1252 C *bis*, 1254 C, 1258 A, &c.

Some curiosities are left over : *in* omitted with rel. where expressed already with antecedent : *in id quod peruenimus* 1223 B, C. There is no corruption here : you find the same in Acts xiii. 2 both O. L. and Vg. (latter *in opus quod adsumsi eos*), and also in Ambst. *quaest.* 123, § 2, *perfectum ad id quod factum est.*

persuadeo c. acc. pers. (also Iren.-lat. Pelag.) 1150 c.

quousque (never *quoadusque*) 1174 A, D.

sanctus spiritus (once) 1258 D : see Souter's note on this in *Quaestiones* (index), p. 535 a, and add Tert. (*bis*) Nouat. Ambst. (comm.) (12 exx.), Aug. (10 exx.) O. L. Acts xv. 2, Vg. Acts ii. 38.

ex subiunctis 1182 c, where Ambst. would have said *ex subiectis*.[1]

---

[1] Cf. *Study of Ambrosiaster*, pp. 138–40.

II

'AMBROSIASTER'[1]

The Name. The name 'Ambrosiaster' was coined, apparently by Erasmus, to indicate a Latin commentary on the Epistles of St. Paul, which he knew to be preserved in manuscripts and printed under the name of Ambrose, who was Bishop of Milan towards the end of the fourth century. It is improbable that he knew of any other attribution, in fact it is practically certain that he did not. The coinage of the name indicated that in his opinion the commentary was not a genuine product of St. Ambrose, but the work of another who pretended to be St. Ambrose. The judgement of Erasmus on this matter of authorship, although not always reliable in similar cases, has been almost universally upheld by later scholars : Ballerini, the last editor of a complete issue of the works of Ambrose, alone maintains Ambrosian authorship. So far then, the name Ambrosiaster cannot be denied a certain fitness, but that the real author of the commentary is in no way responsible for the attribution is a fact of which Erasmus was unaware, and which it has been reserved to our own age to discover. The commentary has only four times, I think, been issued by itself, in editions which have now become rare (Cologne, Jan. 1530, and Mar. 1532 ; Paris, Oct. 1534 ; 1540),[2] and these bear Erasmus' name as that of the editor. The work is still most easily accessible in complete editions of the works of St. Ambrose.

[1] See A. Souter, *A Study of Ambrosiaster* (Cambridge, 1905), for many facts recorded here.

[2] I owe my knowledge of the first and second of these to a kind communication of Prof. E. von Dobschütz.

An examination of the MSS. that have survived, in number roughly about seventy, reveals some interesting facts. The vast majority attribute the work to Ambrose, either with or without titles and honorary epithets, but the oldest MS. of all, that at Monte Cassino, of the sixth century, is anonymous, and the same would appear to be the case with one or two others. If Professor Baxter is right (and I think very likely he is), Augustine refers to an Ambrosiaster note on Galatians as 'Ambrosius' (*epist.* 82, A.D. 405).[1] It is, however, remarkable, that quotations from the commentary on Romans appear in various MSS. of Irish-Latin provenance under the name 'Hilarius', and a quotation from that same part of the commentary is cited as 'sanctus Hilarius' in a work of St. Augustine written about 419 (*Corp. Scr. Eccl. Lat.,* vol. lx (1913), p. 528). A MS. recorded in the medieval catalogue of Bobbio, entitled 'Hilary on Romans', would appear to be a MS. of the same part of the commentary. This palaeographical situation at once suggests that the commentary, as originally issued, was anonymous, and that the attributions are guesses. In favour of this view is the certainty that the later commentaries of Pelagius and Cassiodorus were also issued anonymously. It would appear that these early commentators desired no personal glory, but only to be useful. The really important thing was the scripture text, and their comments were simply appendages to this. Only when the commentators attained some reputation would the name be attached to their commentaries.

In this connexion we must consider another work, which scholars have almost universally combined to attribute to the same author, namely, the *Quaestiones Veteris et Noui Testamenti,* printed, until the Vienna edition of 1908 gave it the honour of a separate volume, in the

[1] *Journ. Theol. Stud.* xxiv. (1922–3), p. 187.

Appendix to the Works of St. Augustine. The MS. tradition of this work attributes it to that Father almost universally, but a MS. of south German provenance, now at Berlin, written about the end of the thirteenth century, attributes a portion of the work to St. Ambrose. The whole of one Question, too, is quoted under Ambrose's name as early as the middle of the fifth century in the *Disputatio Hieronymi et Augustini de Ratione Animae.* Finally, Dom Morin has discovered an extract from the same work, definitely attributed to Ambrose as against Augustine in a glossed thirteenth century MS. of St. Paul's Epistles in the British Museum.[1] There are strong reasons for considering that Questions 101 and 109 were issued also separately and anonymously. Here also, then, the MS. tradition is inconsistent.

There is yet a third work which undoubtedly comes from the same author, namely a fragment of a commentary on St. Matthew published both by Mercati and by Turner in 1903-4. This is anonymous in the sole known MS. And we may perhaps add a fourth work, *Mosaicarum et Romanarum legum collatio*, which tradition attributes to Ambrose.

We thus find that of works which have all come from the same pen, the MS. tradition is sometimes anonymous, sometimes attributes to Hilary, sometimes to Ambrose, sometimes to Augustine. These works must be of no ordinary character to be thus assigned in early times. We shall first consider the evidence for date and place of composition, and then mention recent views concerning the authorship. Afterwards we shall consider the character of the MS. tradition, then the biblical text and the character of the commentary, and finally the style and vocabulary of the author.

---

[1] Harl. 659; cf. *Revue Bénédictine*, t. xxvii (1910), 115.

First then as to the *Date*. This is fortunately easily ascertainable. In the commentary on First Timothy, chap. iii, verse 15, we find the words *ecclesia . . . cuius hodie rector est Damasus*, which show that the passage was written between 366 and 384. The author also mentions the emperors Nero, Vespasian, Domitian, Diocletian, Constantine, Constantius, and Julian, but no later emperor. The manner of the last reference suggests that he wrote some little time after Julian's death (363). Some of these emperors appear in the *Quaestiones*, not the Commentaries, but it is convenient to use the two works together, as they are mutually helpful in fixing the writer's date. In Question 44 it is stated that about 300 years have passed since the destruction of Jerusalem. This brings us to about 370. In Question 115 the devastation of Pannonia by the Quadi and Sarmatae in the year 374 is referred to. In the same document a woman who had had eleven husbands, and a man who had had twelve wives are mentioned. Jerome (in his epistle 123, § 9) refers obviously to the same people, though his numbers do not quite tally, and dates the incident of the funeral of the woman at the period he was assisting Damasus (382-4). The famine mentioned in the same *quaestio* (p. 334) is probably to be identified with that mentioned by Ambrose and Symmachus, of date 382. In Question 114 pagan worship appears in full swing, a state of affairs which would be impossible after 382, in which year Gratian confiscated the property of the temples and deprived the pagan priests of their privileges. In Question 125 Eusebius (no doubt he of Vercelli), who died in 371, is referred to in such a way ('quondam') that he must have been dead for some years. In Question 101 Professor Turner has drawn the veil from a cryptic allusion to a deacon, *qui nomen habet falsi dei*, and has shown that this is a reference to one Mercurius, who is commemorated by Pope Damasus as a faithful helper in his building projects.[1] A letter from Damasus to Jerome, dated by Vallarsi in 384, sends five questions for solution, which are among the first twelve in Ambrosiaster's collection. This can be no accident, and suggests that Damasus was reading the *Quaestiones* at the time: 384 is therefore a *terminus ante quem*. The principal works of our author were written between 366 and 384.

As to the *place* of composition, Father Brewer told me about 1910 that in an unpublished form of the commentary on the Epistle to the Romans there is definite proof that the commentary on that book was, at least in one of its forms, written in Rome itself. With regard to certain of the *Quaestiones* the author is explicit. In Question 115 the words occur ' hic in urbe Roma '. Question 101, also, bears the title DE IACTANTIA ROMANORUM LEUITARUM. Questions 102 'Against the Novatians' and 114 'Against the Pagans' suit Rome better than any other place. Yet there are indications which point to the probability that the author did not reside in Rome all his life. There are some facts which point to a residence for some period elsewhere. Samuel Berger called the text of the Epistles of Paul used by Ambrosiaster the text κατ' ἐξοχήν of Milan. Again, Ambrosiaster seven times uses the phrase *descendere ad inferos*, which suggests a knowledge of the form of Roman Creed in use at Aquileia. But if there are these indications pointing to a residence in North Italy, there are yet more striking signs of connexion with Spain. In enumerating citizens in the provinces he begins with *Hispani: Hispani Galli et Afri* (*Quaestiones*, p. 249, 6), with which compare the way Seneca, an undoubted Spaniard, says (in his *De Ira*, i. 11, § 4) *Hispani Gallique et Asiae Suriaeque molles bello uiri*; and again in the *Quaestiones*, p. 324, 25, where our writer could have mentioned Gaul or Africa or Sicily, he mentions Spain: *ne quis de urbe*

---

[1] *Journ. Theol. Stud.* vii (1905–6), p. 281 f.

Roma transuolet in Hispaniam. Further, he and Priscillian are the only Latin authorities who mention the demon *Saclas* : they both also attack the Manicheans, who were powerful in Spain. It seems permissible to conjecture that the author was acquainted with Spain, had resided in North Italy, but lived principally in Rome.

As to the *identity of the author.* The centuries which have passed since the invention of printing have naturally been prolific in suggestions on the subject of the real authorship of these two great works. Their importance may be gauged partly from the attributions above-mentioned, partly from the opinion of modern scholars of wide learning, who can hardly be charged with prejudice. Harnack says : ' We ought to call him the great unknown : for what ʼWestern expositor of the early period or the Middle Ages is his equal? ' Again, he says : ' Both works are admirable in their kind, and perhaps the most distinguished product of the Latin Church in the period between Cyprian and Jerome.' Jülicher has styled Ambrosiaster the best commentary on St. Paul's Epistles previous to the sixteenth century. All who read much of it cannot fail to be impressed by its qualities. Of many suggestions about the authorship, some very carelessly thrown out, only five have been backed by serious arguments. Hilary the Luciferian deacon was the favourite till a generation ago ; but already in the eighteenth century Jean-Baptiste Morel, one of the greatest patristic scholars who ever lived, had proposed Tyconius the Donatist ; in 1880 Dr. Joseph Langen proposed Faustinus. Neither of these two later suggestions was able to displace Hilary : the arguments were mainly linguistic, and not convincing. In 1899 a suggestion of a different sort was made by one of the most eminent authorities of all time. Dom Morin is fertile in suggestion, and in that year he called attention to various striking resemblances between our writings and those of an obscure person, Isaac, a converted Jew, who was concerned in the opposition to Damasus as pope in 378.[1] From the writings themselves it appears that our author was neither bishop nor deacon, and therefore presumably a layman. What is still more important is his very great interest in Judaism, and this Dom Morin was the first to point out. He is acquainted with Jewish apocrypha and Jewish legends. He knows the customs of the synagogue, and other matters connected with Judaism. If Isaac was the author, this would explain the silence of Jerome, the henchman of Damasus, with regard to him, and this silence needs some explanation. Amongst those who have supported this view of Morin,—and he can count many among his supporters—, Zahn, Turner, and Wittig deserve special mention. Zahn called attention to a remarkable passage in Jerome's commentary on the Epistle to Titus, in which he speaks of ' quendam ex Hebraeis, qui se Romae in Christum credidisse simulabat', giving a stupid explanation of the differences between the Matthaean and Lucan genealogies of our Lord, when it would have been more fitting that he should cultivate Christian charity. Such an explanation occurs in our *Quaestiones*, and is not altogether undeserving of Jerome's criticism. The case for Isaac as author of the Commentaries and *Quaestiones* cannot be better expressed than in the words of Prof. C. H. Turner (*J. T. S.* vii. 367–8):

' But if it be once admitted that the lecturer (or writer) whom (or about whom) St. Jerome heard was identical with the author of the *Quaestiones*, the problem which we set out to face is as good as solved. For we know, on this hypothesis, that he was a Jew : that he made what was in Jerome's opinion an insincere conversion to Christianity : and that he would have done better

[1] M. Rade, *Damasus, Bischof von Rom* (Freiburg i. B. and Tübingen, 1882), p. 31 f., 49 f.

to have studied ethics than exegesis, "justice and mercy and the love of God" rather than "names and numbers". Whatever else is uncertain, it is certain that this description can fit no one but Isaac. Isaac was an ex-Jew: his prosecution of Damasus on a capital charge and in a civil court may well have seemed to the pope's partisans the negation of justice and mercy and the love of God : and if the assertions of the latter party may be believed, his adhesion to Christianity proved in the day of his exile to be only skin-deep—"facto ad synagogam recursu caelestia mysteria profanavit". If, then, it appears that St. Jerome both must have known, and did know, our author's works, his silence can only have been due to a consciously deliberate "boycott" of one whom he felt he had strong and valid reason to disapprove. . . . But assume that Jerome believed the writer of the *Questions* and the *Commentary* to have been a schismatic, a calumniator of the successor of St. Peter, an apostate from the Christian faith, and there was every inducement for him to suppress all mention of the fact that such a man had made serious contributions to theological study, and to let the waters of oblivion flow over them and their author alike.'

Dr. Joseph Wittig of Breslau has ingeniously explained the name Hilarius affixed to the commentary as a kind of pseudonym derived from the meaning of the Hebrew Isaac, 'laughter'. He has also made a serious attempt to fill in the outlines of Isaac's life and literary activity, and these an attempt has been made to amplify in the introduction to the Vienna *Quaestiones*. Against the Isaac hypothesis I know only two difficulties. One is linguistic : there appears to me to be hardly enough resemblance between the language of the tractate on the Trinity ascribed to Isaac in the Paris MS. and freshly edited in 1909 by Zeuschner,[1] and that of the Commentaries and *Quaestiones*. The other difficulty is the assertion of Damasus' pontificate by his great enemy. This objection may have been rightly

---

[1] *Kirchengeschichtliche Abhandlungen*, hrsg. v. M. Sdralek, VIII. Bd. (Breslau, 1909), pp. 97 ff.

got over by Wittig, who supposes a reconciliation with Damasus prior to the composition of the commentary on First Timothy. In some ways this would explain the situation well. Jerome may have had the added motive of jealousy to account for his suppression of the Ambrosiaster.

It was principally this difficulty of language and the identity of name which led me in 1903 to adopt the second hypothesis, ventilated by Morin in that year, that the author was ' Decimius Hilarianus Hilarius, governor of Africa in 377, prefect of the city in 383, and praetorian prefect of Italy in 396'. This man was a Christian and bore the name Hilary: there seemed a chance that, after the rejection of the other Hilaries, he might be the right one. Jerome's silence, however, seems quite fatal to this view, apart from other considerations. He would not have ignored the work of a man with whose daughter he is known to have been on terms of friendship. I think all the reviewers of the *Study of Ambrosiaster* rejected the claims of Hilary the proconsul. More recently a final blow has been struck at this view. The inscription which is our chief authority for the details of this governor's career was published in the *Corpus Inscriptionum Latinarum*, vol. viii, 1219, and there the names ' Decimius Hilarianus' are certain, but the next name ' Hilarius' was due to what seemed a certain restoration, all that appears on the stone in its present state being H, then a vertical stroke, then a gap of three or four letters, then I V S. A better copy was afterwards published as no. 14398 of the same volume,[1] and from it, supported as it is by two other inscriptions, nos. 14346 and 17519 (= Gsell 257), it is clear that the partly missing name should be read as ' Hesperius', not ' Hilarius'. The late Professor Seeck

[1] Cf. also S. Gsell, *Inscriptions latines de l'Algérie*, tom. i (Paris, 1922), no. 259.

of Greifswald, the greatest authority on that period of history, has identified him with certainty as the second son of the poet Ausonius.[1] Thus Dom Morin's second theory falls absolutely to the ground.

Morin continued, however, to grapple with the problem, and in 1914[2] published his third suggestion, supported by his well-known learning and lucidity, that the mysterious author was Evagrius of Antioch. Ambrosiaster's works suggest that he was an aristocrat, that he had a practical knowledge of Roman law, that he was not an ecclesiastic when he composed the greater part of his works, but that he must have become a bishop before his death; that he had seen many countries, and that he had a special knowledge of Egypt. The career of Evagrius is exactly parallel. From 363 he held public positions in various parts of the Empire, and spent ten years in Italy. It was in 373 that he became a *presbyter*. Returning to the East in the same year, he visited Basil at Caesarea in Cappadocia, and subsequently made the acquaintance of Jerome at Antioch. Their relations were friendly until Evagrius in 388 or 389 allowed himself to be chosen schismatic bishop of that city. His tenure of the See was brought to a speedy end by his death.

These arguments are powerfully reinforced by a comparison between the style of Evagrius' translation of Athanasius' *Life of St. Antony* and the works of Ambrosiaster. It cannot be denied that most striking resemblances are to be found. Morin has made a strong case. Evagrius' lapse from orthodoxy is quite a sufficient reason for Jerome's silence about his later literary achievements. In fact, I know no objection to this theory except the fact that the Ambrosiaster works show no interest in mona-

---

[1] Pauly-Wissowa, *Real-Encyclopädie*, Bd. VIII (Stuttgart, 1912–13), 1249 f., where Hesperius' career is exactly sketched.
[2] *Revue Bénédictine*, t. xxxi, pp. 1–34.

chism. The fact that a Greek should write Latin, and be
Latin in his point of view, should offer no difficulty in the
way of accepting Morin's latest hypothesis, for as good
a judge as Prof. E. W. Watson inferred from Ambrosiaster's Latin that he was a Greek by birth.[1]

The Manuscript Tradition of the Commentaries. It is as
true now as it was in 1905 that we must await the publication
of the Vienna edition for a full account of the manuscripts.
The task of editing the commentary offers many difficulties
and must be spread over a number of years. The Vienna
edition will appear appropriately, as will be seen, in three
volumes, the first containing the commentary on Romans,
the second, that on the two epistles to the Corinthians,
and the third, the rest of the commentaries. I am indebted
to Father Brewer not only for the information he most un-
grudgingly gave, but also for the kind permission accorded
to me to state here and now results which in any other
sphere than scholarly research would justly be called sen-
sational. There are three different editions of the commentary on Romans, and two of the commentaries on First
and Second Corinthians, while the remainder of the commentaries survive in one form only. These editions are
all author's editions, and none is to be attributed to a later
editor. 'Ambrosiaster' is to be distinguished from the
vast majority of ancient writers, who issued their works in
one form only. It is an additional argument for common
authorship that of the *Quaestiones* there are also two
author's editions, a third which exists being, in this case,
a medieval compilation from the other two. Briefly the
situation is as follows:

First Edition, issued anonymously, but in some copies
bearing the name 'Hilarius', at least in the case of the

---

[1] *Classical Review*, vol. xxiii (1909), p. 237. More recently Morin has
made a fourth suggestion, *Claudius Callistus siue Hilarius* (cf. *Nuovo
Bollettino*, vii (1901), p. 245), but his paper is inaccessible to me.

commentary on the Epistle to the Romans, contained commentaries on Romans, and all the other epistles except
Galatians, Ephesians, and Philippians. This, in existing
copies, has unfortunately had its biblical text altered to
a form of the Vulgate. I cannot refrain from noting the
curious and independent testimony to the view suggested
in the Vienna *Quaestiones* (p. xii) as to the order of issue of
various parts of the works of Ambst. Noting the absence
of many *quaestiones* connected with the smaller Pauline
Epistles from the second edition of the *Quaestiones*, I inferred that the commentary on these epistles was later
than the earlier edition of the *Quaestiones*. It happens
that Galatians and Philippians are two specially concerned.
It is open, therefore, to the student to argue either way the
priority of the first edition of the *Quaestiones* or the first
edition of the Commentaries, as he prefers. The MSS. in
which this first edition occurs are one at St. Peter's, Salzburg
(saec. ix), which is the archetype of two others, one at Munich
(Freising) (saec. x), and the other at Zwettl (saec. xii).[1]
A fourth is at Cologne (no. xxxiv) (saec. x). It is possible that
Cheltenham 518 (saec. xv), on all (?) epistles (my own discovery), Göttweig 42 (my own discovery), Leningrad, F. v.1.
no. 17 (saec. xi), and a Troyes MS. which contains 1 and
2 Cor. only, belong really to the same form, and it is
certain that a fragment at Verona does.

All these MSS. have the genuine ending to First Corinthians, and the genuine beginning (including the prologue) to
Second Corinthians. My reason for suggesting that the
Cheltenham and Troyes MSS., e. g., also belong really to
the first edition is that they contain the genuine prologue to
2 Cor. and presumably the correct ending to 1 Cor. and the
correct beginning to 2 Cor. also. I did not realize when this
genuine prologue was published over twenty years ago in

---

[1] It is interesting that this MS. also contains Hilary (of Poitiers) on
the Trinity.

the *Journal of Theological Studies* from the Cologne and Troyes MSS. that it carried with it the genuine end of 1 Cor. and the genuine beginning of 2 Cor. In this I was misled by the Benedictines,[1] who give the right end of 1 Cor. and the right beginning of 2 Cor., but the wrong prologue.

The Second Edition, which is that of most MSS., including the later Bodleian 689 (saec. xii), formerly of Merton College and related in character to the MSS. of Vendôme and Chartres, bears the name of Ambrose. Its difference from the first consists in revisions of Romans, and First and Second Corinthians, and in the addition of commentaries on Galatians, Ephesians, Philippians, which were, as we have seen, wanting in the first. In this form, also, the biblical text has been altered to a form of the Vulgate. This class also had in its archetype lost the genuine end of 1 Cor. (namely from xv. 44 (Migne 269 B = 284 B)) and the genuine beginning of 2 Cor., including the prologue, down to i. 5 (Migne 277 A = 292 B). For this missing part was substituted, not as the Benedictine editors say, the corresponding portion of the commentary of Ps.-Jerome, but actually, as has been proved by the collation of three Paris MSS., the genuine uninterpolated Pelagius, into which the repairer of the gap in the archetype has introduced one sentence of his own. The text of this substituted Pelagian portion has been published.[2] The MSS. collated were numbers 1759 (saec. viii-ix), 1761 (saec. ix-x), and 13339 (saec. ix, Rom., 1 and 2 Cor.), and their value is in the order given. No. 1759, a beautiful MS. of Rom., 1 and 2 Cor., is shown by its palaeographical characteristics to belong to Verona or neighbourhood (e. g. $\overline{at}$ = autem, $\overline{ma}$ = misericordia). There is some relationship between 1761 and 13339. By a curious fatality the five MSS. contained in the Royal Library at the time of the publication of the big catalogue

---

[1] *Pelagius's Expositions*, &c., vol. i (Camb. 1922), pp. 51 ff.
[2] Ibid. 53 ff.

are all omitted in the index: hence not one appears in the *Study of Ambrosiaster*. The MSS. are, in addition to those above named, 1760 (saec. x) (Rom.), 1762 (saec. xii) (Rom.), 1763 (saec. xiii) (all).

The Third Edition, which is properly anonymous in origin, and still betrays this fact by the subscription FINIT AD ROMANOS, without name of author, contains a third edition of Romans and a repetition of the rest of the commentaries as in the second edition. It also alone provides the correct Biblical Text. What especially distinguishes this edition from the others, apart from these peculiarities, is the fact that it contains a curious transposition of a portion of the last part of the commentary on First Corinthians to the end of the commentary on Romans. The words FINIT AD ROMANOS are followed by *hucusque sublata discordia* (Migne xvii 276 A of older issue = 290 C of later) and so on to the end of the commentary on 1 Cor. The MSS. of this recension include the elder Bodleian (756, saec. xi, formerly of Salisbury), the Colbertinus of the Benedictines, which is Paris 1761 referred to above, and two other MSS. known to them, viz. a St. Mihiel MS. which still exists, and the Reims MS., now lost.

Unfortunately, however, these three classes do not include all the MSS. There are some, headed by the oldest, the Monte Cassino half-uncial of the sixth century, which are mixed. For instance, that MS. shares the special peculiarities of the third edition in being anonymous and in containing the curious transposition just referred to, but the biblical text has been somewhat vulgatized, and possibly in other respects also it shares rather with the second than the third edition.

It is clear from a consideration of the facts just stated that already within two centuries after its original issue or issues the Ambrosiaster commentary had had some strange experiences in transmission. Cassiodorus appears to have

possessed it anonymous, and yet not to have known that
the Ambrose he had heard of and was searching for was
the very commentary he had in his hands.   But the strange
history of this commentary was not ended by the time of
Cassiodorus' death.   Soon after, probably, a possessor of
the commentaries on Romans, First and Second Corinthians, completed the set by adding a collection of (presumably) anonymous commentaries on the other epistles.
Three MSS., one now of unknown situation, have survived
to testify to his action, one at Amiens, formerly at Corbie,
and another, formerly of Cues on the Moselle, now in the
British Museum (the latter having lost Rom. and 1 Cor.
which it once had).   Both belong to the eighth or ninth
century.   Jacobi and Hort independently proved that the
author of the anonymous commentaries thus used to complete a defective Ambrosiaster was none other than the
great Antiochene exegete, Theodore of Mopsuestia, whose
expositions were rendered into Latin, as Swete thinks, in
Africa in the sixth century.   The same form of 'Ambrosius', partly Ambst., partly Theodore, was used by various
medieval writers, Amalarius (*flor.* 820-40), Sedulius
Scottus (saec. ix med.),[1] his contemporary Hrabanus
Maurus, Lanfranc of Bec (saec. xi) and his younger contemporary Ivo (of Chartres).   There is an interesting
difference in the tradition even here.   Sedulius used
a MS. in which Theodore began with Galatians, but Hrabanus used one where Theodore began with Philippians.

Nor is this all.   Ambrosiaster, to whom Hebrews was
always an anonymous work, not by the Apostle Paul
(a fact pointed out for the first time in 1905),[2] did not write
a commentary on that epistle.   Yet we find in some MSS.,
for example that at Monza, the later Bodleian MS., and
the Vienna MS. 4600, as well as some printed editions,

---

[1] See *Journ. Theol. Stud.* xviii (1916-17), p. 226.
[2] *Study of Ambrosiaster*, p. 171 f.

a commentary on that epistle posing as part of the complete work. It was reserved to the indefatigable Professor Riggenbach of Basle[1] to show that this commentary is none other than that by the Englishman Alcuin, and it is a sign of the backwardness of study in this department that an easily ascertainable fact like this should not have been elicited before. The Benedictines were satisfied when they had found it to be spurious.

Sometimes sets of Pauline commentaries were made up in other ways, such as Ambrosiaster combined with Claudius of Turin, occasionally also Ambrosiaster combined with Haymo of Auxerre (who is sometimes called in later MSS. Remigius).

All the facts hitherto mentioned serve as means to classify the MSS., but we have not yet exhausted these. The regular order of the later epistles in the commentaries is 1, 2 Thess. Col. Tit. 1, 2 Tim., but some MSS. (the Monte Cassino MS. for example) provide a somewhat different order, Phil. Eph. 1, 2 Thess. Tit. Col. 1, 2 Tim. Philem. The commentary on Philemon, too, is often defective, *Cas.* ending at v. 17, while one St. Gall MS. and the Cologne, Le Mans, Padua, both Bodleian MSS., &c., end in v. 22. Finally, there are other distinguishing traits, of course: for example, Father Brewer (died 1922) found interesting interpolations at times in individual MSS., such as the later Bodleian.

The Vienna edition of the commentary on Romans was intended by Brewer to display all three editions, the first and second on the left-hand page, and the third on the right-hand page. What has been added in the second edition was to be made clear by a change of type from what already belonged to the first. Textual variants were to be added on the pages to which they belonged. Mean-

---

[1] *Die ältesten lat. Komm. zum Hebräerbrief* (Zahn's Forschungen, viii. 1) (Leipz. 1907), pp. 18 ff.

time the curious scholar will find some of the differences between the editions in the notes to the Benedictine edition and also on pp. 187–9 of the *Study of Ambrosiaster*.

The present state of the text cannot be called good. The Benedictines had hardly grasped in full the complexity of the problem with which they were faced. Their notes are sufficient to show that there are remarkable variations between the authorities, but are very defective as regards omission and addition. One can get from them no clear idea of the real situation in the manuscripts. Of these they employed altogether thirteen,[1] all in French libraries, but do not appear to have made complete collations of all, certainly not in the modern sense. Confusion has been made worse confounded in the later Migne reprint. These reprints are known to be bad, but the four volumes of Ambrose must be the worst of all, with about 1,000 misprints in each. Further, the Benedictines took great account of what they call the Roman edition of the works of Ambrose. It is not to be denied that this edition has great merits, but as the editors of it believed the commentaries to be by Ambrose, they freely emended the biblical text from parallel passages in the genuine works of that Father: Eph. vi. 12 (*lucta*) and Col. ii. 23 (*saturitatem et diligentiam*) would appear to be examples, cf. Ambr. *Noe*, p. 480, &c. In a good many minor points of order of words and such like we find all examined manuscripts in disagreement with the printed text. There can be no question that some modern editor with ideas very frequently altered the order he found in the manuscripts, an unsound proceeding, especially in the case of such an original and unconventional writer. A very large number of new readings from the manuscripts, undoubtedly correct, have been given in the third and sixth chapters, especially, of the *Study*. A few striking cases may be mentioned here:

---

[1] *Sancti Ambrosii . . . opera*, t. iv (Venetiis 1751), p. 779.

In Rom. i. 4, as printed, reads *dicente Cleopha in Emmaus*: nos putabamus, &c. Now, it was not in Emmaus that Cleophas said this, but on the way to Emmaus; also, there is no scripture authority for the statement that it was Cleophas and not his companion who spoke thus: the better MSS. make all clear by reading *et Emmau* 'and Emmaus': and we remember that in certain Latin Gospels *Emmaus* (*Am[m]aus, Ammaon*) is taken as the name of the second of the two disciples. In Eph. v. 24 *mulier consubstantialis uiro est*: the Bened. note says 'Old editions and some MSS. *quia mulier consubstantia* (so elder Bodl.): Roman edition *consubstantiua* (which is, of course, the right reading): other MSS. *consubstantialis* (clearly an emendation).' The writer never uses *consubstantialis*, but elsewhere has the rarer *consubstantiuus* (seven exx.), which Tertullian has at least three times. The word *dehabeo* (= non habeo) gave trouble to scribes;[1] hence we need not hesitate to restore it with the MSS. *in 1 Cor.* xii. 14, where Migne has *debent*, and *in 1 Cor.* xii. 28, where Migne has *non habet*. In another place, every MS. with which I have ever been acquainted is wrong, save one, the Monte Cassino MS. It is *in 1 Tim.* v. 13, where all read *proximitate* or *proximae* (Bened.) or something like it, but this makes no sense, the proper reading being *proxenetae* (match-makers): the scribes may be excused for not knowing this rare word. The whole passage is *Nuptiarum enim sunt proxenetae, multorum secretorum participes, adulatrices, seruorum querulae.*

List of Manuscripts of the Ambrosiaster Commentaries.[2]

Amiens 87 (saec. viii–ix) (Rom. 1, 2 Cor.) (Corbie).
Avranches 241 (saec. xii) (Rom., incomplete).

---

[1] Feuardent on Arnob. Iun. *Dial. with Serap.* (Migne liii) considers it a coinage of his, apparently.

[2] This list, which is much fuller than that in *Study of Ambrosiaster*,

Bamberg Bibl. 89 (B ii. 20) (saec. xi) (Col. Tit. 1, 2 Tim. Philem. Hebr. Rom. xvi. 19–end).

(Basle A ii. 42 (saec. xvi) (Hebr.).)

Bramshill House, England, iv (saec. xii).

Brussels 971 (5468) (saec. xii) (Gembloux).

   ,,   972 (9372) (saec. xii) (S. Laurence, Liége).

Chartres 34 (109) (saec. x ex.).

Cheltenham, Thirlestaine House, 518 (saec. xv in.).

Cologne xxxiv (saec. x) (Rom. 1, 2 Cor. Phil. 1, 2 Thess. Col. Tit. 1, 2 Tim. Philem. (to v. 22)).

Cologne xxxix (saec. ix) (Rom.).

Florence Laur. plut. xiv dext. cod. 6 (412) (saec. xi) (+ Hebr.).

   ,,   ,,   plut. xv dext. cod. 2 (saec. xi).

   ,,   ,,   Leop. Med. Fesul. cod. xxiii (saec. xv) (Rom.).

   ,,   ,,   Ashb. 60 (saec. viii) (first five quaternions lost: Gal. Phil. Eph. 1, 2 Thess. Col. 1, 2 Tim. Philem. Tit.).

   ,,   Bibl. Centr. Naz. ii. i. 335 (Magl. Cl. xxxix, num. 97) (saec. xii) (Rom. and part of 1 Cor.).

Fulda Aa 18 (saec. x) (Weingarten and Constance).

   ,,   (59 (saec. ix) (Hebr.)).

Ghent 455 no. 129 (159) (saec. x) (1, 2 Cor. Gal. Eph. Phil. 1 Thess. Col. 2 Thess. 1, 2 Tim. Tit. Philem.) (Trèves).

Göttweig 42 (saec. xi–xii) (Rom. 1, 2 Cor. Phil. 1, 2 Thess. Col. Tit. 1, 2 Tim. Philem.).

Ivrea 57 (xliii) (saec. xii).

Karlsruhe Aug. cviii (saec. ix) (Rom. 1, 2 Cor.) (Reichenau).

   ,,   Aug. xcvii (saec. ix in.) (Gal. Eph. Phil. 1, 2 Thess. Col. Tit. 1, 2 Tim. Philem. (Reichenau).

Laon 107 (saec. ix) (Rom.).

Le Mans 229 (saec. xi) (Gal. Eph. Phil. Col. 1, 2 Thess. 1, 2 Tim. Tit. Philem. (to v. 22)) (La Couture).

Leningrad : see Petrograd.

London, Burney 42 (saec. xii) (+ Hebr.) (somewhat mutilated).

   ,,   Harleian, 3063 (saec. viii–ix) (2 Cor. from i. 17–end) (Cues, perhaps Corbie).

pp. 14 ff., has been compiled mainly from the catalogues; the places indicated in brackets are the earlier or original homes of the manuscripts. Where no contents are specified, it is presumed that the set of commentaries is complete.

Monte Cassino 150 (346-242) (saec. vi) (Rom. iii. 9-end, 1, 2 Cor. Gal. Phil. Eph. 1, 2 Thess. Tit. Col. 1, 2 Tim. Philem. (to v. 17)) (Lucullanum near Naples).

Monza $\frac{c-2}{62}$ (saec. ix-x) (+Hebr.).

Munich 6262 (Fris. 65) (saec. xii?) (Freising).

,,   17043 (Scheftl. 43) (saec. x) (Rom.) (Schleftlingen).

,,   27031 (saec. xv).

Orléans 85 (82) (saec. xi) (Rom. Hebr.) (Fleury).

,,   200 (177) (saec. xiii) (Rom.) (Fleury).

Oxford Bodl. 689 (2530) (saec. xii) (+Hebr.).

,,   ,,   756 (2526) (saec. xi) (Salisbury).

Padua Sant' Antonio (Scaff. v N. 94) (saec. ix) (Gal. Eph. Phil. 1, 2 Thess. Col. Tit. 1, 2 Tim. Philem. (to v. 22)).

Paris 1759 (saec. ix in.) (Rom. 1 Cor.).

,,   1760 (saec. x) (Rom.).

,,   1761 (saec. ix-x) (4 quaternions lost) Rom. (last part), 1, 2 Cor. Gal. Eph. Phil. 1, 2 Thess. Col. Tit. 1, 2 Tim. Philem.) (Verona?).

,,   1762 (saec. xii) (Rom.).

,,   1763 (saec. xiii).

,,   13339 (saec. ix) (Rom. 1, 2 Cor. (to xi. 21)).

Petrograd, F. v. 1, no. 17 (saec. xi) (S. Benignus, Dijon).

Rome, Vat. lat. 283 (saec. xi) (Rom.) (Florence).

,,   ,,   ,,   640 (saec. xv) (Gal. Eph. Phil. 1, 2 Thess. Col., Tit. 1, 2 Tim. Philem.).

,,   ,,   Pal. lat. 169 (saec. viii-ix) (1, 2 Cor.) (Lorsch).

,,   ,,   Urbin. lat. 39 (14) (saec. xv) (Rom.).

,,   Vallicell. D. 41.

,,   Basilicana D. 169 (saec. xi) (Rom.).

Rouen 151 (A 195; formerly 215) (saec. xii) (Jumièges) (Peter Lombard?).

St. Gall 101+100 (saec. ix-x) (Rom. 1, 2 Cor. Gal. Eph. Phil. 1, 2 Thess. Col. Tit. 1, 2 Tim. Philem. (down to v. 22)).

,,   330 (saec. ix) (Gal. Eph. Phil. 1, 2 Thess. Col. Tit. 1, 2 Tim. Philem.).

St. Mihiel 16 (saec. x) (Rom.).

Salzburg (saec. ix).

Toulouse 154 (I. 7) (saec. xiii ex.) (Albi?).

Tours 298 (saec. xii) (1 Cor. &c. + Hebr.) (Marmoutier).

Trèves 122 (saec. viii–ix) (Rom.).

Troyes 128 (saec. xii) (Clairvaux).

    ,,   432 (saec. ix–x) (1, 2 Cor. (Col. was before Tit.) Tit. Philem.) (bibl. Bouhier).

    ,,   485 (saec. xi–xii) (Clairvaux).

(,,   785 (saec. xvii) (variae lectiones on 1, 2 Cor. from an ancient MS. of Church of St. Paul, Besançon) (Bibl. Bouhier).

Turin Pas. Lat. cciii (I. i. 5) (saec. xv).

Vendôme 30 (saec. xiii) (Rom. to xvi. 11).

(,,   129 (saec. xii) (Hebr.).)

Verona lxxv (saec. ix) (Gal. Eph. Phil. 1, 2 Thess. Col. Tit. 1, 2 Tim. Philem.).[1]

Vienna 550 (saec. x) (1 Cor. extracts).[2]

    ,,   743 (saec. viii–ix) (Rom.).

    ,,   4600 (saec. xv) (Rom. Hebr.).

Vitry-le-François 2 (saec. xii) (extracts apparently)[2] (Trois-Fontaines).

WOLFENBUETTEL (saec. vi) (Rom. fragments).[3]

Zwettl 33 (saec. xii).

MSS. of Claudius of Turin on the Epistles of St. Paul.[4]

(1, 2 Thess. and 1, 2 Tim. in these MSS. appear to be unaltered Ambrosiaster.)

Monte Cassino 48 (saec. xi in.).

Orléans 88 (85) (saec. ix) (Fleury).

Paris 2394 A (saec. x) (Auxerre).

Hatto MS.[4]

Vercelli 40 (xxxix) (saec. x).

---

[1] Related to Monte Cassino 150 and Paris 1761; Corssen, *Epistula ad Galatas* (Berol. 1885), p. 36.

[2] A good many other MSS. contain extracts, but I have not recorded them.

[3] See Tischendorf, *Anecdota Sacra et Profana* (Lips. 1855), p. 154; Jülicher, *Theol. Lit. Ztg.* xliii. (1918), 71.

[4] See A. Souter, *Pelagius's Expositions*, &c., vol. i (Cambr. 1922), p. 330 f.

The Biblical Text. Much time has been devoted by Ziegler, Corssen, and myself to the study of the Old-Latin forms of the Epistles of St. Paul, and among them the text used by Ambrosiaster as the basis of his commentary. At the time of the publication of the sixth chapter of the *Study*, I was under no illusion as to the permanence and value of the details presented there. I did all that was possible for me, aided by Father Brewer, to present the text as accurately as I could, with the critical material at my disposal. I did not then know, and Father Brewer himself perhaps did not know, that only MSS. of the third edition gave the correct biblical text. It is therefore all the more gratifying to me that I now see the method to have been sound on the whole. I did at least distrust Vulgate readings, where others were present in the MSS., and the chapter, planned as it was by the greatest New Testament textual critic of our time, was commended by another authority, the only reviewer who paid real attention to it, in most flattering terms. The method adopted was a double one. First, the text was tested for Africanisms, by collating it along with all Cyprian's quotations in the *Testimonia*, on to the Latin side of Claromontanus (*d*). Second, it was tested for Europeanisms, by comparing it in all passages where Lucifer's text was extant, on to the Vulgate. Finally, in each apparatus readings which agreed with the Vulgate and *d* respectively against the text adopted for collation purposes, were marked with *vg.* and d_2. The result of this minute study was to show that our text has travelled far from Cyprian's form, and yet seems to have the same ultimate root : it is, however, reasonably close to Lucifer's form, which is identical with d_2. If Cyprian's is the earliest text, it underwent a serious revision to become the arche-type of Lucifer's and Ambrosiaster's, which are probably to be looked on as sister texts. Some may prefer to con-sider Ambrosiaster's a cultured daughter of Lucifer's.

I have always fancied that Ambrosiaster adopted an existing text as the basis of his commentary. It seemed to me that this assumption was the basis of every investigation of it. I was therefore not a little surprised to read in the Commentary on the Thessalonian Epistles, published in 1909 by Von Dobschütz, great in textual criticism as in every other department of New Testament study, the view (p. 52) that 'the three Latin commentaries (Theodore, Ambst., Pelag.) have importance to begin with in virtue of the fact that *they independently translate the Greek text*, and, in particular circumstances, avail themselves of the original also, where they give Old-Latin translations as the basis'. It has always seemed to me that we could recover by textual criticism of the MSS. of Ambst. not a translation which he had made from the Greek, but an Old-Latin codex like *d* or *g*, though not identical with either. Perhaps Von Dobschütz is only speaking loosely, but if not, I would ask how he explains the fact that hardly any readings of Ambst., reliably attested, are absent both from *d* and from *g*. An interesting agreement of reading rather than rendering is shared with D G 88 *dg*, D and R (of vg) Sedul. in 1 Cor. xiv, where verses 34 and 35 appear, not in their usual place, but after verse 40 at the end of the chapter: it is interesting to observe that *m*, which is extant here, does not agree: so that apparently it is only one stratum of the Old Latin which has this peculiarity. An agreement with *g* and Pelag. alone occurs in Col. ii. 18, *extollens se.* In a word, as we saw in dealing with Victorinus, the text used by Ambst. is an European text, perhaps specifically a Milanese text—as Berger would have it, though I cannot think the evidence adequate to establish certainty—of the Epistles of St. Paul, a sister text to that of Victorinus, and belonging to the same class as *d* and *g*: in other words, that type which was readiest to hand in Italy when Jerome set out to make his revision.

The Gospel Text. The quotations from the Gospel harmonize to a considerable extent with the text of *b* (Codex Veronensis); e.g. Lc. xxiv. 13, *cleofas et ammaus* is the order of *b*, and *b* only amongst MSS. Ambst. is not an exact quoter in incidental citations, and his text would have to be compared throughout with all extant O.L. MSS. for more definite data to be given. This task I have never been able to perform in full. I have, however, noted points shared with *ff₂*. In brief, it is the sort of text Burkitt conceives to have been behind the Vulgate revision in the Gospel.[1] Note that Mt. xiii. 17 (*Quaest.*, p. 380) agrees with *e* exactly.

Text of Acts. Here absolute certainty has been reached. Ambst. used a text identical throughout with *gigas* (saec. xiii, at Stockholm). This text was also used by Lucifer and Niceta of Remesiana. There is evidence that Jerome also possessed a codex of this type, though according to Wordsworth and White Jerome did not adopt this, but a different type, as the basis of his revision: to his disadvantage, as the same scholars believe.

Apocalypse. About the text of this part of the New Testament not much can be said, but it is interesting to call attention to the group *gig.* Ambst. Priscill. which join in reading *aeramento turino* as the rendering of χαλκολιβάνῳ against all other authorities known to me in i. 15. Apoc. xiv. 4 (*in 2 Cor.* xi. 2) agrees almost exactly with Primasius' form, having the three agreements *coinquinauerunt*, *permanserunt*, and *uadit*, but there is not the same agreement in the case of the long quotation Apoc. ii. 12-26, 29, which is exhibited in the *Study*, p. 209 f. There the text looks distinctly European; and it may be that Ambst. used an African or Spanish text in his earlier writings, and an European-Italian in his later.[2]

---

[1] Cf. *Study*, 205-7.

[2] See also H. J. Vogels, *Untersuchungen zur Geschichte der lateinischen Apokalypse-Übersetzung* (Düsseldorf, 1920), pp. 230 ff., &c.

Ambst. was, in fact, acquainted with variants in MSS.
On Gen. ii. 7 he speaks of *aliqui codices* (*Quaest.*, p. 425).
On Rom. v. 14 he knows the text both with and without
the negative (so some cursives, *d*, codd. ap. Aug., Orig.).
His appeal against the Greek to the Latin textual authorities in that same verse is well known. He holds that,
where there is disagreement between the Latin of his day,
backed by quotations in Tert. Cypr. and Victorin., the
Greek MSS. have been corrupted, whereas those behind
the texts of those old Latin authors were pure. In other
words he is a declared champion of the Western text in
a pure form, and thus finds many to sympathize with him
to-day. At Rom. ix. 17 he gives variants *reseruaui* (unique),
suscitaui: Rom. xii. 11 *tempori* and *deo* (*domino*) ; 2 Cor.
v. 3 *induti* and *expoliati*: on Gal. ii. 1–2 he advocates the
absence of *et suffocato* in the Apostolic decree (Acts xv. 29) ;
at Gal. ii. 5 he defends the positive. Ambst. holds firmly
to his Latin text against the Greek.

The Character and Method of the Commentary. To
the testimony of Harnack and Jülicher to the character
of the work, already given, a much older testimony
may be added, that of Sixtus of Siena,[1] approved by
Richard Simon : ' breves quidem in uerbis, sed sententiae
pondere graves '. Simon says further : ' There are few
ancient commentaries on the Epistles of St Paul, or on
any part of the New Testament, that can be compared
with him.'

The commentary on each epistle is preceded by a short
argument, giving some account of the community or
person addressed in it, and of its purpose. These prologues, at least in some cases, for example, that to
Philippians, show, like those of Victorinus, use of the
Marcionite prologues, but they are much longer than
these, and much more interesting. The mention of the

---

[1] *Bibl. Sancta*, lib. 4 ; Simon, p. 134.

Symmachiani in the prologue to Galatians suggests that Victorinus was used there : we have seen that he refers to them in his work on that epistle. Owing to a loss of leaves already referred to, most Ambrosiaster MSS. contain the Pelagian prologue to 2 Corinthians instead of the Ambrosiaster prologue, first published in 1902.

In the commentary proper he gives us generally one verse (sometimes two or three) of his Old-Latin copy of the Apostle, and follows this immediately with his note. The comment is generally at least twice as long as the verse commented on, sometimes much longer. Yet it may be said that he is brief, especially if compared with the long-winded Greek commentators : he judiciously avoids the long digressions which are characteristic of them. He does not quit his text. The treatment of the shorter epistles is relatively longer than that of the longer, especially in passages that are concerned with matters of church government.

He shows himself a thorough master of Scripture in the comments which he gives, though, as I think we have already remarked, he is not exact in his shorter quotations. His favourite texts have been collected in chap. iv of the *Study*. His theological views are those of all the churches of his time : in other words he is an orthodox Trinitarian. He follows the ordinary custom of his day, which was to establish the doctrine of the Church on the occasion of certain passages. Concurrently, he refutes the heretics. Those especially mentioned are Photinians, Arians, Cataphrygians (i. e. Montanists), Novatians, Donatists (in the European form *Donatiani*), Manicheans, Marcionites, Symmachians. His theology has some connexion with that afterwards held by Pelagians, but this might be said of almost every earlier catholic writer : Pelagius was in part unjustly attacked. The allegorical method is almost entirely absent. What chiefly attracts us is that Ambrosiaster had a real idea of historical method and of development. He affirms the original identity of bishop and presbyter. He recognizes the difference between the organization of the churches in his own time and that in apostolic times: he tells us more than once that there were not bishops in all places as yet in those times. He is also very suggestive on the early history of the Church of Rome. Probably no other commentator, Greek or Latin, realizes so clearly the attitude of the Jews to Paul and of Paul to the Jews: he is throughout alive to this aspect of St Paul's teaching. There is an independence and an originality about his comments. He is antagonistic to Greek authorities. Frequently we feel a kind of 'saeva indignatio' bursting out, in somewhat unlikely places, as if he were a man that had a special grievance. Schwierholz[1] has tried to correlate these passages with the history of Isaac, and not altogether unconvincingly, though imagination must not get too much rein here. We shall be on safer ground when we see how far these passages are special to particular editions of the commentaries. Of the authors used, Tertullian, Cyprian, and Victorinus of Pettau are mentioned. There is evident use of all three in the *Quaestiones*. Also he knows apocryphal literature: on 1 Cor. ii. 9, the well-known quotation "Things which eye saw not, and ear heard not", &c., is attributed to 'the Apocalypse of Elijah among the apocryphal writings'. Simon Magus' ability to fly (*in Rom.* viii. 38 f.) no doubt comes from some 'Clementine' writing. The apocryphal book about Jamnes and Mambres was known to him (*in 2 Tim.* iii. 8-9): also the *Acts of Paul* (see Schmidt's 2 Ausg., p. 157) and the *Acts of Peter* (p. 141 f.). The note on Rom. xvi. 11 about Narcissus, to the effect that 'in aliis codicibus'

---

[1] *Ambrosiaster-Studien* (Breslau, 1909), pp. 71 ff.

K

he is called a 'presbyter', is from the *Actus Petri cum Simone*, c. 3 (p. 48, l. 7, ed. Lipsius, 1891); that on 2 Tim. ii. 18, 'alia scriptura' about Hymeneus and Filetus, refers to the *Acts of Paul (and Thecla)*[1] (cf. Lipsius, p. 245, l. 4) and those on 2 Tim. i. 15 and iv. 14 are from the same, cc. 1, 4, (Lipsius, p. 235, 3-4 and 238, 4). According to Brewer, also, he has used on 1 Tim. iii. 12-13 the letters of Pope Siricius,[2] though that place has a remarkable likeness to a passage in the letters of Pope Innocent (Coustant, pp. 789 ff.), which would reverse the obligation. Again, Otto Lang in his analysis of the Vatican Greek Catena on First Corinthians (Gr. 762) (Leipzig, 1909), pp. vi-vii, signalizes a number of passages which have some connexion with the material present in Ambst. The authors concerned are Chrysostom[3] and Theodoret.[4] As Latin works were not often translated into Greek, it may be that we have in this catena some of the Greek material used by Ambst. Origen may be a source of all three. It is absolutely certain, too, that our author made use of the works of his greatest contemporary, Hilary of Poitiers, and this makes Augustine's mistake excusable. I cannot as yet produce a passage from the commentaries, but the following from the *Quaestiones* are entirely convincing. *Quaest.* cxxii. 371, 11 *humana eloquia* non sunt idonea *ad res explicandas diuinas* is almost exactly (actually six words out of nine) from Hilary (*De Trin.* Migne, x. 97 c), and again *Quaest.* cxxv, p. 385, 3 *inferior natura* quid in *potiore* sit nescit is from Hil. *de syn.* vi. 19 (495 B) neque enim aliquando *inferior natura* superioris a se *potiorisque* naturae uirtutem consequitur. I have noted, besides, some half-a-dozen in-

---

[1] It is now known that the widely circulated *Acts of Paul and Thecla* is an extract from the *Acts of Paul*.

[2] See *Thes. Ling. Lat.* s.v. *deseruitio*, and compare with *cod. Casin.* of Ambst., which reads *deseruitionis* (Migne *ministerii*).

[3] 199 A 3-5: almost word for word Chr.

[4] 241 D 2-6: Thdrt. very close.

teresting expressions, which I have found both in Hilary and in Ambst.

Features of the Commentary. There are several very distinct kinds of illustration employed by our author. A large number are derived from Government and Law. I have found such in Tertullian (*bapt.* 11), in the Clementine Homilies, and in Ambrose (in *ps.* i, § 13 ; cxviii. *10*, 25, 4), but they do not appear to be common in any other author. The Imperator and his subordinates, who are often coupled with him, may conveniently come first. The interesting alternatives *rex* and *regnum Romanum* also occur. It was not apparently till the fourth century that the Roman antipathy to these terms was got over :[1] we find them in Symmachus and Claudian. 'Among the Romans the *reges* are called Augusti' (p. 144 A Migne). In the prologue to Second Thessalonians he speaks of the 'abolitio regni Romani'. 'Astrologers and natural philosophers excuse themselves for neglect of God, by saying that they use the stars and elements as stepping-stones to Him, just as people obtain an audience of the *rex* through the *comites*. No one is so senseless as to claim that the *comes* should receive the honour due to the *rex* : any who attempted to confer it would justly be condemned for treason.' 'People have to see the *tribuni* and *comites* first, because the King is a mere man, and does not know to whom he ought to entrust state business. To win *God's* favour, one has no need of a helper' (60 D, 61 A). 'The bust of the *Imperator* has authority in his absence, not in his presence' (456 A). 'The armour of the Christian bears the devices of his *Imperator*' (334 B). 'The *Imperator* must have an army: it is a part of his body, having in front of it *tribuni, comites, and magistri*: to all of these the soldiers are inferior' (261 C).

---

[1] The emperor was sometimes called βασιλεύς in Greek ; cf. Synesius, *De Regno*, c. 19. See also Svennung, *Orosiana* (Uppsala, 1922), p. 163 f.

The apostles are the *uicarii* of Christ (210 B, 328 C, 334 A): a bishop is *uicarius* of the Lord (254 A). On 314 B it is asked whether God was in Christ 'quasi in uicario aut legato'. The apostles are the *legati* of Christ (263 A). The man, in relation to the woman, is the *legatus* of Christ (273 B). 'It is custom and law to do no violence to the *legati* of men : how presumptuous and bold it is to inflict not only violence but death on the *legati* of God' (425 A). 'Seeing we cannot reciprocate all God's kindnesses, let us at least faithfully and earnestly carry out his *legatio* (i. e. the duty of his representatives)'[1] (513 D). '*Iuris consulti* or *pontifices, quos uocant sacerdotes*, have decreed fixed days on which cases are to be tried' (214 A). *Fiscalia* or 'imperial dues' are mentioned on 172 A : 'ideo dicit "tributa" praestari, uel quae dicuntur *fiscalia*, ut subiectionem praestent.'

The references to Law in general or to particular statutes are unusually frequent. These would not so much surprise us in apologetic works, but their presence in a commentary must be due to special knowledge of, and interest in, law on the part of the writer. Further, if one may say so, the language is rather that of the *aduocatus* or barrister than that of the *iuris consultus* or solicitor. It runs the whole gamut of legal procedure, from the decision of the magistrate that there is a case, up to the declaration of the verdict and even to the revision of a judgement and the recall of a sentence (for the words used cf. *Study*, p. 178, and note that *reum tenere, reum constituere*, and *sententiam reuocare* are all quoted in the *Vocabularium Iurisprudentiae*, vol. v). Cumont feels no doubt that the author had studied law, and suggests that perhaps he had even occupied some public position before becoming a doctor of the Church. We may remember in this connexion that Isaac pro-

---

[1] The authority of *uicarii* of *praefecti* lapses in the absence of these *praefecti* (456 A).

secuted Damasus on a capital charge in the public courts, and that Evagrius was obviously intimate with court procedure. In *Quaest.* 124, § 6, there is a very interesting passage about the relative merit of devotion to study— presumably legal studies—on the part of a rich and a poor man. In 366 A, B he enumerates adulterers, homicides, perjurers, thieves, sorcerers, and other criminals as punishable by *leges Romanae*, and then points out that the idolatry, blood, and fornication of the Apostolic Decree are crimes unknown to Roman Law. The *leges Romanae* excuse fornication (64 C). He cites (521 B) an edict of Diocletian against the Manicheans, otherwise known only from the Pseudo-Ambrosian *Mosaicarum et Romanarum legum collatio*, which, as we have seen, may be a product of this very author. On p. 110 D he says, ' The Romans therefore know Law, because they are not barbarians : but they grasped natural righteousness partly of themselves, partly from the Greeks : for laws were brought to the Romans from Athens (reference to the xii Tables no doubt), just as to the Greeks from the Hebrews ' (cf. also 185 D). ' A judge must not sit on the left' (458 A). 1 Cor. vi. 6 is rightly explained, as by Ramsay,[1] thus : ' " infideles" aut arbitros, ut adsolet fieri, postulatos significat, aut iudicem publicum, cui dici solet : Hodie dies sacrorum est, ius dici non potest '. On 461 A, 'use of wine was unknown to Roman women in early days, just as that of water is now : such power had the authority of discipline '. On 144 C the use of the corpses of criminals by physicians in early times is mentioned, as a means of ascertaining the causes of diseases and thus profiting the living. On 392 A we hear the principle enunciated : 'ubi holographa manus est, falsum dici non potest.' The note on 1 Tim. iii. 12–13 well illustrates his interest in ecclesiastical law.

But the author appears also to have had a special

---

[1] *Expositor* for 1900, i, pp. 278 ff.

interest in the principles behind law and legal institutions, such as is very rare, if not unique, in his period. Dr. A. J. Carlyle, in his *History of Mediaeval Political Theory in the West*, vol. i (1903), is the first who has given him the credit he deserves. In the commentary on Colossians (iv. 1):

> 'Masters must not forget that God created, not slaves and free, but all free-born. "Slavery is the consequence of man's sin. Man making war upon his fellow-man, makes free-born men captives, and chance determines whether those are to remain slaves or to be redeemed. Before God the *sinner* is the slave: Ham is an example of this, and the ancient writers who maintain that the wise were free and the foolish slaves, really recognized this principle. Masters must remember that their lordship extends only over the body; they have no authority over the mind. God only is the master of that: let them remember this, and only exact just service from their slaves, who are still their equals, not to say their brethren.'[1]

Some of the references previously given will serve as a further illustration. He is interested, too, in the relation of natural law to the Mosaic law, and in the question of woman's relation to man. On the latter subject he frequently states that 'Man is the image of God, but not woman', basing his view on the Pauline statements that the husband is head of the wife, and must not veil his head, because he is the image of God, while the wife must veil hers. This is taken as a proof of the inferiority of the latter and the impossibility of her likeness to God. That man and woman are nevertheless of one substance is not denied.[2]

The author is very emphatic against *Astrology*. Astrologers, spoken of usually as *scrutatores siderum*, but also technically as *mathematici*, are coupled occasionally with the *sophistae Graecorum*, the natural philosophers, scientists,

---

[1] Carlyle, p. 113 f.   [2] *Study*, p. 152.

or pseudo-scientists of the day. A *conquisitor saeculi* (199 A) is defined as 'one who thinks that the universe is managed by conjunctions of stars (or horoscopes), and that births and deaths are decreed by calculations connected with the zodiac'. Again, natural law is a better teacher than 'cursus siderum' and 'calculi signorum' (207 A). On 456 B (*in Col.* ii. 18, 19) they are *puffed up*, examining the movement of the stars, which he (St. Paul) calls *angels*. On 200 D those who examine and observe the movements of the stars are referred to. 'They assign all power to the stars, being enslaved to a carnal view' (452 D). Those who scrutinize the courses of the moon are mentioned on 381 B. The *sapientia carnis* of Rom. viii. 7 is defined as 'in the first place, astrological learning, an invention of men, and second a delight in visible things'. Again (451 C), unbelievers are blind to the fact that all 'sapientia et scientia' is in Christ, because they do not read of 'astrologia' in the Gospels, &c. As I have said, the *sophistae Graecorum* or *sophistae (sapientes) mundi* are simultaneously attacked (282 C, cf. 366 A, B).

He draws illustrations also from *Pagan Religion.* On p. 239 B, 'the pagans call the sun and the moon and the other heavenly bodies the gods of heaven: on the earth they call Apollo, Aesculapius, Hercules, and Minerva gods and lords'. The veiling of the eyes before the pagan mysteries is attacked (271 B), those aimed at being especially those of Mithras: 'apud paganos quibus uelantur oculi, ne quae "sacra" uocant perspicientes, uariis se uanitatibus cernant inludi' (271 B); again he speaks in almost the same terms of the way the pagans are tricked: 'pagani in tenebris mystica sua celebrantes in speleo uelatis oculis inluduntur' (418 B). The worship of the Magna Mater is especially attacked in the following passage (110 A): 'sententia paganorum turpis et foeda est, maxime quae in Phrygia inuenta est, in qua nisi spurcus intersit, sacra-

mentum mutum est et torpescit religio.' Ventriloquism
and the Sibyl are also alluded to (206 B, C). Roman festivals
are referred to on 381 B (*in Gal.* iv. 10): "Ye observe days
and months and seasons and years." 'Those observe
days who say for example: "We must not set out
to-morrow, for nothing should be begun the day after
to-morrow"; and so they are wont to be the more deceived.
These again worship months, who examine the courses of
the moon, saying, for instance: "On the seventh day after
the new moon, tools (or perhaps 'documents') ought not
to be completed"; again: "On the ninth day after the
new moon, you ought not to bring home a slave you have
bought, for instance": and in this way misfortunes are
wont to occur more easily. And they observe seasons
thus, when they say: "To-day is the beginning of spring:
it is a day of rejoicing" (i. e. Hilaria, 25 March): "after
to-morrow it is the Vulcanalia" (23 Aug.); and again they
speak thus: "It is the day after; we must not leave home."
They worship years, when they say: "On the first of
January it is a new year", as if years were not completed
every day: but to keep up the memory of the well-known
Janus with his two faces, they indulge this superstition,
which ought to be far removed from the servants of God.'
Sacred rites (of Mithras) in which one imitated the voice
of a crow and flapped one's arms like a bird's wings are
mentioned on p. 61 C. The worship of Apis and of birds
is alluded to in the same place.

Specially interesting are the references to *the Jews*, and
an exhaustive treatment of these would form an excellent
subject for a paper, which should if possible be written by
a Jew. It is in fact much to be desired that some learned
Jew should make a careful study of the works of the
Ambrosiaster. (It may be mentioned that Isaac finds no
place in the *Jewish Encyclopaedia*.) I can only give a certain
number of the references here. Those in the *Quaestiones* will

be found from my index, pp. 517–18. The writer is interested primarily in the Mosaic Law, but also in the customs of the synagogue and the position of the Jews in the world. His attitude is different from that of other authors who, like him, made the Jews the subject of a polemic. In the commentaries he has the insight to see where Jews are meant, though not explicitly mentioned, and shows from time to time that customs of the synagogue have been taken over by the Church. ' The name *Judaei* dates from the time of Judas Maccabaeus' (58 B). Romans, chap. vii, verse 5, " uitia peccatorum quae per legem ostenduntur" is meant as an attack on the Jews: chap. ix, verses 11 to 13, also refers to them; cf. on verse 28. ' Not a few of the Jews have believed' (155 A). He wrongly confines the reference in the ' altar' of First Corinthians (ix. 13) to Jews, while the ' temples' refer to Gentiles. 1 Cor. ix. 20: "to them that are under the law" is ingeniously referred to the Samaritans:[1] ' legem enim solam accipiunt, id est, quinque libros Moysi.' The ' doctores' of 1 Cor. xii. 28 are defined as those ' qui in ecclesia litteris et lectionibus retinendis (memorizing) pueros imbuebant more synagogae'. 1 Cor. xiv. 30-1, " but if a revelation be made to another sitting by, let the first keep silence, for ye all can prophesy one by one, that all may learn, and all may be comforted", are explained thus: ' this is the tradition of the synagogue which he wishes us to follow, because he is writing of course to Christians, but to Gentile converts, not to former Jews, that they should speak seated, the older men by virtue of their office on chairs, the next in age on benches, and the youngest on the pavement on mats.' (With this passage cf. Philo ii. 458 Mangey, cited by Hort on *James* ii. 2.) Some of the false apostles of 2 Cor. ii. 17 had a zeal for the *traditio Iudaica*. ' Them that are perishing' (2 Cor.

---

[1] This interpretation is found already in Origen: see A. Souter, *Pelagius's Expositions*, vol. i, p. 182, n. 1.

iv. 3) are especially Jews. The long note on Gal. iii. 17-18 may be commended as an excellent example of the author's method. The 'magistri' of Eph. iv. 11 are defined almost exactly as the 'doctores' of 1 Cor. xii. 28, but it is mentioned that the tradition of the Jews in the teaching of children has fallen into disuse among Christians through neglect. In Phil. i. 13 'praetorium' is strangely interpreted as 'Iudaismus', and the 'ceteri omnes' as 'uniuersae ecclesiae gentium'. He is interested in the derivation of *Hebraei*, and several times derives it from *Habraham*, through a postulated intermediate form *Habraei*: he is no better and no worse a philologist than his contemporaries. On Col. ii 16-17 he tells us that the Jews attack the Christians for disdaining to have anything to do with their festivals, or their new moons, or their sabbaths, which they pass in ease, banqueting, and luxury. The opponents of Paul's Gospel in 1 Tim. i. 3-4 are Jews, who will perhaps give the people a delight in the fables the Jews are accustomed to relate about their own origins, Abraham, Isaac, and the other patriarchs, and about circumcision and the law of Moses. On Titus iii. 9 they are stigmatized for pluming themselves on the origin of the patriarchs, when from this they can have no merit with God. And on the same place he makes a reference derived from some apocryphal book, as already hinted. 'Certain Jews', he says, 'had the view that the burial of Moses was concealed, lest he should be called up by sorcerers . . . and that Solomon was helped in the building of the temple by a great host of demons.' The note on First Timothy, chapter v, verse 1, is particularly interesting: 'apud omnes utique gentes honorabilis est senectus, unde et synagoga et postea ecclesia seniores habuit, quorum sine consilio nihil agebatur in ecclesia: quod qua neglegentia obsoleuerit nescio, nisi forte doctorum (the bishops) desidia, aut magis superbia, dum soli uolunt aliquid uideri.' He carefully distinguishes

Jews who have become Christian from those who do not
yet believe (140 c–d), and does not permit Christians who
have come from paganism to insult the children of Israel
(160 A). He proclaims the superiority of converted Jews
to Christians converted from paganism: this superiority is
due to the virtue of Abraham and the other patriarchs
(69 c, 70 c, 75 A, 76 B, c). Twice he declares that it is not
the Jews who confess Christ that are apostate, but those
who deny that Messiah has come, clearly predicted, as he
is, in the Old Testament (75 A, 146 c).

A few further passages illustrating the character of his
exegesis may now be given. Those who know the author
best are most likely to appreciate the value of his contributions. The more he is studied the more this appears.
Some of the following have already been cited by Simon:

Rom. i. 13. Unde dixit 'uocatis sanctis': quid tamen est
'uocatis sanctis'? Si enim iam sancti sunt, quo modo uocantur
ut sanctificentur? Sed hoc ad dei pertinet praescientiam, quia
quos scit deus futuros sanctos, iam apud illum sancti sunt, et
uocati permanent.

Rom. i. 24. 'Tradere' autem est permittere, non incitare aut
immittere ut ea quae in desideriis conceperant, adiuti a diabolo
explerent in opere: nec enim possent huius modi bonum cogi-
tatum habere.

Rom. v. 12. 'Mors' autem dissolutio corporis est, cum
anima a corpore separatur. Est et alia mors, quae 'secunda'
dicitur, in gehenna, quam non peccato Adae patimur, sed eius
occasione propriis peccatis adquiritur: a qua boni inmunes sunt
tantum, quod in inferno erant, sed superiore, quasi in libera.

Rom. viii. 28 "qui secundum propositum uocati sunt". Hoc
dicit quia diligentes deum ac si inperite precati fuerint, non illis
oberit quia propositum cordis illorum sciens deus et ignauiam,
non illis imputat quae aduersa postulant, sed ea adimet (pres.) quae
danda sunt deum amantibus... Hi ergo secundum propositum uocantur, quos credentes praesciit deus futuros sibi idoneos, ut ante
quam crederent scirentur. Note 'propositum' of men, not God.

Rom. viii. 29, 30. "Quos praesciit et praedestinauit." Istos

quos praesciit futuros deuotos, sibi ipsos eligit ad promissa
praemia capessenda, ut hi qui credere uidentur et non permanent in fide coepta, a deo electi negentur, quia quos deus
elegit apud se permanent. est enim qui ad tempus eligitur, sicut
Saul et Iudas, non de praescientia, sed de praesenti iustitia.
"Conformes fieri imaginis filii sui." Hoc dicit, quia ideo prae-
destinantur in futurum saeculum, ut similes fiant filio dei, sicut
supra memoraui. "Ut sit ipse primogenitus in multis fratribus."
Recte 'primogenitus', quia ante omnem creaturam non factus
sed natus est; ad cuius exemplum deus homines in filios sibi
adoptare dignatus est. est et 'primogenitus' in regeneratione
spiritus. est et 'primogenitus' ex mortuis, uicta morte ascendens
in caelos. 'primogenitus' igitur in omnibus frater noster dicitur,
quia homo dignatus est nasci: dominus uero est quia deus noster
est, sicut dicit propheta Hieremias: *hic deus noster.* "Quos
autem praedestinauit, illos et uocauit." 'Vocare' est cogitantem
de fide adiuuare, aut compungere eum quem sciat audire. "Et
quos uocauit, ipsos et iustificauit; quos autem iustificauit, hos
et magnificauit." Hoc dicit quod supra, quia quos praesciit deus
aptos sibi, hi credentes permanent, quia aliter fieri non potest
nisi quos praesciit deus, ipsos et iustificauit, ac per hoc et magnificauit illos, ut similes fiant filio dei. de ceteris quos non praesciit
deus, non est illi cura in hac gratia, quia non praesciit. ac
si credant aut eligantur ad tempus, quia uidentur boni, ne
iustitia contempta uideatur, non permanent ut magnificentur,
sicut et Iudas Scarioth, aut illi LXXII, qui electi, post scandalum
passi, recesserunt a saluatore.

Rom. ix. 5 . . . "Christus secundum carnem, qui est super
omnia benedictus in saecula: amen" de saluatore dicit . . .
quando enim nulla paterni nominis fit mentio, et de Christo
sermo est, non potest differri, ne deus dicatur . . . siquis
autem non putat de Christo dictum, 'qui est deus', det personam de qua dictum est, &c., in the same vein.

Rom. ix. 11 an important note on God's foreknowledge.

Eph. iv. 11–12 on church offices, a subject greatly interesting
to Ambst. Let us quote a part of it:

Inter istos post episcopum plus esse intellegitur, qui propter
reseratum occultum scripturarum sensum profetare dicitur, prae-
sertim quia futurae spei uerba depromit, qui ordo nunc potest
esse presbyterii. nam in episcopo omnes ordines sunt, quia

primus sacerdos est, hoc est princeps sacerdotum, et propheta et euangelista et cetera adimplenda officia ecclesiae in ministerio fidelium. tamen post quam in omnibus locis ecclesiae sunt constitutae et officia ordinata, aliter composita res est quam coeperat. primum enim omnes docebant et omnes baptizabant, quibuscumque diebus uel temporibus fuisset occasio. nec enim Philippus tempus quaesiuit aut diem quo eunuchum baptizaret, neque ieiunium interposuit, neque Paulus et Sileas tempus distulerunt quo optionem carceris baptizarent cum omnibus eius, neque Petrus clericos habuit aut diem quaesiuit, quando Cornelium cum omni domo eius baptizauit, nec ipse, sed baptizare iussit fratribus qui cum illo ierant ad Cornelium ab Ioppe; adhuc enim praeter septem diaconos nullus fuerat ordinatus. ut ergo cresceret plebs et multiplicaretur, omnibus inter initia concessum est et euangelizare et baptizare et scripturas in ecclesia explanare: at ubi omnia loca circumplexa est ecclesia, conuenticula constituta sunt et rectores et cetera officia in ecclesiis sunt ordinata, ut nullus de clero auderet, qui ordinatus non esset, praesumere officium quod sciret non sibi creditum uel concessum. et coepit alio ordine et prouidentia gubernari ecclesia, quia si omnes eadem possent, inrationabile esset, et uulgaris res et uilissima uideretur. hinc ergo est unde nunc neque diaconi in populo praedicant, neque clerici uel laici baptizant, neque quocumque die credentes tinguntur nisi aegri. ideo non per omnia conueniunt scripta apostoli ordinationi quae nunc in ecclesia est, quia haec inter ipsa primordia sunt scripta. nam et Timotheum presbyterum a se creatum 'episcopum' uocat (quia primi presbyteri 'episcopi' appellabantur), ut recedente eo sequens ei succederet. denique apud Aegyptum presbyteri consignant ('confirm'), si praesens non sit episcopus. sed quia coeperunt sequentes presbyteri indigni inueniri ad primatus tenendos, immutata est ratio, prospiciente Concilio ut non ordo, sed meritum crearet episcopum, multorum sacerdotum iudicio constitutum, ne indignus temere usurparet, et esset multis scandalum. in lege nascebantur sacerdotes ex genere Aaron leuitae; nunc autem omnes ex genere sunt sacerdotali, dicente Petro apostolo *quia estis* inquit *genus regale et sacerdotale*; ideoque ex populo potest fieri sacerdos. "In aedificationem corporis Christi." Ecclesiae ordinationem ad compaginationem humani generis in professionis unitate dicit compositam, ut diuersi dignitate in Christo omnes sint unum, unum caput habentes Christum, hoc est auctorem uitae.

Phil. ii. 10–12, one of the longest theological notes in the commentary.

The notes on the Pastoral Epistles are full of important observations on church government, which I think have not been hitherto adequately noticed in any published work except Professor C. H. Turner's contribution on 'The Organization of the Church', chapter vi, of *The Cambridge Mediaeval History*, vol. i, pp. 154 ff.

Ambrosiaster's Theology. A comprehensive work on the theology of Ambrosiaster will be written when the Commentaries are satisfactorily edited. A writer who influenced both Augustine and Jerome, not to speak of Pelagius and many another author, is not without importance from the theological point of view. And his importance in this regard is becoming increasingly recognized, as will be seen not only from general works like Harnack's *History of Dogma*, but also from special studies like those of Buonaiuti[1] and Mundle.[2] In this section a few of the more important topics will be briefly considered.

Ambrosiaster has not penetrated deeply into St. Paul's doctrine of Grace, but christological problems interest him greatly. Like many another he attaches great weight to Trinitarian teaching, and he is much influenced by the necessity to oppose such heretics as the Novatians and the Manicheans. For him, as for other orthodox writers of the fourth century, Christ is God: for example, in Romans ix. 5 'God, blessed for ever', God is identified with Christ, and in many another passage of St. Paul, where 'God' is mentioned, the comment says that Christ

[1] E. Buonaiuti, *La Genesi della dottrina agostiniana intorno al peccato originale* (Roma, 1916).

[2] W. Mundle, *Die Exegese der paulinischen Briefe im Kommentar des Ambrosiaster* (Inaug. Diss.) (Marburg in Hessen, 1919), pp. 71–94. To him I am very much indebted.

is meant. The identity of Father and Son is vigorously asserted, and Christ and the Spirit are also identical. His christology has almost a docetic ring. The power of God and Christ to suffer is minimized as much as possible, and the real humanity of Jesus is not understood by Ambrosiaster.

Yet Ambrosiaster cannot ignore the fact that Christ is in the Pauline system subordinated to God (cf. *in Rom.* viii. 34; *in 1 Cor.* xv. 24, 28). By the subordination of the passage in First Corinthians Christ in no way gives up his lordship: the Son will always rule with the Father, but he is *deus de deo*, as the Nicene creed puts it, and the subordination of the Son to the Father is in no way to be compared with the subordination of created things to the Son. These utterances may have a polemical purpose, may in fact be directed against the Photinians, who are often named, but it is not possible for us definitely to say. The kenosis passage in the Epistle to the Philippians offers difficulties to Ambrosiaster. The exaltation of Christ he cannot understand, as according to him Christ lost nothing by taking on our humanity, and already possesses equality with God. He feels that the contrary belief would involve him in Arianism.

Ambrosiaster's teaching on the Trinity shows that he regarded the doctrine as the principal element in Christian belief, after the Godhead of Christ. It forms the contents of the *expositio fidei* communicated to the Thessalonians (*in 1 Thess.* iii. 9); it is the foundation of Christian teaching, which the Colossians should not abandon (*in Col.* ii. 6 f), and the substance of the hidden wisdom of which Paul treats in First Corinthians, chapter ii. Ambrosiaster finds reference to the Trinity in various unsuspected places. The 'secret of the Trinity' (*trinitatis mysterium, mysterium trinitatis*) is perhaps oftener referred to in him than in any other author.

If we turn to his understanding of Paul's doctrines of justification and redemption, it is instructive to observe how an exegete, who is as yet untouched by the great Pelagian controversy, views these momentous matters. He is relatively nearer to Pelagius than to Augustine. He has not grasped the idea that before God man must always be the receiver and the favoured, never the giver or benefactor. Ambrosiaster, like many another, is obsessed by the idea that we can acquire merit with God, and the associated idea that certain labours on our part are necessary to gain it.

By *fides* Ambrosiaster understands (*in 1 Cor.* xii. 3) the facts forming the content of belief, and not the belief itself. The 'righteousness of God' is shown in His keeping of his promise, but *in Rom.* iii. 31 very acutely seems to identify it with 'mercy'. Fulfilment of the Law is identified with belief, and this fact renders Ambrosiaster's exegesis of the Epistle to the Romans unsatisfactory. He distinguishes in fact three laws, divine law, natural law, and the law of deeds (this last from the Old-Latin translation of Gal. iii. 19), by which is meant the ceremonial law. He thus fails to understand the Apostle's argument. When he uses the expression *sola fide*, he, like other early writers, refers merely to the forgiveness of sin offered at baptism.[1]

He does not really understand the doctrine of justification by faith, as is clear from his comment that only *fides* can establish a *meritum* (*in Rom.* iii. 20; iv). Abraham's faith was all the more to his credit that he had been shown no miracle, and in his day most men were unbelievers. Belief becomes almost a work of supererogation.

Freedom from the law is thus considered to mean freedom from the ceremonial law. The comment on

---

[1] Loofs, *Leitfaden zum Studium der Dogmengeschichte* (ed. 4) (Halle a. S. 1906), p. 387: cf. also Buonaiuti's treatise (cited p. 78, n. 1).

Rom. xiii. 9 is positively naïve: 'he who loves his
neighbour fulfils the law of Moses: the command to love
one's enemies *also*, belongs to the new law.' The Mosaic
Law, so far as its moral part is concerned, is still in full
force and is only excelled by the new law of Christ. 'All
things are lawful for me' (1 Cor. vi. 12) is thus weakened
to mean 'all things are lawful for me that are lawful for
my fellow-apostles'.

On the subject of sin Ambrosiaster seems to speak
with two voices. On the one hand writers on the history
of Christian dogma, like Harnack and Seeberg, are
perfectly justified in regarding him as a forerunner of the
Augustinian doctrine of inherited sin:[1] his famous note
on Romans v. 12 is quoted by Augustine himself. The
consequence of the Fall is bodily death—inherited guilt
seems to be once only spoken of (*in 1 Cor.* xi. 10)—and it
is certain that even in Ambrosiaster's view the Fall
developed fatal consequences for mankind. But he
frequently distinguishes between the first death and the
second death.[2] The second death is eternal damnation,
which is a punishment of personal sins, from which the
good are free. But even the *boni* live merely in the upper
part of hell. For the devil has obtained the power over
all the dead, and can hinder their resurrection to eternal
life (*in Rom.* v. 12; *in Col.* ii. 14). Thus the Law was given
by God to bring men back again into obedience to Himself,
and it has really fulfilled its purpose. The Jews come off,
therefore, very well in Ambrosiaster's system: all they
needed was forgiveness of sin.

As regards the flesh, he admits (*in Rom.* vii. 22) that it is
by inheritance that all flesh is subject to sin, but as he
denies that the soul is inherited, he nullifies his view of
inherited sin. The soul, according to him, remains

---

[1] Cf. also the treatise of Buonaiuti referred to above.
[2] *Study*, p. 155.

essentially unaffected by the corruption of human nature
that dwells in the flesh.   At Rom. vii. 25 the freedom of
the *animus* is expressly brought into prominence, and the
activity of the Holy Spirit is expressly confined to *co-*
operation.   The ' grace ' of Rom. vii. 25 is for him nothing
but the *lex fidei*.   The sinful corruption of man consists in
this, that he cannot resist the temptations of the flesh,
while the redeemed can resist them with the help of the
Holy Spirit.   Ambrosiaster has not grasped the idea of
a complete inward transformation.   The relation of flesh
and spirit is conceived by him predominantly as a difference
of degree, instead of that of two mutually exclusive
categories.   The sinful nature of the flesh is thus minimized,
and sin itself is put down to the devil's account.   With him
the devil takes the place of the Pauline *peccatum*, which
Paul himself conceives as half personal, half impersonal,
and yet Ambst. cannot emancipate himself altogether from
the Pauline teaching.

His attitude to this subject is made yet clearer by
his view of redemption and forgiveness.   Redemption and
forgiveness have absolutely nothing to do with one another.
Redemption means emancipation from the power of the
devil, while forgiveness of sins is God's work and gift,
which stands in no direct relation to Christ's death.
Redemption means that Christ has broken the devil's
power and has made resurrection possible for the souls
held fast by him in the underworld.   The devil and his
satellites acquired this power by making Adam sin.   This
power God does not seek to take away from the devil
by force.   He sends Christ on to the earth to preach
forgiveness of sins to men.   When the devil sees that the
object of Christ's preaching is to reconcile God and man,
he fears for his own supremacy, puts Christ to death
stupidly, from rage at His goodness, and thus becomes
guilty of the sin of murder, since Christ, as sinless, is not

subject to death. Christ can now, descending to the underworld, contend with him for the dominion over the dead, not only with power, but also with justice. By a battle which takes place in the underworld the dead are freed and can ascend to heaven.[1] Christ's death was not an act of God to ensure forgiveness of sins to men, but was merely permitted by Him. Christ's mediatorial work is viewed merely as the communication to men of the true knowledge of God and forgiveness of sins. Thus God and man were reconciled before his death, and redemption has to do, not with God, but with the devil.

Forgiveness of sin, bestowed by God on man, is communicated to the believer through baptism. Thus baptism and faith are combined in true Pauline fashion. The man thus inwardly changed in baptism is by this fact bound over to a moral change of life. Ambrosiaster is very fond of referring *gratia* to the forgiveness of sin in baptism, even if it be not absolutely restricted to this. The Spirit, however, does not appear as the all-working power, but He only helps man's action. Pauline mysticism is as it were materialized when our exegete defines the putting on of Christ as the being called Christian (*in Gal.* iii. 27). He is not clear on the question whether we have power to refrain from sin ; thus he stands about half-way between Pelagius, who positively asserts that we have, and Augustine who denies this. Deadly sins can be avoided by constant prayer (*in Eph.* vi. 18). From certain passages we see Ambrosiaster's acquaintance with the institution of penance in the early Church. Ambrosiaster does not, like Paul, regard the moral life as the necessary consequence of redemption. The new life of the Christian is taken always to mean the life beyond, the reward of the Christian

[1] A synthesis of the notes on Rom. iii. 24, viii. 3 ; 1 Cor. ii. 8, xv. 57 ; 2 Cor. v. 21 ; Gal. i. 4 ; Eph. v. 2 ; Col. ii. 14–15 ; 1 Tim. ii. 6–7 shows his attitude, briefly described above.

if he keeps himself pure from sin. The Holy Spirit is given to the Christian only when he is free from sin, which is an un-Pauline view. Ambrosiaster has a clear understanding, but he lacks the necessary religious experience to grasp the deeper truths of St. Paul. God's foreordaining is with him, as with Pelagius, weakened to mean foreknowledge. At Phil. ii. 13 he goes absolutely counter to the true sense in saying that God helps our good efforts; that it is ours to will, His to bring to pass!

Style and Language. The style of Ambrosiaster is in general plain, and even at times rough. There is no beauty and rarely any eloquence about it. It is fairly obvious that the author cannot have had what we should call a rhetorical training. This fact one gathers not only from a general impression, but also by a detailed method, which is now receiving the prominence it deserves. Prof. Watson has said in the course of a review [1] of the Vienna edition of the *Quaestiones* that the author was a foreigner, in other words a Greek, by birth, because he pays no attention to the rules for the composition of rhythmical prose. He has a very interesting vocabulary, being altogether more colloquial than cultivated contemporary writers. This will appear in the sequel. Some of his phrases and words may now be quoted, all of which occur also in the *Quaestiones*.

Scriptural quotations are introduced by *inter cetera ait*, &c., *hinc est unde . . . (ait) inquit, unde . . . ait (inquit)*. The present participle *dicens* is in such cases very common, in nom. or abl. case generally, also *teste* and *testante*. He seems never to have *infert* (Hier. Ps.-Hier., &c.)=Origen's ἐπιφέρει. Following a quotation we find *hoc dicit quia* (*quoniam*), *hoc dicit ut*, &c., explaining the import of quotations.

Some of the same features as were noted in Victorinus

---

[1] *Classical Review*, vol. xxiii (1909), p. 237.

are also to be noted here, almost in equal abundance, e. g. a pair of nouns or adjectives or adverbs almost synonymous, where one might be regarded as sufficient. The difference between the two authors lies in this, that Victorinus affects the doubling of verbs more than nouns, adjectives, and adverbs, while it is quite the other way with Ambrosiaster. The genitive of equivalence is another feature of Ambst. : *aemulatio zeli*, &c. : a similar use is found in Greek ; cf. Eusebius, vol. i (ed. Heikel), p. liii. A further feature of Ambst. is the use of the ablative absolute of personified abstract nouns, with the present participle of intransitive verbs : compare also the employment of another noun in apposition instead of the participle. Examples of the first use are : *dictante iustitia* (191 C), *paenitentia subsequente* (219 C) : of the other *teste uirtute* (a favourite expression), *teste conscientia sua* (137 C, suggested by Rom. ix. 1).

The use of particles is also quite distinctive : for example, the rare word *adubi* (= ubi), of which the *Thesaurus* gives a very defective account. It always goes with *autem* in Ambst. The *Thesaurus* has no examples from Ambst., though the word occurs fifteen times in his writings, —and none from Theod. Mops.-lat., though he has it five times. *Quid est ut* occurs in the sense of *quid est cur*, for which the nearest analogy I can find is *quid causae est ut* in Ambst., and also sporadically in Hier. and fairly often in Aug.[1] Reduplication of inferential particles, already referred to under Victorinus, is a characteristic (and it is none too common in Latin), especially *ideo ergo*. *Si quo minus*, a rather rare equivalent for 'but if not', εἰ δὲ μή, is not infrequent.[2] Ambst. seems to use it much oftener than

---

[1] Cf. *non est ut* Aug., *De nat. et orig. animae* i. 11 § 13 *bis* (see also p. 37 f. above).

[2] See now *Novum Testamentum S. Irenaei* (Oxford, 1923), p. cvii ; Koffmane, *Gesch. d. Kirchenlateins* (Breslau, 1879-81), p. 132 ; Burkitt, *The Old-Latin and the Itala*, pp. 41 ff. ; add Tertullian, *adu. Prax.* 1 ex. ; Ioh. xiv. 11 *ap.* Tert. *adu. Prax.* 24 ex.

any other writer. *Cum quando* = quando is found only in Tertullian and Hilary[1] outside our author, in whose commentary it occurs four times, and in the *Quaestiones* twice: *per id quod* also is frequent.

Other words are :

abdico 'reject' : abdicatis Iudaeis 146 A.

absolutum est 'it is clear' : 86 c, &c.

adaeque : 496 c.

addisco (= disco): addiscere spiritalia 56 D, &c.

apophoretum 'a gift' : 404 B, 405 B.

apparentia (never *apparitio*) : 276 A, &c.

brutus : sensu bruta caro 321 A.

certus quia : eight examples in comm.

coimaginari : 160 B.

condignus (c. dat.): 3 exx. This construction is commoner than might appear from bad editions of authors.

conlocare meritum (*sibi*) *apud deum* : 9 (11) exx.: plural also in Anon. in Math. ; [Ambr.] *sacr.* i. 2, 4 ; Cassiod. *in Rom.* ix. 18 (cf. Ulpian in *Vocabularium Iurisprudentiae*).

consubstantiuus (never *consubstantialis*).

corrigo (intr.) : 10 exx. : common in Pelag., also in Bened. *reg.*

coruscus (subst.).

credentes and *diffidentes*, for 'believers' and 'unbelievers' often (see Koffmane, pp. 53 ff.).

crementum (opp. *detrimentum*) : 94 c, &c.

dehabeo = non habeo : three times. Also in Arnob. Iun. *Confl. Arn. et Serap.* at least twice : see also lexx.

de non esse : remarkable tmesis = non de esse. The only parallels I know[2] is *inter* non est Gal. ii, 6 ap. *De Indur. Cord. Pharaonis*, Itin. Aether. (once). Perhaps some compounds of *sum*, as MSS. suggest, were not fully formed. Also *de non fieri.*

dilucido (four times).

dissimulo ab : very frequent : rather rare outside.

emendo intr. (5 exx.) Pelag. Caesar.-Arel.

----

[1] Tert. *carn. resurr.* 10 pr. *bis* ; cf. also *C. S. E. L.* lxv, p. 302 *bis* ; Löfstedt, *Beiträge* (1907), 33 ; *Spätlat. Studien* (1908), 30 ; C. Weyman in *Berl. Phil. Woch.* 1917, col. 1166 ; Th. Stangl, *ibid.*, col. 970.

[2] But see more in E. Löfstedt, *Philol. Komm. z. Peregr. Aetheriae*, 186 ff.

genus = modus: *hoc genere, eodem genere*: especially *duplici genere*.

**impraescius* (add to lexx.) (twice); also *impraescientia*.

incarnandus, of Jesus, who came into the world *incarnandus* 151 A (twice *Quaest.*).

magia (sing. fem.) once.

maior and other comparatives, with gen. after: on analogy of Greek (cf. Stolz-Schmalz, *Lateinische Grammatik*, ed. 4, p. 385).

melioro (often): 95 B, &c.

multifarie intellegere (Hil.) 3 exx.

nudis uerbis (twice) (cf. Niceta, and Weyman's note in review of Burn's *Niceta* in *Archiv f. lat. Lexikogr.*, Bd. xiv. 489 f.).

nunc usque (four times): Aug. also [1] (never *usque nunc* in Ambst.).

permitto: *crucifigi (&c.) se permisit* (Hil.). (Seven times Ambst.).

possibilitas (once).

proficio ad (of growth in a bad direction) often.

pseudo enim *apostoli* (once or twice): an ignorant person regarded each part as a separate word.

remissa (plur.) (twice) (also Pelag. Ps.-Hier., in addition to authors noted in *Study*, p. 136 [2]).

renascibilitas (once).

sanctimonium 521 A (never *sanctimonia*).

spurcus (subst.) (twice).

in subiectis = 'in what follows', for *in sequentibus*, &c.

subsequor: *paenitentia subsequente*.

tractare apud se (also Caesarius) (one ex.). Hier. says *tractare secum*.

transpungo: 121 C, *transpuncta sententia*.

uicem reddere: to give 'tit for tat'. Two exx. of a nom. sing. *uices* were recovered from Ambst. in this phrase, a form otherwise known only from the contemporary Schol.-Iuv.[3]

Curiosities of Diction. Our examination of Ambrosiaster may conclude with a list of some curiosities of his diction, a list made possible by use of the Monte Cassino edition of the Monte Cassino MS. Most of these interesting features have been obliterated in the ordinary printed editions, based as they are on later MSS. than the *Casi-*

---

[1] See also *Nouum Testamentum S. Irenaei*, p. cix.

[2] Cf. also C. H. Turner, *Eccl. Occ. Mon. Iur. Ant.* i, p. 356.

[3] See *Classical Review*, xvii (1903), p. 55.

nensis. Yet other forms chronicled below (under *ageo*, &c.) are not to be regarded as Ambrosiaster's, but as early instances of corruptions found everywhere in the seventh and eighth centuries.

Abnveo (2 conj.)

In 1 Cor. ix. 15 debitum enim obsequium *abnuet* ab his sibi inpendi.

Adnveo (2 conj.)[1]

In Rom. viii. 28 non illis imputat quae aduersa postulant, sed ea *adnuet* quae danda sunt deum amantibus.

Acceptilo

In 2 Thess. iii. 17 ut sub nomine eius epistula *acceptolari* (sic cod.) non possit, quae non fuerit manu eius subscribta.

Advlescenta

Tit. ii. 4 ut instituant adulescentulas uiros suos diligere.

,, ,, 6 iuniores similiter hortare continentes esse.

1 Tim. v. 2 adulescentulas ut sorores in omni castitate.

        expos. adulescentas ut sorores admonet edocendas.

,, ,, ,, 11 iuniores autem uiduas deuita.

        expos. prohibet *adulescentas* uiduas in hac suscipi professione.

,, ,, ,, 14 uolo itaque iuniores nubere.

        But this last verse reads, in the *Quaestiones Veteris et Noui Testamenti cxxvii*, p. 414, l. 22, of my edition, thus: uolo *adulescentas* nubere.

It can hardly be doubted that the copy of the Epistles of St. Paul used by 'Ambrosiaster' had *adulescentas* in the text of 1 Tim. v. 2, 11, 14. We have thus three examples of this very rare word to add to the three given in the *Thesaurus.* Two of the three there given are from the Munich fragments of an Old-Latin version of the Pentateuch edited by Ziegler. So doubtful were the *Thesaurus* editors about the form *adulescenta*, which was no doubt unliterary, that they placed an interrogation mark before it. Not only do

---

[1] Cf. *Quaest.* 41 (p. 67, u. 22 ed. S), and *Thes.* s. v. *abnueo.*

the new examples confirm the old, but they incidentally furnish a fresh proof that the Pauline commentary and the *Quaestiones* come from the same pen.

Aegrimonium

In Rom. xv. 7 dum infirmitates nostras accepit et *aegrimonia* nostra portauit (cf. Esai. liii. 4, Matth. viii. 17).

Ageo (*dub.*) [1]

In Gal. ii. 19 qui non *aget* (present) quae mundi sunt uel erroris, mortuus mundo est.

Amnego (Abnego)

Tit. ii 12 *amnegantes* impietate et saecularibus desideriis.

Arma (-ae) *fem.*

In 2 Cor. vi. 7 *arma* iustitiae perimit iniquitatem.

Callosus

In Rom. v. 6–7 cum pro *callosis* debitoribus tarde aliquis fidem suam obligare se patiatur.

Caro (*adv.*)

In 1 Cor. vi. 20 *caro* empti sumus.

,, ,, vii. 23 tam *caro* empti sumus ut a nullo redimi potuisse- mus nisi a Christo.

In Eph. v. 5 quae res facit ut *caro* uenundentur, ne pauperes uiuant.

Cieo (*perf.* Cievi)

In Col. i. 22 misericordia et prouidentia dei *cieuit* eos.

Confideo (2 conj.) (*dub.*) [1]

In 2 Cor. x. 16 manifestum est quia uir prudens non in his *confidet* neque gloriam sperat, quae aliorum laboribus con- stant.

Consubstantialitas

In Col. i. 15 haec est unitas et *consubstantialitas* patris et filii, ut inuicem sint.

---

[1] Our doubts as to some of these *-et* forms are confirmed by *tradet* (*in 2 Tim.* ii. 20), where assuredly *tradit* is meant.

Dehabeo

In Rom. xv. 17–19 in tantum ut *de* non *habeat* aliquid diuinae uirtutis (for *dehabeo* cf. *Study,* 98, and for the tmesis, *de non esse, de non fieri, Study,* 100: also pp. 20, 86 above).

Depeto

In 1 Tim. iii. 2 qualis episcopus debeat esse describit, ut nemo episcopatum *depetat.*

Diffido *perf.* Diffidi

In Rom. xi. 11 non sic *diffiderunt* ut numquam iam crederent.

Dignitosus [1]

In Rom. xi. 21 illos qui praerogatiua patrum *dignitosi* erant.

„ „ xvi. 5 ut ostendat et *dignitosos* credere.

In Cor. vii. 35 utile uero, quia *dignitosum* est aput deum, et leue in saeculo.

In 1 Tim. v. 20 quando uident *dignitosum* uirum erroris causa corripi.

Dominica Dies

In 1 Cor. xv. 7 post dies octo resurrectionis suae, id est *dominica die.*

Ĕdeo

In 1 Thess. ii. 20 dum bona conuersatio proficit magistro, fructus sui *edet* laborem.

Ex

In Rom. x. 18 teste Raab ex-meretrice.

„ „ xvi. 23 omnes ecclesias aut certe Iudaeorum et ex-gentilium.

In Gal. ii. 2 Barnaba et Tito, uno *ex* Iudaeorum, et altero (-um *Cas*) *ex* gentili.

Exoperor

Phil. ii. 12 cum timore et tremore uestram ipsorum salutem *exoperamini.*

Expilator

In Rom. vii. 24–5 gradus fabricauit Adam, per quos ad filios eius *expilator* ascendat.

(*al. codd.* exspoliator).

---

[1] This account amplifies that in *Study,* p. 101.

Extendo

In 1 Cor. i. 1 ostendat . . . esse Christum filium, esse et deum patrem, non unionem, cum *extenditur*[1] filium dici.

Extorris

Act. xxvi. 24 ap. *in 2 Cor.* xi. 6 multae litterae te faciunt *extorrem* (= Gk. τὰ πολλά σε γράμματα εἰς μανίαν περιτρέπει).

Firmis[2]

In Gal. iv. 14 iniuriae apostoli temptatio erat Galatarum, in qua *firmes* inuenti sunt, non dubitantes de fide.

In Col. i. 11-13 *firmes* et stabiles sunt.

Gratifio

In 2 Tim. 1. 17-18 solent quidam personis magis quam causis seruire, uolentes *gratifieri* maioribus.

> Perhaps a passive of *gratifico*, but perhaps merely the two words *grati fieri* made by mistake into one.

Ima (-ae) *subst. fem.* = ima pars

In 2 Cor. vii. 5 miserunt eos in *imam* carceris.

„   „   „ 7 ut nec *imam* carceris nec plagarum dolorem con-putaret scissi corporis.

> This use comes from his Bible (Acts xvi. 24 ; see Codex Bezae and Lucifer in Wordsworth and White's critical apparatus).

In Col. i. 11-13 attollens nos de *ima* tartari.

Impudoratus

2 Tim. ii. 15 operarium non *impudoratum*, recte tractantem uerbum ueritatis. So also Pelagius, and the exposition of Ambst. confirms it.

Inordinatio

In 2 Cor. xii. 21 *inordinationis* nomen facit crimen.

Instructura

Eph. ii. 21 in quo omnis *instructura* conpacta crescit, &c.

Interpola (*masc.* 'a corrupter')

In 2 Thess. iii. 17 propter *interpolas* et adulteratores scripturarum.

---

[1] Perhaps corrupt: others *ostenditur*.

[2] Cf. the much commoner *infirmis*: in Gal. iv. 19 uelut per abortum nati, deformati et *infirmes* inuenti sunt.

INVEHOR (*met.*) c. acc.

In 1 Cor. i. 20 tam Iudaeos quam gentiles *inuehitur.*

MAGNIANIMIS [1]

In 1 Thess. v. 14–17 hos qui moderati sunt in *magnianimes.*

MORTICINA (*subst. fem.*; *scil.* caro)

In Rom. ix. 32 aut tetigisset aliquam *morticinam* ('carrion').

MUNERATIO

In 2 Cor. vii. 7 sic hoc aestimans quasi *munerationem* tribulationum.

NANCISCOR (NANCTUS *passive*)

In Eph. iv. 31 *nancta* occasione.

OBLECTABILIS

In Col. ii. 9 quae ad praesens sunt et cernuntur oculis, suauia et *oblectabilia* uidentur.

OBSECROR (*depon.*) [2]

In 1 Cor. iv. 16 o beniuolentiam sancti apostoli, qui *obsecratur* filios ut imitentur patrem!

In 2 Cor. i. 11 cuncti deo gratias referant, cum cessat temptatio; aut cum oritur, simul *obsecrentur.*

In 2 Cor. ii. 10 ideo *obsecratur* (apostolus) ut dimittant illi (with about half a dozen MSS.).

2 Cor. vi. 1 adiuuantes autem et *obsecramur* ne in uacuum, &c.

In 2 Cor. x. 1 ideo ergo absens *obsecratur* et modestiam Christi interponit.

OBSECUNDOR (*depon.*)

In Rom. v. 14 ut, abolitis peccatis prioribus, uni deo *obsecundaretur* genus humanum.

---

[1] This type, not infrequent in good MSS., is ignored or almost ignored by lexica; cf. *pusillianimis* (1 Thess. v. 14 ap. Ambst.); *unianimis.*

[2] A list of rare deponents (not including this) is given by E. Löfstedt, *Philologischer Kommentar zur Peregrinatio Aetheriae* (Uppsala and Leipzig, 1911), pp. 214 ff. He mentions *oror = oro, supplicor = supplico. obsecror* occurs in the glossary 'Abolita' (C. G. L. iv. 183, 31 *testantur* obsecrantur uel iurant aut pręcantur).

Observo a[b]

In Gal. ii. 2 ut *ab* his tantum *obseruarent,* id est *a* sanguine et
fornicatione et idololatria.

,, ,, ,, cum iubentur *a* sanguine *obseruare.*

,, ,, ,, ut *obseruarent* se *a* sanguine edendo cum carne.

,, ,, ,, ut *obseruent* se *ab* idololatria, *a* sanguine (sicut Noe)
et *a* fornicatione.

,, ,, ,, et *a* suffocato *obseruandum.*

It is probable that this idiom comes straight from Ambst.'s
copy of Acts, for there (xv. 29) e and Pacian have *a quibus
obseruantes* (for the usual *abstinentes*) *uos.*

Occideo

In Eph. v. 2 inmeritus qui *occidetur,* placet deo, non quia
occidetur, sed quia usque ad mortem iustitiam conseruauit.

Offeret (= *offert*)

In Eph. v. 2 qui iuste occiditur, diabolo se *offeret.*

Pauso

In Rom. viii. 19 ut tunc demum etiam ipsa creatura possit discingi
ab officio seruitutis et *pausare in otio.*

That this is the true reading is confirmed by *Quaest. Vet. et
Nou. Test. cxxvii,* no. 127, §4 (p. 400, u. 20): aut totus
enim operatur aut totus *pausat in otio.*

Perparuus

In 2 Cor. ix 6 huic parco *perparua* messis est, quia cum dubita-
tione seminat.

Perscruto

In Gal. iv. 10 qui cursus lunae *perscrutant.*

Plaudeo

In 2 Cor. xii. 10 *plaudet* ergo cum illi insultatur, et surgit cum
premitur.

Praememoro

In Gal. i. 12 sicut *praememoraui.*

Praestigium

In Col. ii. 12 ut perseuerent in abrenuntiatione pompae et
praestigii (*scripsi* : *cod.* praestigiis) satanae.

PROXENETA ('a go-between')

In 1 Tim. v. 13 quid est enim ut ea 'loquantur quae non oportet'? nuptiarum sunt *proxenetae*,[1] multorum secretorum participes, adulatrices, seruorum querulae.

PROXIMO (*adv.*)

In 1 Cor. vii. 30 scientes enim et *proximo* finem mundi.

PSALMIGRAFUS

In Rom. x. 17 quod enim *psalmigrafus* de creatura dixit.

„ „ xv. 3 *psalmigrafus* ex persona eius uerba facit ad deum patrem.

In 1 Cor. ix. 9 et *psalmigrafus* 'homines', inquit, 'et iumenta saluabis'.

PUTRAMEN

In 1 Cor. iv. 14 id agit ut medicus salutaris, qui *putramina* abscidens, dolorem inlatum spe et blanditiis mitigat, ut aeger se curari permittat.[2]

QUALISUIS

In 1 Cor. xii. 4 qui dicit dominum Iesum, in sancto spiritu dicit, *qualisuis sit*.

„ „ „ „ in loco ordinis officii ecclesiastici positus gratiam habet, *qualisuis sit*.

In 2 Cor. vii. 1 ceteri, *qualesuis sint*, inmundi sunt.

REFRIGERO (*intr.*)

In Tit. iii. 14 iubet sumptus illos necessarios dari ab his qui crediderunt, ut *refrigerarent*.

RELEVIO [3]

In Rom. vi. 15 eruti a lege quae illos habebat obnoxios, et *releuiati* et reparati.

RESPONSATOR

Tit. ii. 9 seruos dominis suis subditos esse, in omnibus optimos, non *responsatores*.

---

[1] The other MSS. read *proximae, proximitate,* &c., cf. p. 56.

[2] The whole passage is rather like a recollection of Cyprian *De lapsis* 14 (247, 20 ff. H.).

[3] Cf. *alleuio* side by side with *alleuo*, and *angustio* with *angusto*. The ordinary form *releuo* occurs, for instance, at *in Rom.* vii. 24-5.

Robustitas

In Col. i. 10 mentis fida dicatio et *robustitas* fidei.

Sonus (-us) *4 decl.*

1 Cor. xiv 7 si distinctionem *sonus* non dederint.

Strumentum

In Rom. ix. 21 alia (uasa) quae *strumento* sint culinarum.
In Gal. iv. 10 septima luna *strumenta* confici non debent.

Sufferet (= *suffert*)

In 2 Cor. xi. 19 hic enim sapiens sustinet imprudentes qui patientia tua *sufferet* eos ut possint proficere.

 (For the parallel forms *offeret = offert*, see above, and *auferet = aufert*, see *Thesaurus* s. v. *aufero*.)

Superficium

In Eph. ii. 22 fideles *superficia* sunt templi dei.

Tribueo

In Eph. iv. 28 ad meritum proficit cum quis de proprio *tribue* egenis.

Verberator

1 Tim. iii. 4 non obnoxium uino, non *uerberatorem*.

Vivefacio

In Col. i. 19 ut et faceret et reformaret, et lapsa erigeret et mortua *uiuefaceret*.

III

JEROME

Eusebius Sofronius Hieronymus,[1] best known to us by his third name, which has crumbled down in French and English to Jerome, was born about the year 347 at Stridon on the north-eastern frontier between Italy, Dalmatia, and Pannonia, therefore not far from the north of the Adriatic and the city of Aquileia. His family was possessed of considerable property, and it was possible for him to receive the highest education at Rome, where he was a pupil of the great rhetorician Donatus. His parents were Christian, at least in name. At Rome Jerome became an enthusiastic student of Latin literature : it was only later that he learned Greek, and then Hebrew. It was in Rome that he acquired his marvellous Latin style, which is not unworthy of comparison with that of the best days. There also he was baptized. A residence at Trèves, where he spent some time after his secular studies were completed, served to confirm him in the Christian faith, and started him on a course of serious study of Christian literature, which was to last unbroken for fifty years.

The tastes thus acquired grew upon him in subsequent residence at Stridon and neighbouring places, where he enjoyed the intercourse of others like-minded with himself, and at the same time adopted ascetic views. This period of his life unhappily terminated, he started on his first journey eastwards, visiting Athens and Thrace, and crossing Asia Minor to Cilicia and Syria. He reached

---

[1] The best modern biographies are by G. Grützmacher, *Hieronymus, eine biographische Studie zur alten Kirchengeschichte*, 3 vols. (Leipzig and Berlin, 1901–8), and F. Cavallera, *Saint Jérôme, sa vie et son œuvre*, première partie, tomes i et ii (Louvain and Paris, 1922).

Antioch in the autumn of 374, where he was again happy
in congenial society. There he suffered illness and be-
reavements; there also, probably, he had the dream which
led him to give up the reading of profane authors, so dear
to him. He wrote an allegorical commentary on Obadiah,
of which he was afterwards ashamed, and came in contact
with eastern monachism. A wave of enthusiasm for the
ascetic life was passing over some of the best spirits of
the time, and Jerome was swept away by it to the solitude
of Chalcis, about fifty miles south-east of Antioch. He
was somewhat disillusioned by the life there, and adopted
the remedy of hard work. Being dissatisfied with the
Greek and Latin translations of the Old Testament, he
began to learn Hebrew under the tuition of a converted
Jew. At the same time he studied Greek thoroughly, got
manuscripts copied for his use and for the enlargement of
his library, and continued to write both literary works and
letters. Involved in theological controversy, he returned
to Antioch, and had the advantage of attending the lectures
of Apollinaris of Laodicea there. Not earlier than the
latter part of 378 he proceeded to Constantinople, where
he was privileged to hear another master, Gregory of
Nazianzus, to whom he always refers afterwards as his
teacher *par excellence*, and to make the acquaintance of
his namesake, Gregory of Nyssa. All the while he was
perfecting his knowledge of Greek and writing in his
native language. He was also much exercised by the
problem of translation from Greek into Latin, and it is to
this period we owe his important translation of Eusebius'
Chronicle. It would be impossible to exaggerate the significance of the Constantinople period (379–382) in Jerome's
development, for there he became gripped by Origen,
and resolved to make known to the West some of that
writer's exact and voluminous learning.

The Council of 382 brought Jerome back to Rome as

interpreter to two Eastern bishops, and Pope Damasus almost at once associated him with himself in the rule of the Church. The secretarial services of the young scholar were much appreciated by the bishop of Rome. Not less was his learning valued, for the pope frequently consulted him on biblical difficulties, such as the meaning of the word *Hosanna* and the parable of the prodigal son. Having found his first judgement of Jerome confirmed, Damasus entrusted him with the task of preparing a revision of the Latin New Testament text or texts at that time in use in the West. The Gospels were revised according to the text of ancient Greek manuscripts, and as few alterations were made in the Latin as possible, to avoid offence to the susceptibilities of readers accustomed to the old renderings. The current form of Latin Psalter was also similarly revised by him. The papal influence made Jerome a *persona grata* in the higher Christian society of Rome, and in particular an adviser on biblical matters to several ladies of the time, with whom his friendship continued unbroken throughout their lives. This devotion to study was no affectation on their part, but a serious passion which led them into lives distinguished by austerity and self-denial. There can be no doubt, at the same time, that these noble ladies exercised a refining influence on Jerome's character.

We need not linger over the ascetic propaganda of this period, which occupied Jerome almost as much as his biblical studies. Jerome had had some hopes of succeeding Damasus (died December 11, 384), but Siricius was elected, and *he* was not interested in Jerome. All influences converged to send him back to the East, and to the East he went in August 385, never to return. He travelled for about a year before he eventually settled, in summer 386, at Bethlehem. Many sacred sites had been visited, and the personal acquaintance of the blind exegete, Didymus of Alexandria, was probably the most inspiring result of these long journeys. From 389 till the end of his life Jerome was the head of a monastery for men, founded by his Roman friend Paula, who at the same time became abbess of a neighbouring nunnery. There he occupied himself in ceaseless study and authorship, and it is with part of the literary fruit of this period that we are concerned, the commentaries on four Pauline Epistles.

An eminent Belgian scholar has recently summed up Jerome's character and achievements so well that I cannot do better than quote his words : ' It was not easy to draw a faithful portrait of this man who combined the greatest faults with the finest qualities. A passable theologian, but of a strict orthodoxy; with little originality of mind, but of a prodigious memory and vast erudition ; irascible and vindictive, but at the same time generous and tender ; a controversialist always formidable, but sometimes unjust ; overwhelming his adversaries not only with good argu-ments, but also with insults and nicknames ; a stylist of the first rank, but with some faults in taste ; always active, or rather in eruption ; detested by some of his contemporaries and petted by others, especially by some women ; is it surprising that posterity has some difficulty in judging him impartially ?   It is indisputable that he has rendered the greatest services to the Church.   In the first place he has kept very high the ideal of Christian perfection ; in the midst of the corruption of the dying paganism, in the midst of the laxity which naturally followed the triumph of Christianity, he preached the asceticism and renunciation of which he was himself an example, not without harshness or exaggeration.   Further, he revealed the sacred books to the West ; it is an uneasy question how many centuries the Latin world would have had to wait for a suitable text of the Bible if Jerome had not been there.' [1]

[1] Dom Donatien de Bruyne in *Revue Bénédictine*, t. xxxvi (1924), *Bulletin d'ancienne littérature chrétienne latine*, p. 85 f. in a review of Cavallera's biography of St. Jerome.

The difficulties of the task had long deterred Jerome, and but for the insistence of Paula and her daughter Eustochium these commentaries would never have seen the light. Only four commentaries in all were accomplished, and these were on the following epistles: Philemon, Galatians, Ephesians, Titus; in this order, as we learn from Jerome himself, who also tells us that they were produced within the period of a few months.[1] Cavallera is perhaps right in assigning them to the period 389-392,[2] as Jerome's *De Viris Illustribus*, written in 392, furnishes a *terminus ante quem*, and the commentaries show considerable development from earlier writings.

The text used here is that which is to be found in the seventh volume of Vallarsi's second edition, published at Venice in 1769; the edition in Migne's Patrology is a mere reprint of this, and there is nothing more recent or better. Vallarsi's edition is most readable and, so far as one can at present judge, represents Jerome's work very faithfully. References to Scripture are not always recorded in it, and the orthography is occasionally erroneous, but it is quite premature to suggest what other improvements may be possible. The only person who appears to have looked into the manuscripts in recent times is Dr. Peter Corssen, of Berlin, who, in studying the Vulgate text of the Epistle to the Galatians, took the trouble to examine the biblical text in certain MSS. of Jerome's commentary on that epistle.[3]

I have made as complete a list of extant MSS. as I can, and I append it here. The Epistles contained in each MS. are named, except in cases where I am unable to state the exact details. The manuscripts used by Vallarsi are asterisked.

---

[1] Grützmacher, i, pp. 60 ff. ; ii, pp. 18 ff. ; Cavallera, i (1), pp. 138 ff. ; Hier. *in Gal.* praef. ; *in Eph.* praef. ; *in Tit.* i. 10–11 ; *in Philem.* i.

[2] Cavallera i (2), p. 27. Dom Chapman favours 387 (*J.T.S.*, xxiv (1922–23), p. 38, n. 1).

[3] In his *Epistula ad Galatas ad fidem optimorum codicum Vulgatae* (Berol. 1885), p. 37, he enumerates five manuscripts he had studied.

Admont 490 (saec. xiii) (Gal. Eph.).

Angers 285 (276) (saec. x) (defective).

    295 (286) (saec. xii) (Tit. Philem.).

Avranches 71 (saec. xii) (Gal. Eph. Tit. Philem.).

Bamberg B. vi. 14 (saec. xiii) (extract).

Berne 314 (saec. xi) (Philem.).

Brussels 1024 (5504–12) (Gembloux) (saec. xi).

Cambridge, University Library, Ff. iv. 31 (saec. xv) (Gal. Tit. Philem. Eph.).

Cambridge, University Library, Kk. i. 17 (saec. xiii) (Tit. Philem.).

Cambridge, Trinity College, B. 10, 5 (saec. viii) (extracts from Gal. cf. James, *Catal.* i, p. 293). (Durham.) See London, Cotton.

Cesena, Bibl. Malatest. (saec. xv) (Gal. Eph. Tit. Philem.).

Cheltenham 21163 (Libri 744?) (probably Quaritch, *Catal.* 290, June 1910, item no. 355), = Sotheby, *Catal.* 20th and 21st Nov. 1912 (saec. xi) (Gal. Eph. Tit. Philem.). Schenkl, 3410.

    6546 (saec. ix) (extracts from Tit.).

Cologne lviii (Darmst. 2052) (saec. ix) (Eph. Tit. Philem.).

Cramer-Klett, Frh. von (S. Maximin, Trèves, A 56) (Gal. Eph.).

Douai 242 (saec. xii) (Gal. Tit.).

    241 (saec. xii) (Eph. Philem.).

Florence, Laurentian : Leopold. Medic. Fesul. cod. xxxiii (saec. xv) (Gal. Eph. Tit. Philem.).

    Laur. plut. xix cod. vii (saec. xv) (Gal. Eph. Tit. Philem.).

    ,,   ,, xv dext. cod. i (S. Croce 160) (saec. xii) (Gal. Eph. Tit. Philem.).

    ,,   ,, xv dext. cod. ii (S. Croce 155) (saec. xi) (Gal. Eph. Tit. Philem.).

    ,,   ,, xviii dext. cod. ix (saec. xiii) (Eph. Tit. Philem.).

    ,,   ,, xiv dext. cod. vi (S. Croce 148) (saec. xi) (Tit. Philem.).

    San Marco (now Laur.) (saec. xi–xii) (Gal. Eph. Tit. Philem.).

Geneva 17 (Petau) (saec. xv) (Philem. Gal. Eph.).

Göttweig 35 (saec. xii) (Gal. Eph.).

Heiligenkreuz, 103 (saec. xii) (Gal. Eph. Tit. Philem.).

Karlsruhe, cod. Aug. lxxxi (saec. ix in.) (Eph. Tit. Philem.).

Leningrad (Petrograd, St. Petersburg), Q. v. 1, no. 46 (saec. x) (Eph.), cf. Staerk, vol. ii, plate 65.

London, B. M., Cotton, Vitell. c. viii (saec. viii, part of Cambridge, Trin. Coll., above) (extracts from Gal.).

„ Harl. 3030 (saec. x) f. 181 v. (Eph.).

„ „ 3049 (Durham) (saec. xv) f. 120 v. (Tit.).

„ 3. B. 1 (Rochester) (saec. xii) f. 91 v. (Tit. Philem.).

Lambeth 361 (saec. xv) (Gal. Eph. Tit. Philem.).

Mantua, Commonalbibl. C. v. 2 (Polirone) (saec. x–xi).

Metz 79 (saec. xi in.) (Gal. Eph. Tit. Philem.).

Milan, Ambrosian, C. 118 Inf. (saec. ix) (Eph. Tit. Philem. Gal.).

Modena, Estense (=Vienna 13697 (suppl. 2609), formerly Buda-Pesth National Museum, from library of Matthias Corvinus). (saec xv = 1488) (Gal. Eph. Tit. Philem.), cf. S. B. Wien. Akad. clix, 6. Abh. (1908).

Monte Cassino 291 (saec. xi) (Gal. Eph. Tit. Philem.) (cf. Lowe, *Beneventan Script*, p. 348).

Montpellier, École de Médecine 141 (Buherianus C. 53) (saec. viii–ix) (Eph.).

Munich, Staatsbibl. 3101 (saec. xvi) (Gal.).

„ 6285 (Freising 85) (saec. x) (Gal. Eph. Tit. Philem.).

„ 13038 (Ratisbon) (saec. ix in.) (Eph. Tit.).

„ 14388 (S. Emmeram E. 11, in Ratisbon) (saec. ix et x) (Eph. Tit.).

Universitätsbibl., Cod. MS. 12 (saec. xv = 1491) (Gal. Eph. Tit. Philem.).

Novara 84 (lvi) (saec. xiv) (Tit.).

Oxford, Balliol College, 157 (saec. xv) (Gal. Eph.).

Merton „ 26 (saec. xv) (Gal. Eph. Tit. Philem.).

New „ 62 (saec. xiii in.) (Philem. Gal. Eph.).

Paris, B. N. lat. 1639 (saec. xii) (Gal. Eph. Tit. Philem.).

„ „ 1760 (saec. ix–x) (Gal.).

„ „ 1762 (saec. xii) (Gal. Eph. Tit. Philem.).

„ „ 1827 (saec. xiv) (Gal. Eph. Tit. Philem.).

„ „ 1850 (saec. xiii) (Gal. Eph. Tit. Philem.).

„ „ 1854 (S. Martial, Limoges) (saec. ix) (Gal. Eph. Tit. Philem.).

„ „ 1855 (S. Amand) (saec. xiii) (Gal. Eph. Tit. Philem.).

Paris, B. N. lat. 1856 (saec. x) (Tit. Philem.).

   ,,   ,, 1857 (saec. xiii) (Philem. Gal. Eph.).

   ,,   ,, 2453 (saec. xii) (Tit. Philem.).

   ,,   ,, 2666 (saec. xiii) (Philem.).

   ,,   ,, 9531 (saec. x) (Gal. Philem.).

   ,,   ,, 13354 (S. Germain-des-Prés) (saec. x) (Eph.).

   ,,   ,, 14850 (saec. ix) (Gal.).

   ,,   ,, 17378 (saec. xii) (Philem. Gal. Eph.).

   ,,   ,, 18071 (saec. x) (Tit. Philem.).

   ,, nouv. acq. lat. 1459 (Cluni) (saec. x) (Gal. Eph. Tit. Philem.), cf. L. Delisle, *Inv. des mss. de la Bibl. Nat., Fonds de Cluni* (Paris, 1884), p. 105 f.

Arsenal 295 (389 T. L.) (Fontenay, dioc. Autun) (saec. xii) (Gal. Eph. Tit. Philem.).

   ,,   351 (398 T. L.) f. 106 (Chaalis, dioc. Senlis; later S. Martin-des-Champs) (saec. xii) (Tit.).

Mazarine 737 (907) (Grands Augustins, Paris) (saec. xiii) (Gal. Eph. Tit. Philem.).

Reims 82 (E 246) (saec. xii) (Gal. Eph. Tit. Philem.).

Rome, Vat. lat. 337 (saec. xv) (Gal. Eph. Tit. Philem.).

   ,,   ,, 338 (saec. xii) (Tit. Philem.).

   ,,   ,, 339 (saec. xv) (Gal. Eph.).

*,,   ,, 340 (Corbie) (saec. ix) (Gal.).

   ,,   ,, 6072 (saec. xi ex.) (Tit. Philem.).

   ,,   ,, 7636 (saec. xv a. 1446) (Gal.).

   ,, Urbin. lat. 52 (olim 96) (saec. xv) (Tit. Philem.).

   ,,   ,,   ,, 55   ,,   (saec. xiv) (Gal. Eph.).

   ,,   ,,   ,, 522   ,,   (saec. xi) (Eph. Gal.).

Angelica 504 (D. 8. 8) (saec. x–xi) (Gal.).

Vallicell., A 8 (saec. xii–xiii) (Tit. Philem.).

   ,, E 42 (saec. xiii in.) (Tit. Philem.).

**Vittorio Emmanuele, 1565 (Sess. xcvi) + 1372[3] (Sess. xxxix[3]) (Nonantola?) (saec. ix) (Gal. Eph. Tit. Philem.).

Rouen 449 (A. 343) (saec. xii) (Tit. Philem.).

St. Gall 128 (saec. ix) (Gal.).

     129 (saec. ix) (Eph. Tit. Philem.).

St. Mihiel 16 { (saec. xii) (fragment of Eph.). { (saec. x) (Tit.).

St. Omer 652 (St. Bertin) (n. d.) (fragment of Gal.).
Toulouse 158 (saec. xii) (Tit. Philem.).
Troyes 420 (Clairvaux) (saec. xii) (Gal. Eph. Tit. Philem.).
Utrecht 102 (Eccl. 223, antea 284 t.) (saec. xv) (Gal. Tit. Philem.).
　　　　　101 (Eccl. 372, antea 291 k) (saec. xv) (Eph.).
Valenciennes 86 (79) (saec. xii) (Gal. Tit. Philem.).
Vendôme 134 (saec. xii) (Eph.).
Venice cod. 17 membr. (saec. xv) (Philem.).
Verona lxii 60 (saec. viii–ix) fol. 2 (extracts from Gal.).
　　　　lxxiv (saec. ix) (contents ?).
Vienna 742 (theol. 185) (saec. xi) (Philem. Gal.).
　　　　844 (Salisb. 138) (saec. xv) (Tit. Philem.).
　　　　1002 (Salisb. 179) (saec. x) (Gal. Eph.).
　　　　13697 (suppl. 2609): see under Modena.
　　　　1163 (saec. xii) (Eph., text only).
Wolfenbüttel 28 Weissenb. (saec. x) (Gal.).[1]
　　　　　13 Weissenb. (saec. x) (Eph. Tit. Philem.).[1]
York Cathedral xvi 1, 1 (= 36) (saec. xvi) (Gal.).

If we pass now to the Biblical text employed by Jerome as the basis of his comments, our conclusions must be rather tentative. The limited number of manuscripts employed by Vallarsi will make us cautious, and the case of the Commentary on St. Matthew's Gospel will make us suspicious. For Professor C. H. Turner has made it clear that Jerome did not always, as we might infer from the printed editions, present the *lemmata* in full. ' It seems ', he says, ' that Vallarsi, whether with or without MS. authority, habitually prolongs the *lemmata* beyond the point at which our (Worcester) fragments and the other MSS. which I have consulted conclude them, and the passages thus inserted are of course borrowed from the Vulgate '.[2] If this was done in the case of the Gospel commentary, it may also have been done in the Epistles.[3]

---

[1] See Th. Gottlieb, *Die Weissenburger Handschriften in Wolfenbütte* (S. B. Wien. Akad. clxiii, 6. Abh. (1910)).

[2] *Early Worcester MSS.* (Oxford, 1916), p. xv.

[3] Corssen notes the omission of Gal. ii, 17–18.

So far as the text of Galatians is concerned, Dr. Corssen examined five old manuscripts of the commentary,[1] and his results may here be summarized. He points out that Jerome does not always quote particular passages of the Epistle in the same fashion throughout. It must be remembered under what conditions the commentaries were produced, and that he certainly carried a great deal of Scripture in his memory. One or two of Corssen's examples will illustrate the situation: Gal. iv. 14 *suscepistis* (MSS. of comm.), as contrasted with *excepistis* (Vg.): Gal. v. 25 *si spiritu uiuimus, spiritui obtemperemus*, as contrasted with the Vulgate *si uiuimus spiritu, spiritu et ambulemus.* But in Gal. iii. 1 we find that *praescriptus*, the true Vulgate reading, is given also by three out of the five manuscripts of the commentary, as against the ordinary reading *proscriptus.* Corssen's verdict will hardly be disputed, that the text quoted in Jerome's commentaries is nearer to the Vulgate than is either the Victorinus text or the Ambrosiaster text.[2] Both the Jerome commentary text and the Vulgate are farther away from the 'Western' text of the Greek manuscripts D and G than any other Latin texts known, including in these latter parallel passages in the works of Jerome. Corssen's illustrations of this fact may be repeated, with the texts brought up to date. Gal. ii. 1–2, 12–14, are quoted in Epistle 112 (= *C. S. E. L.* lv, p. 376); Gal. iii. 10, 19 in Epistle 121 (= *C. S. E. L.* lvi, pp. 31, 32):

Vulg.	*Hier. in comm.*	*Hier. in aliis scriptis*
ii. 1–2		
deinde	dehinc	*om.*
iterum ascendi	rursum ascendi	ascendi iterum
contuli cum illis	contuli cum eis	exposui eis (illis)
	in gentibus	inter gentes
	seorsum	separatim
ii. 12–14		
	subtrahebat et segregabat se	subtrahebat se et segregabat
	simulationi eius consenserunt	consenserunt cum illo

---

[1] *Epistula ad Galatas*, p. 37.   [2] Corssen, *op. cit.*, p. 52.

P

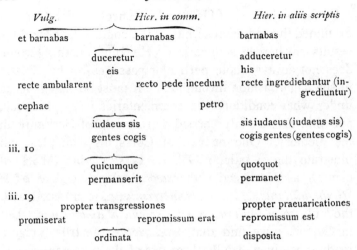

Vulg.	Hier. in comm.	Hier. in aliis scriptis
et barnabas	barnabas	barnabas
	duceretur	adduceretur
	eis	his
recte ambularent	recto pede incedunt	recte ingrediebantur (in-grediuntur)
cephae		petro
	iudaeus sis	sis iudaeus (iudaeus sis)
	gentes cogis	cogis gentes (gentes cogis)
iii. 10		
	quicumque	quotquot
	permanserit	permanet
iii. 19		
	propter transgressiones	propter praeuaricationes
promiserat	repromissum erat	repromissum est
	ordinata	disposita

Of all the nineteen variants in the third column, only five have not been found in any other Old-Latin text such as that of Victorinus or Ambrosiaster. The text in Jerome's commentary appears, in fact, to be a sort of half-way stage between the Old-Latin and the Vulgate: it is a partial revision made by St. Jerome from the Old-Latin, with the help of Greek MSS.

Recently the question has been re-examined by Dom John Chapman.[1] He accepts Corssen's conclusion, as just stated, for *Galatians*, but extends the inquiry farther. Jerome was always cautious in textual matters, and often leaves a reading in the text, though he criticizes it in his commentary. Some examples of this practice of his may be given:

Gal. i. 16: The Old-Latin *acquieui* is retained in the text, though the Greek ($\pi\rho\sigma\alpha\nu\epsilon\theta\epsilon\mu\eta\nu = contuli$) is recognized as better (p. 398 C, cf. p. 402 E).

Gal. v. 7 *nemini consenseritis* is perhaps retained by him in the text, but he points out that corresponding words are absent both from Greek MSS. and Greek commen-

---

[1] *J. T. S.*, vol. xxiv (1922-3), pp. 36 ff. The question has also been independently studied by the present writer.

tators on St. Paul, and therefore ought probably to be omitted.

Eph. i. 14 *adoptionis* is retained in the text, though he recognizes that *adquisitionis* is a better rendering (and is actually found in certain Old-Latin authorities).

Tit. iii. 15 *domini nostri* is kept, though he tells us that the Greek MSS. are without the expression.

Philem. 6 *euidens* is kept, but *efficax* is given in the comment as a better rendering.[1]

Jerome takes no trouble to introduce harmony with the text of the *lemma* into the quotations of the same passage made in the body of the notes. Some of these differences are due to hurried recollection of an Old-Latin form, others are doubtless due to literal translation from his Greek commentators. As an exhaustive study of the text of the four Epistles in Vallarsi's edition would be wasted labour, and the task would have to be performed over again after the publication of the Vienna edition of the commentaries, we can now pass to a study of the commentaries themselves.

Of all ancient Latin Christian writers probably none takes us more into his confidence on the subject of his methods than Jerome. From the lengthy prefaces to these commentaries we can gain much information. His claim to have no Latin predecessor can only be allowed if we follow him in rejecting Marius Victorinus as useless[2] and if we assume that he was ignorant of Ambrosiaster.[3] He

---

[1] Other passages are *in Gal.* v. 4 (p. 481 B–C); ii. 3-5 (p. 400 B ff.); iii. 1 (p. 418 C); v. 7 (p. 487 A); 8 (p. 487 C ff.); 13 (p. 494 A); 21 (p. 509 E); *in Eph.* i. 6 (p. 552 C); 10 (p. 556 D); iii. 14 (p. 599 C); v. 22-23 (p. 654 C); *in Tit.* iii. 1 (p. 729 E); 10-11 (p. 737 E); *in Philem.* 1 (p. 749 E); 20 (p. 759 E).

[2] See above, p. 22.

[3] Jerome's ignorance or pretended ignorance of this work is one of the puzzles of the Ambrosiaster question. Von Dobschütz (*Eberhard Nestle's Einführung in das griechische Testament*, 4te Aufl., Göttingen,

therefore had to depend on Greek commentators and on
the personal studies of all kinds he had pursued up
to the time of composition. He names among Greek
commentators Origen, whom he follows more than any
one else, and very closely. He used also, he tells us,
Didymus, Apollinaris, Alexander, Eusebius of Emesa, and
Theodorus of Heraclea, commentators on Galatians; and
Origen, Didymus, and Apollinaris for Ephesians. He does
not say explicitly what commentators he used for Titus
and Philemon, but we may safely infer that Origen was
his principal source for the commentaries on these
epistles also.

The use made of Origen can be to a very considerable
extent tested by confrontation with actual fragments of
that writer in the original Greek, but it will be well to
give some account of the others meantime, before we
proceed to examine the borrowings from Origen.

Alexander is probably the Valentinian of that name
mentioned by Tertullian in his *De Carne Christi* (written
between 208 and 211). No fragments of this writer
survive.[1]

Theodorus of Heraclea (flourished 340-356). No single
fragment of his work has survived.[2]

Eusebius of Emesa in Syria (died about 360). Eusebius
wrote ten volumes on Galatians. Very brief citations
from them are to be found in Cramer's *Catena*.[3] Of these
thirteen short notes[4] it is possible that the following had
some influence on Jerome's commentary:

1923, p. 116) is inclined to identify Marius Victorinus with Ambrosiaster.

[1] C. H. Turner in Hastings' *Dictionary of the Bible*, vol. v, p. 489.

[2] Turner, p. 497 f.

[3] Turner, p. 498. J. A. Cramer, *Catenae Graecorum Patrum in
Novum Testamentum*, tom. vi (Oxonii, 1844), pp. 32 ff.

[4] Enumerated by Turner, p. 498.

Eusebius (Cramer, p. 32).

αἱ δεξιαὶ τὴν ὁμόνοιαν δηλοῦσι.

Hier. *in Gal.* ii. 9.

ex quo perspicimus propterea dexteras datas . . . (ut) circumcisorum et habentium praeputium esset una communio.

Eusebius (Cramer, pp. 62 f.).

ἵνα τὴν υἱοθεσίαν ἀπολάβωμεν.

στοιχεῖα δέ φησι τὰ νόμιμα.

Hier. *in Gal.* iv. 4–9.

recipimus igitur adoptionem filiorum dei.

elementis . . . mundi, lege uidelicet . . . Moysi (p. 453 B ; cf. 454 B).

Eusebius (Cramer, p. 65).

τὰ οὖν ἐμὰ πάθη καὶ οἱ διωγμοί, ὦ Γαλάται, ὑμέτερος ἦν πειρασμός.

Hier. *in Gal.* iv. 14.

contumelias et persecutiones et plagas . . . hanc fuisse temptationem uel maximam Galatis.

Eusebius (Cramer, p. 68).

νῦν τὰ ἐναντία ἀκούοντες, σκηνὴν καὶ παιγνίον ἐνομίσατε τὰ κατ᾽ ἐμέ.

Hier. *in Gal.* iv. 20.

mutabat uocem suam, et in histrionum similitudinem ('factus' si quidem 'est theatrum mundo et angelis et hominibus' (= 1 Cor. iv. 9)) habitum in diversas figuras uertebat et uoces.

The result of this part of our investigation is almost negligible.

Of Didymus of Alexandria (*ca.* 310–99) not a single fragment on any of our Epistles survives.[1] But Jerome tells us that he personally consulted Didymus on biblical questions.[2] In view of Jerome's high opinion of Didymus, it is very probable that recollections of Didymus' teaching are embodied in these expositions.

The latest of the Greek commentators on the Epistles actually named by Jerome is Apollinaris[3] (the younger) of Laodicea (in Syria), who died before 392. Of this writer also, probably because of his heretical opinions, no frag-

---

[1] Turner, p. 499 f.

[2] *Praef. in Eph.* p. 539 f.

[3] That this is the correct Latin form is proved by the evidence of the best MSS. of Jerome's *Chronicle* and *Epistles*, &c.

ments have survived in Greek, but a good deal of his matter must be latent in Jerome's commentary on Ephesians. Professor Turner's judgement will not readily be gainsaid: 'of the residuum of Jerome's commentary on the Ephesians, after the Origen matter has been sub-tracted, much certainly came from Apollinaris.'[1] Turner has identified the following two fragments:[2] Jerome, *c. Rufinum* i. 24, 25:

(a) 'In tertia (expositione) quid Apollinaris simpliciter ex-planaret'=*Comm. in Eph.* ii 7: alius uero hoc quod ait 'ut ostenderet in saeculis superuenientibus abundantes divitias gratiae suae in bonitate supra nos in Christo Iesu', ad illam intellegentiam transferet quod non simus merito nostro, sed gratia eius saluati, et maioris bonitatis indicium sit pro pecca-toribus magis quam pro iustis mori: 'pro bono enim forsitan quis audeat interire'; et daturus nobis sit quae 'nec oculus uidit nec auris audiuit nec in cor hominis ascenderunt', quae omnia ex parte iam dederit in Christo Iesu, quia nullum absque Christo bonum dici potest: (b) 'in tertia quid Apollinaris contra illius (*i.e.* Origenis) uadens dogmata sentiret'=*Comm. in Eph.* iii 1: licet quidam alium sensum in hoc introducant quod Paulus praedestinatus et sanctificatus 'ex utero matris suae' ad praedicationem gentium ante quam nasceretur, postea uincula carnis acceperit.

Origen of Alexandria and Caesarea (lived from about 184 till about 253) produced a series of Greek textual and exegetical works on the books of the Old and New Testa-ment, which for number and quality has never been surpassed. The extreme hostility with which certain of his theological opinions were pursued about a hundred and fifty years after his death, has led to the loss of most of his works in the original Greek. Certain of these, however, have been preserved in old Latin translations by Jerome and Rufinus. In his earlier period Jerome was

---

[1] Turner, p. 500.
[2] Turner, p. 500, n. §: see also Turner, p. 495.

an enthusiastic admirer of Origen, and in his later life tried to explain away an enthusiasm as natural as it was creditable. The catalogue of Origen's writings preserved in Jerome's letter to Paula (*epist.* 33, § 4)[1] shows that he wrote on the Epistles, afterwards explained by Jerome, the following works:

On the Epistle to the Galatians 15 books (or rather 5 books[2]).
,,   ,,   ,,   ,,   7 homilies (called *tractatus*, Hier. *praef. in Gal.*).
,,   ,,   ,,   Ephesians 3 books.
,,   ,,   ,,   Titus   1 book.
,,   ,,   ,,   ,,   1 homily.
,,   ,,   ,,   Philemon 1 book.

This catalogue is supplemented by the preface to Jerome's *Galatians*, where he mentions that the tenth (and last) book of Origen's *Stromateis* or *Stromata*[3] is occupied with a clause for clause explanation of that Epistle, and that Origen had also written 'excerpta' (= scholia). There is no doubt that a very large part of Jerome's commentary on Galatians is taken direct from Origen, though he is sometimes abridged in the process. Some evidence of this indebtedness may now be presented.

On Galatians iv. 28 (p. 474 c) Origen's reading *uos . . . estis* is quoted from him by name. One passage of the tenth book of Origen's *Stromateis* is translated exactly by

---

[1] Ed. I. Hilberg (*C. S. E. L.* liv (1910), pp. 255 ff.). Vallarsi and the older editors leave out nearly the whole of the catalogue, which was apparently transcribed by Jerome from Eusebius (Turner, p. 490).

[2] 'Quinque' of the preface of Hier. *in Gal.* is confirmed by an Athos MS. which indicates where each volume commenced (Turner, p. 493).

[3] This strange title was doubtless borrowed from his predecessor Clement of Alexandria. The meaning of the word ('miscellanies', literally 'striped bags for holding bedclothes') is best discussed by Hort and Mayor, *Clement of Alexandria, Miscellanies, Book vii* (London, 1902), introduction, chap. i.

Jerome on Gal. v. 13–23. The exposition of these eleven verses covers two columns and a half in Jerome's Latin. Origen's exposition is referred to by name on iv. 28 (p. 474 c). His reading of v. 24 is stated (p. 513 D). Cramer's *Catena* on the Galatian Epistle contains no extracts ascribed to Origen by name, and no one has yet compared the anonymous extracts with Jerome's commentary in order to discover what common matter they share.

The situation in 'Ephesians' is quite different. For in 1902 an exact edition of the Origen material in Cramer's *Catena* was published by the Rev. J. A. F. Gregg.[1] The comparison of this with Jerome will give some idea of Jerome's indebtedness.

Origen, p. 101 Cr.

εἰ ἡ διὰ πρόθεσις τὸ ὑπηρετικὸν ἐμφαίνει.

Hier. pp. 543–4.

si 'per' praepositio ministerium eius per quem res agitur ostendit (the rest follows Origen, but not closely).

Origen, p. 102 Cr.

ὅρα οὖν εἰ μὴ ὥσπερ ἐν τῇ Ἐξόδῳ ὄνομά φησιν ἑαυτοῦ ὁ χρηματίζων Μωσεῖ τὸ ὁ ὤν, οὕτως οἱ μετέχοντες τοῦ ὄντος γίνονται ὄντες ... ἐξελέξατο γὰρ ὁ θεὸς τὰ μὴ ὄντα, φησὶν ὁ αὐτὸς Παῦλος, ἵνα τὰ ὄντα καταργήσῃ. καὶ ζητήσει τις πῶς τὰ ὄντα καταργεῖ. ἀλλὰ ἀκούωμεν ἐπιφέροντος αὐτοῦ τὸ ὅπως μὴ καυχήσηται πᾶσα σὰρξ ἐνώπιον τοῦ θεοῦ.

Hier. p. 545.

quidam curiosius quam necesse est putant ex eo quod Moysi dictum sit 'Hoc dices filiis Israhel: "Qui est misit me",' etiam eos qui Ephesi sunt sancti et fideles, essentiae uocabulo nuncupatos. ... iuxta eundem apostolum *elegisse deum ea quae non erant, ut destrueret ea quae erant.* ipsam etiam scripturam quae in testimonium adducta est, ita edisserunt, ut destructionem eorum quae erant, ex consequentibus intellegamus : *ut non,* inquit, *glorietur omnis caro in conspectu dei.*

[1] *J.T. S.,* vol. iii. 233–44, 398–420, 554–76.

Origen, pp. 102-3.

τὰς ἐν Λευιτικῷ καὶ Δευτερονομίῳ εὐλο-
γίας . . . οὐ τετεύχασι δὲ σωματικῶς
τῶν εὐλογιῶν, φέρ' εἰπεῖν, οἱ προφῆται·
οὐ γὰρ ἐδάνεισαν ἔθνεσι πολλοῖς
ἄνθρωποι περιελθόντες ἐν μηλω-
ταῖς, ἐν αἰγείοις δέρμασιν, ὑστε-
ρούμενοι, θλιβόμενοι, κακουχού-
μενοι, ἐν ἐρημίαις πλανώμενοι
καὶ ὄρεσι καὶ σπηλαίοις καὶ ταῖς
ὀπαῖς τῆς γῆς, οὐδὲ εὐλόγηνται ἐν
πόλει ἢ ἐν ἀγρῷ· ἀλλ' οὐδὲ αἱ
ἀποθῆκαι αὐτῶν εὐλόγηνται.

Hier. p. 546-7.

benedictiones illae quae in Leui-
tico . . . externis gentibus fene-
rare, plena esse horrea frumentis,
benedictos esse in urbibus, benedictos in agris, et cetera his
similia, in prophetis non uide-
bimus expleta, hominibus qui in
melotis et in caprinis pellibus
errauerunt, in egestate, in an-
gustia, in desertis montibus, in
speluncis et cauernis petrarum.

. . . (Deut. xxviii. 12; Heb. xi. 37-8; Deut. xxviii. 3, 5).

These illustrations will suffice to show what the situation is throughout. Those who wish to pursue the
subject farther will find the Jerome references at the foot
of Gregg's pages. The closeness with which Origen has
been followed at points has enabled Professor Turner
occasionally to restore corruptions of Origen's text from
Jerome's translations or adaptations.[1]

Another means of identifying Origenian material in the
Jerome commentary on *Ephesians* is furnished by statements of Rufinus made later in controversy. Rufinus
adduces about twenty passages from Jerome's commentary
to show that he had taken over portions of Origen's commentary without confuting them.[2] The passages are these:

In Eph. i. 4 (548 c–549 A) alius uero qui deum iustum conatur
ostendere ... ante quam humiliarer ego peccaui, et cetera
his similia. (Rufinus i 25–30, 36).

i. 5 (551 c–D) inuadunt itaque in hoc loco occasionem ...
nisi causae praecesserint quae iustitiam dei probent.
(Rufinus *ibid.*).

i. 12 (558 c–E) si *sperauimus* tantum dixisset *in Christo* et
non praemisisset *ante* ... benedicti sumus in caelestibus.
(Rufinus *ibid.*).

[1] Two instances on Cramer, p. 119 (Gregg, § viii, p. 242); another on
Cramer, p. 151 (Gregg, § xii, p. 407), &c.

[2] Turner, p. 494 f.

Q

In Eph. i. 17 (563 c–d) quod uero ait *In agnitione eius* . . . et cetera his similia. (Rufinus *ibid.*).

i. 21 (556 c–567 a) si autem sunt principatus et potestates . . . et dominatione fiat. (Rufinus i. 35).

i. 22-3 (568 c) potest ita (itaque *Hier.*) responderi . . . purgasse perhibetur. (Rufinus i. 36–8).

i. 22-3 (569 d- e) non solum hominum . . . ecclesia intellegi potest. (Rufinus *ibid.*).

ii. 1–5 (573 c) nos uero dicimus . . . adposita sit ad malitiam. (Rufinus i. 37).

ii. 7 (576 a–d) quod nos qui quondam lege tenebamur . . . iuxta sedentium uoluntatem incipient gubernari. (Rufinus i. 34).

ii. 10 (577 d–e) et diligenter obserua quia . . . factura primum locum tenet, deinde plasmatio. (Rufinus i. 38).

ii. 15–16 (582 b–c) et haec quidem iuxta uulgatam interpretationem . . . drachmis quae saluae fuerant copulauerit. (Rufinus i. 36–8).

ii. 15–18 (582 d–583 a) quod autem ait *ut duo conderet in semet ipso* . . . habitaturus est in nouo mundo. (Rufinus i. 36–8).

ii. 15–18 (583 b–d) instaurationem noui hominis tunc plene perfecteque complendam . . . *fiat uoluntas tua sicut in caelo et in terra.* (Rufinus i. 39).

iii. 1–4 (587 b) quia in pluribus locis lectum est uinculum animae corpus . . . per eum praedicatio compleatur. (Rufinus i. 40).

iv. 3–4 (608 e–609 b) quaeritur quo modo una spes . . . et isti in nobis unum sint. (Rufinus i. 41).

iv. 16 (618 c–620 a) in fine rerum cum deum facie uidere . . . in *caelesti Hierusalem,* quam in alio loco apostolus *matrem* sanctorum uocat. (Rufinus i. 42).

iv. 25 (627 e–628 c) propter quod Paulus ipse perfectus . . . in thalamum sponsi et penum regis inducat. (Rufinus ii. 2).

v. 28–9 (659 a) foueamus igitur . . . quod nobis in caelestibus repromissum est. (Rufinus i. 22).

vi. 20 (682 b–c) alius uero propter corpus humilitatis . . . spiritus dei habitat in nobis. (Rufinus i. 40).

There can be no doubt that Origen was employed for

the commentary on Titus also. Nothing of the original Greek of Origen's commentary survives, but Jerome reproduces on Tit. iii. 10, in abridged form, an exposition of Origen's that Rufinus quotes in full in his own Latin version of it.[1]

A similar indebtedness to Origen on Jerome's part can be proved for the Philemon commentary also. The comment on verse 5, translated fully in Rufinus-Pamphilus, occurs in an abbreviated form in Jerome's commentary on that verse. Also, an allegorical interpretation of verse 23 with regard to Epaphras' captivity, quoted by Rufinus[2] as from Origen, is found also in Jerome's commentary on the passage.

These would seem to be the only passages where meantime we can give absolute proof of Jerome's direct dependence on Origen's commentaries on these Epistles, but there are one or two passages that seem clearly dependent on other works of Origen.

Hier. *in Gal.* iii. 1 (p. 418 c): Legitur in quibusdam codicibus : '*Quis uos fascinauit non credere ueritati?* Sed hoc quia in exemplaribus Adamantii non habetur, omisimus. 'Adamantius' was a surname of Origen (cf. Hier. *epist.* 33, 4 'Adamantium nostrum'), and the reference must be to copies of the Epistle to the Galatians, once the property of Origen, preserved at Caesarea.

The following no doubt come ultimately from Origen's *Hexapla* :

Hier. *in Gal.* iii. 14 (p. 435), where Septuagint, Aquila, Symmachus, Theodotion and the Hebrew are quoted at length.

Hier. *in Gal.* vi. 18 (p. 535 A); Fratres germani, quod AMEN uerbum significat Hebraeum. 'Amen' enim Septuaginta interpretes 'fiat', Aquila, Symmachus et Theodotio 'fideliter' siue 'uere' interpretati sunt,

---

[1] Rufinus-Pamphilus, *Apologia pro Origene*, c. 1 ; Turner, p. 496.
[2] *Apologia*, i. 40 ; Turner, *loc. cit.*

but the parallel case of *in Eph.* v. 4 (p. 642 A), which looks
equally 'hexaplaric', actually comes immediately from
Origen's own commentary, as the extant Greek [1] proves,
and it is, therefore, probable that at *Gal.* vi. 18 the same
is true. The next passage also comes either from the
Hexapla direct or through the medium of Origen's commentary on Titus :

> Hier. *in Tit.* ii. 11–14 (pp. 725-6) (à propos of the meaning
> of περιούσιος and Ps. cxxxiv 3–4) pro eo quod est 'in possessione'
> in Graeco scriptum est εἰς περιουσιασμόν, quod quidem Aquila
> et Quinta Editio εἰς περιούσιον expresserunt, Septuaginta uero
> et Theodotio περιουσιασμόν transferentes, commutationem sylla-
> bae fecere, non sensus. Symmachus igitur pro eo quod est in
> Graeco περιούσιον, in Hebraeo SGOLLA, expressit ἐξαίρετον, &c.

The following passage is the most explicit of all :

> Hier. *in Tit.* iii. 9 (pp. 734 E, 735 A) unde et nobis curae fuit omnes
> Veteris Legis libros quos uir doctus Adamantius (= Origenes)
> in Hexapla digesserat, de Caesariensi bibliotheca [2] descriptos,
> ex ipsis authenticis emendare, in quibus et ipsa Hebraea
> propriis sunt caracteribus uerba descripta, et Graecis litteris
> tramite expressa uicino : Aquila etiam et Symmachus, Septua-
> ginta quoque et Theodotio suum ordinem tenent. Nonnnulli
> uero libri, et maxime hi qui apud Hebraeos compositi sunt,
> tres alias editiones additas habent, quam Quintam et Sextam
> et Septimam translationem uocant, auctoritatem sine nomini-
> bus interpretum consecutas. haec immortale illud ingenium
> suo nobis labore donauit, &c.

If we study Origen's commentaries on other biblical
books, such as that on ' Romans ', preserved in Rufinus'
abridged and modified version, we can often see the same
mind at work behind Jerome's Latin. For instance, it
seems to me most probable that mention made by Jerome
of any Greek Christian works or writers, whose date is
prior to Origen, is taken over direct from Origen. The

---

[1] Cramer, p. 191 (Gregg, xxiv, pp. 559–60).

[2] Cavallera (p. i, t. ii, p. 88 f. note H) has collected Jerome's references to this library.

following must be a fairly complete list of such, in chronological order, with the references appended :

1. (First) Epistle of Clement (about a. d. 95). Hier.
in Eph. ii. 1–5 (p. 571 D) De quibus et Clemens in epistula
sua scribit : 'Oceanus, et mundi qui trans ipsum sunt.'
This is from c. 20 § 8 of the Epistle : ὠκεανὸς ... καὶ οἱ μετ'
αὐτὸν κόσμοι. Hier. *in Eph.* iv. 1 (p. 606 A) Cuius rei et
Clemens ad Corinthios testis est scribens : 'Vinculum
caritatis dei qui poterit enarrare'? This is from c. 49 § 2 of
the same : τὸν δεσμὸν τῆς ἀγάπης τοῦ θεοῦ τίς δύναται ἐξηγή-
σασθαι; Jerome had no need to use the Latin translation
of Clement's Epistle, even if it were known to him.[1]

2. The well-known 'Agraphon' of uncertain date : Hier.
in Eph. iv. 31–2 (p. 637 D) ut probati trapezitae : *ibid.* v. 10
(p. 646 C) in morem prudentissimi trapezitae ; *in Philem.*
4–6 (p. 753 E) probandis numismatibus callidus trapezita.
We did not need the evidence of the catenist (Cr. 187, Gr.
xxii. 37, Cr. 195, Gr. xxv. 47) to prove that the Ephesian
comments come from Origen, for the saying γίνεσθε δόκιμοι
τραπεζῖται is as a matter of fact a great favourite with
Origen. He used it on Eph. iv. 25 a (Cr. 182, Gr. xix. 61),
where Jerome did not take it over, and Harnack has given
a long list of examples of its use from other exegetical
works of Origen.[2]

3. References to Ebion or Hebion, the Jewish Christian
writer, who is characterized by Hier. *in Gal.* iii. 14
(p. 435 E) as 'Ebion ille haeresiarches semi-christianus et
semi-iudaeus' : see also *in Gal.* i. 1 (p. 375 B) ; v. 3
(p. 480 A) ; *in Eph.* iv. 10 (p. 614 D) ;[3] *in Tit.* iii. 10–11
(p. 737 D).

---

[1] The catenist has omitted both these references to Clem. *epist.*
[2] A. v. Harnack, *Der kirchengeschichtliche Ertrag der exegetischen
Arbeiten des Origenes: II. Teil: Die beiden Testamente mit Ausschluss des
Hexateuchs und des Richterbuchs* (Texte und Untersuchungen, xlii (4))
(Leipzig, 1919), p. 40.
[3] The catenist has nothing corresponding to this section.

4. Anecdote of the life of the Apostle John, to the effect that in extreme old age he could say nothing to the congregation of Ephesus and neighbourhood but 'Filioli ; diligite alterutrum' (Hier. *in Gal.* vi. 10, pp. 528 E, 529 A). This recollection comes from an unknown source.

5. Reference to Tatian the Encratite (flourished second half of second century) is made (Hier. *in Tit.* praef.) as rejecting some of the Pauline Epistles, but believing especially in the authenticity of the letter to Titus, in spite of its rejection by Marcion and others.

6. Basilides the Gnostic (of uncertain date in second century) is condemned along with Marcion in the preface to the commentary on Titus (pp. 685–6).

7. The Gnostic Valentinus (worked in Rome about 136 to 165) is frequently referred to : *in Gal.* v. 12 (p. 493 D) along with Marcion for rejection of the God of the Old Testament ; so again *in Eph.* iii. 8–9 (p. 593 D) :[1] at *in Eph.* iii. 14–15 (p. 602 B) he is attacked with reference to 'saeculorum suorum probolas atque coniugia', which he regarded as specially supported by that passage of St. Paul : *in Eph.* iv. 5–6 (p. 610 D), where Valentinus is reproved for arguing that there are two baptisms, the passage is to be found in the catenist (πρὸς τοὺς ἀπὸ Οὐαλεντίνου δὲ δύο διδόντας βαπτίσματα χρηστέον τῷ ῥητῷ ἐν βάπτισμα), and its Origenian origin is thus confirmed : *in Tit.* iii. 10–11 (p. 737 D) he appears in a list along with Marcion, Apelles, Ebion, Montanus, and Manichaeus : in the preface to the commentary on Philemon (pp. 743–4) he is found in the same company, where the contemptuous remark is made that Valentinus, Marcion, and Apelles believe that one power created an ant, worms, gnats, and locusts, while another created the sky, the earth, the sea, and the angels.

8. Iulius Cassianus the Docetist and Encratite is mentioned (*in Gal.* vi. 8, p. 526 A) for his views on the nature

---

[1] This part is not used by the catenist.

of Christ and on marriage. The reference is no doubt to his work Περὶ ἐγκρατείας ἢ περὶ εὐνουχίας.

9. The references to Marcion (flourished at Rome from about 140) are very numerous, and no one who knows Origen's works well will doubt that here we are on Origen's tracks.[1] Some of the references concern Marcion's handling of the Pauline text. Hier. *in Gal.* i. 1 (p. 375 D) notes that Marcion left out the words 'et per deum patrem';[2] *in Gal.* iii. 1 (p. 418 A); *in Gal.* iii. 6 (p. 422 E) notes that Marcion left out vv. 6-9, 'Sicut Abraham credidit deo . . . qui ex fide sunt, benedicentur cum fideli Abraham';[3] *in Gal.* iii. 13 (p. 434 A); *in Gal.* iv. 4-5 (p. 448 E) the Docetic reading of Marcion and others, 'factum per mulierem', is rejected;[4] *in Gal.* iv. 25-6 (p. 473 D) it is pointed out that Marcion and Manichaeus did not excise the passage in which the phrase 'quae quidem sunt allegorica' occurs, because they thought that it was hostile to catholic views; *in Gal.* v. 12 (p. 493 D), referred to above in connexion with Valentinus; *in Gal.* vi. 6 (p. 523 D) Marcion's interpretation of this verse is quoted. *In Eph.* ii. 19-22 (p. 584 A) it is pointed out that this passage may be used to controvert Marcionite and other heretical views, and this portion of Jerome is a very literal translation from Origen, as we can see from the corresponding section in Origen, fortunately preserved by the catenist,[5] though the actual reference to Marcion has

---

[1] I am glad to be able to point to the entirely independent investigation of Harnack, *Der kirchengeschichtliche Ertrag der exegetischen Arbeiten des Origenes, II. Teil* (Leipzig, 1919), pp. 141-68 (= Anhang: *Origenistisches Gut von kirchengeschichtlicher Bedeutung in den Kommentaren des Hieronymus zum Philemon-, Galater-, Epheser- und Titusbrief*).

[2] Tertullian, *Adu. Marc.* v. 2, makes no reference to this peculiarity of Marcion's text.

[3] Tert. *op. cit.* v. 3, is less explicit.

[4] No mention in Tert. *op. cit.* v. 4.

[5] Cramer, p. 151 (Gregg, § xii, p. 407).

not survived among his extracts; *in Eph.* iii. 8-9 (p. 593 D)
the ditheism of Marcion, Valentinus, and others is attacked;[1] *in Eph.* v. 9 (pp. 645 E and 646 B) is of the same
tenor, but the catenist leaves out Marcion's name and
generalizes;[2] *in Eph.* v. 31 (p. 660 c) Marcion is convicted
of illogicality in interpreting this passage of Christ and
the Church, though the passage comes from the Old
Testament, which according to him has nothing to do
with Christ.[1] *In Tit.* praef. (pp. 685-6) attacks Marcion
and Basilides for rejecting the Epistle to Titus among
others; *in Tit.* iii. 10-11 (p. 737 D), referred to above under
Valentinus. *In Philem.* praef. (pp. 743-4) is referred to in
the same place.

10. Apelles, Marcion's pupil, is mentioned in the two
passages just cited.

11. Montanus, the founder of the Cata Phrygas heresy
(died about 175) is not known to have been a writer, but
he is mentioned for his opinions. *In Eph.* v. 5-6 (p. 589 B)
his view that the patriarchs and prophets spoke in a trance
and did not know what they were saying, is rejected:[1]
in Tit. i. 6 (p. 697 B) the ascetic views of Montanus and the
Novatians in regard to marriage are proved unsound; *in
Tit.* iii. 10-11 (p. 737 D) he appears in the catalogue of early
heretics along with those already mentioned.

Even yet we have not exhausted the Origenian material
that can be drawn from Jerome's commentaries. There
can be little doubt that most of the passages referring to
Greek philosophers also come from him. It is true that
Jerome supplements these from Cicero, whose philoso-
phical works were well known to him, as to the majority
of educated Romans under the Empire, but the occasion
for referring to Greek philosophers was no doubt given
by Origen in all or most of the passages. Origen, as an

---

[1] All this part is absent from the catenist.
[2] Cramer p. 194 (Gregg, § xxv, p. 562).

Alexandrian, inherited a strong interest in the Platonic teaching and in Philo, who combined study of Plato with an equally enthusiastic study of the Old Testament in Greek. In the preface to the third book of the commentary on Galatians (pp. 487-8) there is a remarkable sentence: 'Quotus quisque nunc Aristotelem legit! quanti Platonis uel libros nouere uel nomen!' (How few now read Aristotle! How many know either the books or the name of Plato!) He is speaking relatively to the number of those who know about the apostles. The Stoic definition of *benignitas* quoted at *in Gal.* v. 22-3 (p. 511 E) does not seem to come from a Latin source; it must therefore come from a Greek source, and that source can hardly be other than Origen. The same is true of the definition of *bonitas* ad. loc. (p. 512 A).[1] The Stoic distinction between *sapientia* and *prudentia* is given at *in Eph.* i. 9 (p. 554 D): though the catenist knows nothing of this, a reference to the passage he preserves will show that Jerome has made use of Origen at this point.[2] That Origen did, as a matter of fact, quote Stoic definitions of ethical and other terms is proved by the note the catenist has preserved on *Eph.* iv. 30.[3] 'A certain Cynic philosopher' is quoted *in Eph.* v. 3-4 (p. 640 A).[4] Stoic cosmological views are alluded to *in Eph.* iv. 5-6 (p. 611 B).[4] The term 'sphaera' as used by 'philosophers' is mentioned *in Eph.* iv. 10 (p. 614 A),[4] as identical with 'caelorum circuli'. *In Eph.* iv. 17-9 (p. 621 E) contains the passage 'quidam philosophorum ἀναλγησίαν, id est indoloriam, praedicauit'.[4] The reference is no doubt to

---

[1] The Stoic distinction between *gaudium* and *laetitia* is referred to below in connexion with Cicero.

[2] Cramer, p. 112 (Gregg, § v, p. 239). The definition of *sapientia* is very like that which Cicero (*De off.* ii. 5) quotes from 'ueteres philosophi'.

[3] Cramer, p. 185 (Gregg, § xxi, p. 555, with Prof. Clement Webb's note).   [4] This passage is absent from the catenist.

Epicurus, or an Epicurean.[1] *In Eph.* vi. 10 (p. 669 B) it is
mentioned that the philosophers put 'fortitudo' among
the four (cardinal) virtues, and that this 'fortitudo' is
clearly 'animi', not 'corporis'. *In Eph.* vi. 12 (p. 675 E)
philosophers say that the clouds are not more than two
(Roman) miles distant from the earth.[2] *In Tit.* i. 2-4
(p. 691 B) the opinion of certain philosophers is cited, that
there is no present time, but only past and future. *In
Tit.* iii. 9 (p. 735 E) Aristotle is referred to as the first of
dialectics, and *in Tit.* iii. 10-11 (p. 737 C-D) the earlier
sense of 'haeresis' is well illustrated thus : 'haeresis
Graece ab *electione* dicitur, quod scilicet unus quisque id
sibi eligat quod ei melius esse uideatur. philosophi quoque
Stoici, Peripatetici, Academici, Epicurei illius uel illius
haereseos appellantur.'

It may be that references to Greek non-Christian literature and mythology also come in great part from Origen.
Epimenides is several times referred to as the author of the
gibe against the Cretans in the Epistle to Titus (e. g. *in
Gal.* iii. 1, p. 416 D; *in Eph.* v. 14, p. 647 E, 648 A;[2] *in Tit.*
i. 12-14, pp. 706-7). The reference to Demosthenes and
Polemo in the preface to the third book of the commentary
on Galatians (pp. 485-6) may be original in Jerome. The
intelligent remark is made in the preface *in Eph.* (pp. 539-
40) that the Diana worshipped by the Ephesians was not
the huntress who holds the bow, and is highgirt, but 'illa
multimammia quam Graeci πολύμαστον uocant', &c. No
doubt it was Origen's learning that led to the classic
remark (*in Eph.* v. 14, p. 647 E, cf. *in Tit.* i. 12-14, pp. 706-
7) about Paul's use of lines of Aratus, Epimenides, and
Menander. The story of the Lapithae and the Centaurs
is alluded to *in Eph.* v. 18 (p. 651 B).[2] Jupiter is 'uerna-
culus' of Crete according to the story (*in Tit.* i. 5, p. 693 D).

---

[1] Cf. Cic. *Fin.* ii. 11, where Cicero coins *indolentia*, with an apology.
[2] This passage is not represented by the catenist.

Callimachus is referred to as a possible author of the
attack upon the Cretans, though Epimenides is preferred
(*in Tit.* i. 12-14, p. 707 C): all this part must be based on
Origen, with the exception of the interesting reference to
Latin translations of Aratus.[1] The quotation from Aristo-
phanes, *Clouds* 1503, ἀεροβατῶ, καὶ περιφρονῶ τὸν ἥλιον,
assigned to ' apud Graecos quidam ', is doubtless from one
of Jerome's Greek authorities (*in Tit.* ii. 15, p. 728 D).
Here our investigation of the Greek authorities, such as it
is, must end, and we turn to the consideration of the
matter contributed by Jerome himself from sources other
than Greek commentators and their writings, and first let
us take Greek [2] writings quoted by him direct.

In Eph. v. 3-4 (p. 641 B) makes a quotation from the
' Hebraicum Euangelium ', these words, addressed by the
Lord to his disciples: ' et numquam laeti sitis, nisi cum
fratrem uestrum uideritis in caritate.' This book appears
to have been a non-heretical but divergent form of our
Matthaean Gospel. Jerome says he translated it both into
Greek and into Latin.[3] The Neo-Platonist Porphyrius
(lived from 233 to 304) is alluded to once or twice: *In
Gal.* i. 16 (p. 391 C) Jerome rejects Porphyrius' view that
St. Paul avoided 'flesh and blood' (namely, Peter, James,
and John) because he had been already taught of God and
therefore did not want human teaching, and *in Gal.* ii. 11–
13 (p. 409 B) it is mentioned that Porphyrius made capital
out of the dissensions of Peter and Paul. Celsus and
Porphyrius were probably the most distinguished anti-
Christian disputants of the earlier centuries. *In Gal.* i. 18
(p. 394 E) rejects the view of ' Clemens in Periodis Petri '

---

[1] See below, pp. 127, 129, 132.

[2] One is Hebrew (or Aramaic).

[3] See *The Apocryphal New Testament*, by M. R. James (Oxford,
1924), pp. 1 ff. Harnack (*op. cit.*, p. 161) thinks Jerome took over the
above reference from Origen.

that Paul's object in going to see Peter was to find out
whether he was bald-headed or not! In the view of some
scholars, a work with this title was a source lying behind
both the Clementine Homilies and the Clementine Recog-
nitions.[1] The following allusion is one about which one
would be glad to know more (*in Gal.* iii. 14, p. 436 A):
'Memini me in Altercatione Iasonis et Papisci, quae
Graeco sermone conscripta est, ita repperisse: λοιδορία
θεοῦ ὁ κρεμάμενος, id est: maledictio dei qui appensus est.'[2]
In Gal. vi. 11 (p. 530 B) contains a vague reference:

> 'In hoc loco uir apprime nostris temporibus eruditus miror
> quo modo rem ridiculam locutus sit: "Paulus" inquit,
> "Hebraeus erat et Graecas litteras nesciebat, et quia necessi-
> tas expetebat ut manu sua epistulam subscriberet, contra
> consuetudinem curuos tramites litterarum uix magnis apicibus
> exprimebat, etiam in hoc suae ad Galatas indicia caritatis
> ostendens, quod propter illos id quoque quod non poterat
> facere conaretur."'

The idea that the letters were rather shapeless is expressed
in an anonymous passage in the catenist,[3] but the real
author of the whole of this statement has not been discovered. Perhaps Didymus may be intended. Athanasius (295–373) is named *in Tit.* iii. 10–11 (p. 737 E) as
supporting the reading *post unam et alteram correptionem.*

The mention of various heretics of date subsequent to
Origen may very well be due to Jerome himself. I have
noted the following: Novatus (flourished 250) (*in Tit.* i. 6,
p. 697 B); Sabellius (about the same date) (*in Eph.* iv. 5–6,
p. 609 D; iv. 11–12, p. 615 A); Manichaeus († about 277) (*in*

---

[1] W. v. Christ, *Griechische Litteraturgeschichte*[5] (München, 1914),
§ 922, p. 1015.

[2] Vallarsi, *ad loc.*, notes that this work is mentioned also at the
beginning of Jerome's *Quaestiones Hebraicae in Genesin*: see his note.

[3] τὸ δὲ "πηλίκοις" ἐμοὶ δοκεῖ οὐ τὸ μέγεθος, ἀλλὰ τὴν ἀμορφίαν τῶν γραμ-
μάτων ἐμφαίνων λέγειν κτλ. (Cramer, p. 90). The passage comes from
Chrysostom, with whom Eusebius of Emesa and Theodoret agree
(see Swete on Theodore of Mopsuestia *ad loc.*).

Tit. iii. 10–11, p. 737 D); Arius (to the Westerns 'Arrius',[1] † 336) (*in Eph.* iv. 5–6, p. 610 C; *in Tit.* ii. 11–14, p. 724 E; iii. 10–11, p. 737 D); Photinus († 375) (*in Gal.* i. 11–12, p. 385 E; *in Eph.* iv. 10, p. 614 D); Macedonius (*flor.* 360) (*in Eph.* iv. 5–6, p. 610 C); Eunomius (*flor.* 361) (*in Eph.* iv. 5–6, p. 610 C; *in Tit.* ii. 11–14, p. 724 E; iii. 10–11, p. 737 D).

The preceding paragraphs may have created the impression that Jerome's [2] commentaries are not much more than compilations from earlier Greek expositions. But this impression would be unjust. It is abundantly true that he has used earlier Greek writers, and has thus preserved valuable exegetical material that would otherwise have been lost; but there are many signs that he was primarily a Latin. In spite of his desire to suppress his early enthusiasm for the Latin classics, his great knowledge of them breaks out from time to time. The references, also, to his Latin predecessors in Christian authorship are not few, and though we cannot deny that a pundit like Origen might have made use of such a writer as Tertullian, we shall not likely be wrong in following the usual assumption that, while Latins borrow from Greeks, Greeks never borrow from Latins. We shall take the references to Latin literature in chronological order.

P. Terentius Afer (*ca.* 190–159 B.C.): *In Gal.* iv. 15–16 (p. 462 D): 'similis est huic illa sententia nobilis apud Romanos poetae: OBSEQVIVM AMICOS, VERITAS ODIVM PARIT (= Ter. *Andr.* 68 (= i. 1–41)).

M. Tullius Cicero (106–43 B.C.). Jerome, in spite of his longing to be 'Christianus' rather than 'Ciceronianus', could not free himself from the influence of the noblest of

---

[1] The Greek Ἄρειος, with the accent on the first syllable, was equated with the well-known Latin gentile name *Arrius*, which also had the accent on the first syllable.

[2] The work of A. Lübeck, *Hieronymus quos noverit scriptores et ex quibus hauserit* (Leipzig, 1872), is inaccessible to me.

all men and writers of the republican period. *In Gal.*
iii. 1 (p. 416 E): 'Graecos leues apud C. Caesarem suggillat
Tullius dicens: AVT LEVIVM GRAECORVM AVT IMMANIVM
BARBARORVM (= pro Ligario Oratio 4, § 11), et pro Flacco
INGENITA inquit LEVITAS ET ERVDITA VANITAS (= pro L.
Flacco oratio, fragm. in fine editionis Clarkianae).[1] In the
preface to the third book of the commentary on Galatians
he twice refers to Cicero, and mentions that it is fifteen
years since a copy of any of Cicero's works has been in
his hands. The distinction made by the Stoics between
'gaudium' and 'laetitia' (*in Gal.* v. 22, p. 510 E) appears
to be derived from Cicero *Tusc. Disp.* iv. 6 § 13, as a comparison of the two passages suggests:

<table>
<tr><th>Hier.</th><th>Cic.</th></tr>
<tr><td>gaudium . . . Stoici quoque qui distinguunt inter uerba subtilius, aliud quid esse aestimant quam laetitiam. *gaudium* quippe esse aiunt elationem animi super his quae digna sunt exultantis: *laetitiam* uero effrenatam animi elationem quae modum nesciat, et in his quoque quae uitio sunt mixta, laetetur.</td><td>cum ratione animus mouetur placide atque constanter, tum illud *gaudium* dicitur; cum autem inaniter et effuse animus exultat, tum illa laetitia gestiens uel nimia dici potest, quam ita definiunt: sine ratione animi elationem. (Cf. also *De Fin.* iii. 10 § 35; *Tusc.* iv. 31 § 66.)</td></tr>
</table>

At *In Gal.* v. 26 (p. 517 C) we have these words: 'uideas
plerosque (quod etiam Tullius ait) libros suos de contemnenda gloria inscribere, et causa gloriae proprii nominis
titulos praenotare.' This passage is clearly a reference
to Cicero, *pro Archia Poeta*, 11 § 26: 'ipsi illi philosophi
etiam in eis libellis quos de contemnenda gloria scribunt,
nomen suum inscribunt,' or *Tusc. Disp.* i. 15 § 34, where
the words are almost identical:[2] 'nostri philosophi nonne
in eis libris ipsis quos scribunt de contemnenda gloria, sua

---

[1] Clark notes that the same quotation is made by Hier. *epist.* 10, § 3 (p. 37, u. 14, ed. Hilberg): it appears to be otherwise unknown.

[2] As Reid notes, on the *Pro Archia* passage.

nomina inscribunt?' Somewhat earlier in the same note
(*in Gal.* v. 26, p. 515 c) Jerome says: 'quantas habeat defi-
nitiones et significantias *gloria*, et philosophorum innume-
rabiles libri et Ciceronis duo uolumina quae de gloria scripsit, indicio sunt.' Cicero's *De Gloria* has, of course,
perished.[1] He is referred to as a model of Latin style in
the preface to the commentary on Ephesians (p. 537 f.).
A portion of the note *in Eph.* i. 9 (p. 554 D): 'sapientiam et
prudentiam esse diuersas Stoici[2] quoque opinantur,
dicentes: "*sapientia* est rerum diuinarum humanarumque
cognitio; *prudentia* uero tantum mortalium"', is in part
very like Cicero *De Officiis* ii. 2 § 5; '*sapientia* est, ut
a ueteribus philosophis definitum est, rerum diuinarum et
humanarum causarum quibus eae res continentur, scientia'.
At *In Tit.* i. 12–14 (p. 706 E) it is mentioned that Cicero
translated the 'Phaenomena' of Aratus into Latin; a large
portion of this translation is still extant.[3]

The polymath, M. Terentius Varro (116–27 B.C.), to whom
both Tertullian and Augustine were so much indebted for
information about Roman religion, is referred to in the
preface to the second book of the commentary on Galatians
thus: 'Marcus Varro, cunctarum antiquitatum diligentis-
simus perscrutator, et ceteri qui eum imitati sunt, multa
super hac gente (i.e. Galatis) et digna memoria tradiderunt.'
Jerome then goes on to say that he has determined not
to introduce uncircumcised men into God's temple, that
it is a long time since he ceased to read pagan authors,
and that therefore he will quote Lactantius instead. Of
Varro's great work, *Antiquitates*, few fragments are preserved, and for the survival of these we are indebted in
great part to Christian authors.

---

[1] The few surviving fragments may be seen in C. F. W. Müller's
Teubner edition of Cicero, partis iv vol. iii (Lips., 1879), pp. 330–2.

[2] See earlier in this chapter, p. 121.

[3] Ed. C. F. W. Müller, partis iv vol. iii (Lips., 1879), pp. 360–82.

M. Caelius Rufus († 48 B.C.) is hinted at in one place: see under Quintilian.

C. Sallustius Crispus (86–35 B.C.) is three times used. The sentence *in Gal.* iii. 1 (p. 416 D), 'uanos Mauros et feroces Dalmatas Latinus pulsat historicus', can hardly be anything but a reference to Sallust, *hist.* fragm. ii. 39 (ed. Maurenbrecher, fasc. ii (Lipsiae, 1893, p. 73)), though it comes to Jerome through the medium of Tertullian, *De Anima* 20 (see below). The same sentence in Sall. *Cat.* i. 2, 'animi imperio, corporis seruitio magis utimur' is twice alluded to by Jerome: *in Gal.* v. 16 (p. 500 A), 'secundum sententiam historici "animi imperio, corporis seruitio magis" uiuere': *in Eph.* v. 33 (p. 662 C): '"animi" quippe, ut ait Crispus, "imperio, corporis seruitio magis utimur"'.

P. Vergilius Maro (70–19 B.C.) became a school author at once, and no later Latin writer is unaffected by him. Jerome quotes him, or refers to him, in these passages: *In Gal.* iii. 1 (p. 417 D), 'unde et quidam e gentilibus: "nescio quis teneros oculus mihi fascinat agnos" (= *Ecl.* 3, 103)': in the preface to the third book of the commentary on Galatians, 'Maro' is coupled with 'Tullius' and pagan authors generally, in the statement that it is more than fifteen years since he had any of them in his hands, and that if he remembers any of them, it is 'quasi antiqui per nebulam somnii'; and then he tells the famous story that Virgil licked his books into shape as bears do their young. This story he may have got from A. Gellius, *Noctes Atticae* xvii. 10 § 2 (*ca.* A.D. 130–) (quoting the sophist Favorinus, of Arles): 'Amici familiaresque P. Vergili in his quae de ingenio moribusque eius memoriae tradiderunt, dicere eum solitum ferunt parere se uersus more atque ritu ursino' &c.: *in Eph.* iv. 6 (p. 611 B–C); '(Zenonem) secutus Vergilius ait:

> "deum namque ire per omnes
> terrasque tractusque maris" (= *Georg.* iv. 221–2), et reliqua;

et:
> "principio caelum ac terras camposque liquentes
> lucentemque globum lunae Titaniaque astra
> spiritus intus alit, totamque infusa per artus
> mens agitat molem et magno se corpore miscet".
>
> (= Aen. vi. 724-7) '.

Q. Horatius Flaccus (65–8 B.C.) is quoted once: *In Eph.*
v. 20 (p. 653 C–D) 'quem ut Flaccus in lyrico carmine ait:

> "si fractus inlabatur orbis,
> impavidum ferient ruinae" (= *Carm.* iii. 3, 7-8).'

T. Livius (59 B.C.–A.D. 17) is probably the source of the allusion to Hasdrubal's wife. The epitome [1] shows that her death was narrated in Book li: 'ultimo urbis excidio cum se Hasdrubal Scipioni dedisset, uxor eius, quae paucis ante diebus de marito impetrare non potuerat ut ad uictorem transfugerent, in medium se flagrantis urbis incendium cum duobus liberis ex arce praecipitauit.' This dramatic incident is alluded to by various other ancient writers,[2] but they all probably hark back to Livy. Jerome's words are these, *in Eph.* v. 25-7 (p. 656 C): 'quamuis sui inuicem maritus et coniunx amore teneantur (qualis illa uxor memoratur Hasdrubalis, quae capto uiro in patriae se iecit incendium, et ceterae quae uiris mortuis superuiuere noluerunt),' &c.

Germanicus Caesar (B.C. 15–A.D. 19) [3] is mentioned as one of the translators of the *Phaenomena* of Aratus, *in Tit.* i. 12-14 (p. 706 E).

M. Fabius Quintilianus (*ca.* A.D. 35–*ca.* A.D. 95) is the

---

[1] Ed. O. Rossbach (Lips. 1910), p. 63.

[2] See Drakenborch's edition of Livy, tom. v (Lugd. Bat. 1743), p. 1007: Val. Max. iii. 2, ext. 8; Appian, lib. 131, and others, enumerated more fully in Pauly-Wissowa's *Real-Encyclopädie*, Bd. vii. 2477. The other Christian references are Tert. *ad mart.* 4; Hier. *adu. Iouin.* i. 43 (t. ii, p. 310 B–c).

[3] It has been suggested that some one else, with the same names, is the real author.

S

probable source of the passage *in Gal.* v. 19–21 : 'pulchre quidem non ignobilis orator, cum ebrium de somno describeret excitatum, ait: "NEC DORMIRE EXCITATUS, NEC VIGILARE EBRIUS POTERAT".' The reference is to M. Caelius Rufus, Cicero's contemporary, and Quintilian *Inst. Orat.* iv. 2 § 124 '(illa M. Caeli in Antonium descriptio)...neque dormire excitatus neque uigilare ebrius poterat'.[1] Jerome was of course well acquainted with Quintilian, to whom he refers by name in the preface to the third book of his commentary on Galatians, as a model of eloquence, bracketing him with the Greek, Polemo.

C. Suetonius Tranquillus (A.D. 70–140 ?) is probably the source of the anecdote at *in Gal.* vi. 10 (p. 528 D) : 'Titus, filius Vespasiani ... tantae dicitur fuisse bonitatis ut, cum quadam nocte sero recordaretur in cena quod nihil boni die illa fecisset, dixerit amicis "hodie diem perdidi".' Suetonius, *Divus Titus* 8, reads thus: 'recordatus quondam super cenam quod nihil cuiquam toto die praestitisset, memorabilem illam meritoque laudatam uocem edidit: AMICI, DIEM PERDIDI.' It is recognized that Jerome's additions to Eusebius' *Chronicle* depend in great part on Suetonius. As a matter of fact, Jerome tells this very anecdote in his *Chronicle*,[2] and a comparison of the language used there shows that he depends directly on Suetonius for it. Jerome in fact seems to have taken little trouble to avoid repeating himself.

A. Gellius (*ca.* A.D. 130–) : see under Virgil, above.

Q. Septimius Florens Tertullianus (*ca.* A.D. 160–240) : *In Gal.* i. 8–9 (p. 383 cf.) : 'eleganter in hoc loco uir doctissimus Tertullianus aduersus Apellem et eius uirginem Philumenem, quam angelus quidam diabolici spiritus et peruersus impleuerat, hunc esse scribit angelum cui multo

---

[1] I owe this identification to a note of the late Prof. John E. B. Mayor († 1910), made in his copy of Vallarsi.

[2] 214th Olympiad, p. 271, ll. 5 ff., ed. Fotheringham.

ante quam Apelles nasceretur, spiritus sancti uaticinio sit
"anathema" per apostolum prophetatum.' This is a reference to Tertullian's *De Carne Christi*, c. 6:[1] 'Apellen, qui
. . . in uirginem Philumenen spiritu euersus est . . . et
angelo quidem illi Philumenes eadem uoce apostolus
respondebit qua ipsum illum iam tunc praecinebat, dicens:
"etiam si angelus de caelis aliter euangelizauerit uobis
quam nos euangelizauimus, anathema sit"' (= *Gal.* i. 8).
Tertullian, *De Anima*, 20, is used at *in Gal.* iii. 1 (p. 416 D).
Jerome's words are: 'uanos Mauros et feroces Dalmatas
Latinus pulsat historicus'; Tertullian's: 'Sallustius uanos
Mauros et feroces Dalmatas pulsat.' The language makes
it clear that it was from Tertullian, and not from Sallust
direct, that Jerome took the words. In the preface to the
commentary on Ephesians, Tertullian is referred to in
connexion with Cyprian, the argument being that Cyprian's
admiration for Tertullian did not keep him from authorship of his own. There is an interesting allusion at *in Tit.*
i. 6 (p. 697 C): 'scripsit et Tertullianus *De Monogamia*
librum haereticum, quem apostolo contraire, nemo qui
apostolum legerit, ignorabit.'

Caecilius Cyprianus, qui et Thascius († 258): *in Gal.*
v. 19–21: 'scripsit et beatus Cyprianus librum *De Zelo et
Liuore* ualde optimum, quem qui legerit, non dubitabit
adnumerare operibus carnis inuidiam.' For the reference
in the preface to the commentary on Ephesians, see under
Tertullian.

Nouatus (Nouatianus) (flourished about 250): see above,
under heretics.

Caecilius Firmianus, qui et Lactantius (flourished 300–
20). In the preface to the second book of the commentary on Galatians these words occur: 'Lactanti nostri
(= Christian, in opposition to the pagan Varro) quae in

---

[1] p. 436, ll. 4 ff., ed. Oehler.

tertio ad Probum uolumine[1] de hac gente opinatus sit, uerba ponemus: "Galli", inquit, "antiquitus a candore corporis Galatae nuncupabantur, et Sibylla sic eos appellat: quod significare uoluit poeta, cum ait: tum lactea colla auro innectuntur (= Verg. *Aen.* viii. 660–1), cum posset dicere ' candida': hinc utique Galatia prouincia, in quam Galli aliquando uenientes, cum Graecis se miscuerunt: unde primum ea regio Gallograecia, post Galatia nominata est."' *In Gal.* iv. 6 (p. 450 E): ' multi per imperitiam scripturarum (quod et Firmianus in octauo ad Demetrianum Epistularum libro facit) asserunt spiritum sanctum saepe patrem saepe filium nominari.' As it appears that there were only two books of Letters to Demetrian, the reference is an unsolved difficulty, the work being of course lost.[2] In the preface to the commentary on Ephesians Lactantius finds his place in the golden chain, Tertullian, Cyprian, Lactantius, Hilary, none of whom was deterred from writing by admiration for his immediate predecessor. *In Eph.* iv. 26 (p. 628 E) contains the following passage: ' Firmianus noster librum *De Ira Dei* docto pariter et eloquenti sermone conscripsit, quem qui legerit, puto ei ad irae intellectum satis abundeque posse sufficere.'

Rufius Festus Auienus (300 ?–350 ?) is mentioned as the most recent of the Latin translators of the *Phaenomena* of Aratus, *in Tit.* i. 12–14 (p. 706 E): ' IPSIUS ENIM ET GENUS SUMUS, quod hemistichium in Phaenomenis Arati legitur, quem Cicero in Latinum sermonem transtulit, et Germanicus Caesar, et nuper Auienus, et multi, quos enumerare perlongum est.' Avienus' works were splendidly edited by Alfred Holder (Innsbruck, 1887).

---

[1] This was a collection of epistles in four books, now lost (M. Schanz, *Gesch. d. röm. Litt.* iii³ (München, 1922), § 761, p. 426): the fragment in *C. S. E. L.* xxvii (Vindob. 1893), p. 155.

[2] Cf. Schanz, *loc. cit.*: *C. S. E. L.* xxvii, pp. 156 f.

C. Marius Victorinus (flourished 353) is mentioned by Jerome as his only Latin predecessor in commenting on the Epistles of St. Paul: see above, chapter 1.

Hilarius of Poitiers (+ 366): in the preface to the second book of the commentary on Galatians (pp. 427-8): 'non mirum est stultos et ad intellegentiam tardiores Galatas appellatos, cum et Hilarius, Latinae eloquentiae Rhodanus, Gallus ipse et Pictauis genitus, in hymnorum carmine Gallos "indociles" uocet.' The particular hymn no longer survives.[1] Hilary is mentioned in the preface to the commentary on Ephesians (see above under Lactantius).

A then recent poet is referred to at *in Gal.* v. 19-21 (p. 508 B–C): 'pulchre quidam de neotericis, Graecum uersum transferens, elegiaco metro de inuidia lusit, dicens:

IUSTIUS INVIDIA NIHIL EST, QUAE PROTINUS IPSUM
AUCTOREM RODIT EXCRUCIATQUE ANIMUM.'

This couplet seems to have escaped the collectors of ancient Latin verse; at least it is absent from Baehrens's *Fragmenta Poetarum Romanorum* (Lips. 1886).

Shortly after this (p. 508 E), he refers to a work of his own: 'licet me quidam in eo libro quem de seruanda uirginitate scripsi, reprehendendum putent quod dixerim adulescentulas ita uinum debere fugere ut uenenum, non me sententiae paenitebit.' The reference here is to Epistle xxii (written in 384), addressed to Eustochium, which in certain manuscripts bears the sub-title 'de uirginitate seruanda': the passage occurs in § 8 (1): 'hoc primum moneo, hoc obtestor, ut sponsa Christi uinum fugiat pro ueneno.'[2]

Some of the most interesting parts of the commentaries recount personal experiences. *In Gal.* ii. 11-13 (p. 408 B–C), he tells how, when a youth at Rome learning public speaking, he used to rush away from the rhetorical school

---

[1] Cf. ed. Feder, *C. S. E. L.* lxv (Vindob. 1916), p. lxx.
[2] Ed. Hilberg, *C. S. E. L.* liv (Vindob. 1910), p. 154, uu. 12 ff.

to the real law courts, and listen to eloquent pleaders contending against one another with such bitterness that they often forgot about the case, and turned to personal insult and cutting gibes. *In Gal.* lib. ii. praef. (p. 427 f.), he speaks of the religious zeal of the Roman Christians of his day, how eagerly they rush to church and the graves of the martyrs, how their 'amen' sounds like the thunder of heaven and shakes the empty pagan temples. In the immediately following passage he tells how the visitor to Achaia will still see the same faults that Paul charged against the Corinthians. A little later in the same preface he illustrates the foolishness of the Galatians from his own experiences of the schismatic city Ancyra, metropolis of Galatia, and from the various Phrygian heresies. He also makes the oft-quoted remark that the Galatians, in addition to the universal Greek, speak a language of their own which is almost the same as that spoken at Trier, where he had long lived. Now and again (e. g. *in Gal.* iii. 14, p. 436 A) he speaks of his Hebrew teacher, and draws lessons from his instruction. *In Gal.* iv. 6 (p. 451 D), quoting our Lord's command in the Gospel to call no one 'father' but God, he says he does not know why in monasteries we either call others by that name, or allow others so to address us. *In Gal.* iv. 17–18 (p. 464 D–E), he illustrates the defection of the Galatians from the Apostle, after his presence was withdrawn from them, by church experience of his own day. When an eloquent or pious teacher arouses a congregation, we see all active in almsgiving, fasting, purity, care for the poor, and such-like virtues: but when he is gone, their energy flags, and all their beneficent activities come to an end. *In Gal.* iv. 27 (p. 474 C), he tells how seldom one comes across a Jew of mark in any city, while Christians abound everywhere: a little later (*in Gal.* iv. 29–31, p. 475 E) he appeals to history to show that the Jews have persecuted the Chris-

tians much more than the Gentiles have. In the preface to
the commentary on Ephesians (pp. 539, 540), he tells how he
went to Alexandria, particularly in order to consult Didymus
personally about difficult passages throughout Scripture.
In Eph. v. 14 (p. 648 D), he says he knows that he heard
a certain person (*quendam*) discussing this passage in
church, who declared that the words were uttered to
Adam, who was really buried at Calvary, where Christ
was crucified; that the place was called 'Calvary' because
the head of a man of old had been buried there, and that
the Lord was really hanging above this grave when crucified. The text was thus read by this exegete: 'Arise,
Adam, thou that sleepest, and arise from the dead, and
Christ will touch thee.'[1] *In Eph.* v. 32 (p. 661 A), he tells
what the eloquent and learned scripture student, Gregory
of Nazianzus, said to him when he was discussing this
passage with him. *In Tit.* i. 5 (p. 694 C), he comments on
the practice by which ecclesiastical appointments go to
unsuitable persons, not to those distinguished for purity
of life: 'nunc cernimus plurimos hanc rem beneficium
facere, ut non quaerant eos qui possunt ecclesiae plus
prodesse, in ecclesiae erigere columnas, sed quos uel ipsi
amant uel quorum sunt obsequiis deleniti uel pro quibus
maiorum quispiam rogauerit et, ut deteriora taceam, qui ut
clerici fierent, muneribus impetrarunt': compare *in Tit.*
i. 5 (p. 694 A–B). May we see in such passages an indica-
tion of Jerome's soreness on the subject of the succession
to Damasus? *In Tit.* iii. 9 (p. 735 C) contains a passage
of peculiar interest, where he tells how he had heard
a certain Jew, who pretended that he had been converted
to Christianity at Rome, discussing the genealogies of our
Lord in the Gospels of Matthew and Luke, and arguing
that from Solomon to Joseph they agreed neither in numbers
nor names: 'qui cum corda simplicium peruertisset, quasi

---

[1] Cf. Athanasius' *De Incarnatione*, § 25.

ex adytis et oraculo deferebat quasdam, ut sibi uidebatur, solutiones, cum magis debuerit iustitiam et misericordiam, et dilectionem dei quaerere, et post illa, si forte occurrisset, de nominibus et numeris disputare.' There is clearly keen personal feeling behind this, and the venerable Professor Theodor von Zahn, of Erlangen,[1] long ago suggested that the reference is to Isaac, an ex-Jew, who took a leading part in the prosecution of Damasus on a capital charge. Many scholars have accepted his further argument that the reference is to the mysterious Ambrosiaster, who certainly discusses questions of this very kind.[2]

Among the most interesting passages in the commentaries are those where Jerome advises or attacks bishops and presbyters. Here again personal feeling seems to underlie what he says. *In Gal.* iv. 13 (p. 458 E): 'these words call us to humility, and crush the conceit of bishops, who, as if seated on some lofty watch-tower, scarcely deign to see mortals and to address their fellow-slaves. Let them learn from the Apostle that even the erring and foolish Galatians are called "brethren"': compare *in Tit.* i. 6 (p. 698 D): i. 7 (p. 699 B). *In Eph.* vi. 4 (p. 666 B) contains a bitter attack on bishops and presbyters who train their sons in pagan literature and make them read comedies and sing the obscene verses of low-comedy actors, though the boys are perchance being educated at the expense of the Church; and then in his graphic way he shows how a teacher of literature or a professor of rhetoric may be spending on his household, or on the pagan temples, or on filthy women of the street, monies that have been contributed by Christian virgins, or widows, or other poor people who sacrifice all their substance. The identity of

---

[1] *Theologisches Literaturblatt*, Bd. xx (1899), pp. 313 ff.: see p. 45 f. above.

[2] Ps.-Aug. *Quaest. Vet. et Nov. Test.* 56; app. N.T. 7 (*C.S.E.L.* l. (Vindob. 1908), pp. 101 ff., 432 f.).

presbyter and bishop is proclaimed in absolutely definite language at *in Tit.* i. 5 (p. 694 E): 'idem est ergo presbyter qui et episcopus,' and then follow the usual Scripture proofs of this undeniable fact (Phil. i. 1; Acts xx. 28; Hebr. xiii. 17; 1 Petr. v. 1-2).[1] At *in Tit.* ii. 15 (p. 728 E) he insists on the duty, not merely of the bishops, presbyters, and deacons, but of the lesser clergy, the exorcists, readers, and sacristans, to give a clear lead to the whole congregation in manner of life and speech.

Without having exhausted in any way the interest of Jerome as a commentator on St. Paul's Epistles, we must now take leave of him. Among all the ancient Latin commentators on the Bible he stands supreme. Though his commentaries were rapidly produced, not painstakingly copied out by his own hand, but dictated to an amanuensis, sometimes at the rate of a thousand lines a day,[2] though he is fully conscious of their defects,[3] and though he writes in a plain every-day style,[4] the commentaries hold their commanding position, because their author approached his task with a well-furnished mind and a perfectly trained pen, with a knowledge of Greek and Hebrew as well as Latin,[5] with a determination to use the very best authorities at his command, with a fine care for the diction of Scripture in the three languages, and for the true text, both Greek and Latin, of the Epistles, in the study of which he does not

---

[1] Jerome (cf. also *epist.* 69, § 3; 146, § 1) is not, of course, alone in this teaching: cf. Ambst. *in 1 Tim.* iii. 8-10; *Quaest.* 101 (*Study*, pp. 156 f.); Theod.-Mops. *in Phil.* i. 1 &c., with Swete's note; a modern reference is Jo. Evelyn's *Diary* at 20 Feb., 1676.

[2] *Praef. in Eph.* lib. ii, pp. 585-6. This means 1,000 lines of the length of the Virgilian hexameter.

[3] He speaks of his *imbecillitas* and *imperitia*, in Gal. praef. pp. 369-70.

[4] Cf. *praef. lib. iii in Gal., praef. lib. ii in Eph.*

[5] Cf. in particular *in Eph.* v. 14 (p. 648 A): 'ego certe secundum paupertatulam meam omnes editiones ueterum scripturarum ipsaque Hebraeorum uolumina diligenter euentilans, numquam hoc scriptum repperi.'

disdain to regard the seemingly unimportant matter of punctuation; and, above all, with a live intellect and a real Christian faith. Our investigation has indeed shown, what the author himself never disguised, that his work is compilation, but the whole has passed through his mind and bears the stamp of his peculiar genius.

In view of the excellence of M. Henri Goelzer's work, *Étude lexicographique et grammaticale de la Latinite de Saint Jérôme* (Paris: Hachette, 1884), it would be superfluous to illustrate Jerome's language here. When the Vienna edition of Jerome's works is complete, a new edition of the illustrious Member of the Institute's work might perhaps be profitably undertaken, but not till then.

IV

AUGUSTINE

THE name of Augustine (or Austin, as our fathers with more loving familiarity called him) is one for which my love and reverence have steadily grown as the result of thirty years' study. It is not easy to refrain from bowing the knee before the stately row of folios enshrining what remains of his astounding wisdom and learning. For me, at least, he is the greatest Christian since New Testament times, and even if he be not the greatest of Latin writers, he is assuredly the greatest man that ever wrote Latin. It is impossible to point to any Latin author who has exercised so profound an influence on succeeding ages, and this he has done by a wonderful combination of gifts, tenderness of heart, passionate love and devotion, tireless industry, spiritual insight, biblical learning, and consummate eloquence.

To appreciate Augustine aright one must know something in the first place of the environment amidst which he grew up. Into the question of the original inhabitants of the district now called Tunis one need not enter. But about the beginning of the last millennium before Christ, settlers came from Tyre in Phoenicia, founded the city of Carthage, and ruled the country continuously till 146 B.C. The Semitic civilization thus established made a lasting impress on the country. The Punic language, a sister language of Aramaic and Hebrew, persisted in the less civilized parts of Africa down even to Augustine's time, and we can trace it clearly in the names of many of the towns, such as Thamugadi, Thubursicum, and Mileu, which are as un-Latin as they could be. Apart from such influences as these, the province was very thoroughly romanized, and was one of the two chief senatorial provinces in the Empire, governed by an ex-consular proconsul appointed by the Senate.

St. Paul had laid down the plan by which Christianity was to become the religion of the Roman Empire, and it was therefore inevitable that before long the new faith should come to the province called 'Africa'. It is natural to suppose that it came to Africa from Italy, either directly or through Sicily. In any case it found a Semitic soil ready prepared for it. The marvellous spread of Christianity in Africa can only be due, I think, to this, though the martyrdoms of the Scillitans, Perpetua and Felicitas, and later Cyprian himself, are factors that must not be overlooked: for no other country in the West, not even Italy, was christianized so extensively within such a comparatively short space of time. A hundred years before Augustine was born there were already eighty-seven churches in the province,[1] and the number must have been greater in his day. It was then in a well romanized, Latin-speaking country, in the veins of whose inhabitants much Semitic blood flowed, where, too, Christianity had been preached with wonderful success for three hundred years, that Augustine first saw the light of day.

He was born at Tagaste, in the Numidian part of Africa, on November 13, 354. Of his parents, Patricius, his father, was pagan, while his mother, Monnica, was Christian. His elementary education was obtained in his native town and

---

[1] The names of the bishops are preserved in the Cyprianic 'Sententiae Episcoporum', C. S. E. L. iii (Vindob. 1868), pp. 435-61 ; much better edited by Hans von Soden in the Göttingen *Nachrichten* for 1909 ; cf. also C. S. E. L. li (Vindob. 1908), pp. 177, &c., 303-67.

developed in the larger town of Madaura, the birthplace of
the fascinating writer Apuleius. In his sixteenth year he
was sent to Carthage, the capital of the province, for what
we should now call his university education. As 'a lad
o' pairts', to use the old Scottish phrase, he found a patron
in Romanianus, who did for him what his recently widowed
mother's resources were unable to achieve. Like most of
his contemporaries, he spent a somewhat dissolute youth,
but was influenced for good by the high moral tone of
Cicero's *Hortensius*, a work now unhappily lost. From
the age of nineteen to twenty-eight he was a follower of
Manicheism, a powerful rival of Christianity. In this
period of his life he received a mastership in his native city,
which he soon abandoned for further study at Carthage.
There he began to feel dissatisfaction with Manichean
doctrine. Discontent sent him to Rome in his thirtieth
year. At the beginning of 384 he obtained a professorship
of public speaking at Milan. There he was powerfully
influenced by Archbishop Ambrose, and *his* influence,
backed by a mother's prayers, helped to bring about his
dramatic conversion to Christianity in the latter part of
the summer of 386. He gave up his public position and
devoted the rest of his life to the Faith, into which he was
baptized at Easter 387.

Later in the same year his mother died, and after a year
in Rome he returned to his native land, never afterwards
to leave it. At first he spent most of his time in philo-
sophic discussion with his friends, and it was much against
his will that he accepted ordination as a presbyter in Hippo
Regius, where, after about four years (in 395), he became
co-bishop, and a little later, on the death of his colleague,
bishop of the church there, a position which he held continuously till his death on August 28, 430.

His life in Hippo was one of ceaseless activity. As

bishop, he not only preached constantly, but supervised settlements of ascetics, both men and women. His pen was never idle. He began authorship while still in his twenties, but it is not till about the year 400 that his works become of supreme importance to the Church. To that period belong his *Confessions*, addressed to God, now one of the world's classics, where he sees himself as God saw him, and traces his life to the time of conversion; and his *De Consensu Euangelistarum*, which shares with Eusebius' *Canons* the honour of being the greatest early work on the Synoptic Problem. After the turn of the century comes one of the longest, most careful, and most important of his works, his *De Ciuitate Dei*, which marks the end of the old world and the beginning of the Middle Ages, just as Dante's *Divina Commedia* closes the Middle Ages and opens the avenue to the modern world. These are amongst his most important works, but we have over four hundred of his sermons, the longest of which took perhaps not more than ten minutes to deliver; the collection of about two hundred and fifty letters, most of which deal with Christian doctrine, and were addressed to correspondents, famous or little known, spread over all parts of the ancient world; a large group of dogmatic writings; a still more impressive group of polemical writings, setting forth at the same time the truth, as he understood it, against the Manicheans, against the Donatists, against the Arians, and above all against the Pelagians; a very interesting collection of writings on moral questions, such as falsehood, continence, wedlock; and biblical expositions.

To the class of biblical expositions belong his massive works *Enarrationes in Psalmos* and *Tractatus in Iohannis Euangelium*. Either of these works alone would have given him an immortal reputation. He lavishes on them all the wealth of his learning and genius. But it is with

shorter and less important works that we are here concerned, his two slight works on the Epistle to the Romans
and his brief exposition of the Epistle to the Galatians.

Augustine was peculiarly fitted to deal with the Epistle to
the Romans, as it was a well-known passage in that Epistle
that led to his conversion. I mean of course verses 13 and
14 in chapter xiii: 'not in chambering and wantonness . . .
but put ye on the Lord Jesus Christ, and make not provision
for the flesh, to fulfil the lusts thereof.' But he quailed
before the task, as one to which even *he* was unequal.
There are, it is true, abundant expositions of particular
sections of this Epistle scattered throughout his works,
and later compilers did not hesitate to take advantage of
the fact. Cassiodorus, in the middle of the sixth century,
used Augustine very largely to counteract the teaching of
Pelagius' commentary on that Epistle, which he revised.
Again, in the same century, before Cassiodorus' time,
a certain Peter of Tripoli put together a commentary from
the works of Augustine, which Cassiodorus expected to
acquire. This work seemed to exist in at least one manuscript,[1] but it is only Florus after all. Unprinted is a
commentary on all the Epistles of St. Paul, which the
greatest man of his age, the Englishman now known as
the Venerable Bede, compiled from Augustine's writings
in the early part of the eighth century. In the following
century a deacon of Lyons, named Florus, did the same
thing, and, curiously enough, it is his work that is in print
under the name of Bede.

But from Augustine himself we have on the Epistle to
the Romans, as I have said, only two short works; the
*Expositio quarundam Propositionum ex Epistula ad Roma-
nos*, which, as he tells us himself,[2] grew out of a conference

---

[1] Rome, Vaticanus latinus, 4950 (saec. xi); Wilmart, *R.B.* 1926, p. 31.
[2] *Retr.* i. 23.

he had with certain brethren, who had asked him particular
questions about the Epistle, while he was still a presbyter
at Carthage. His answers he preferred to put into a book.
This work, written about the beginning of 394, like the
other two with which we have to deal, must not be judged
as we should judge a work of his maturity, but the group
nevertheless marks a real stage in the saint's progress, as
Wundt has recently argued in a convincing way.[1] If the
study of Cicero's *Hortensius*, the adoption of Neoplatonism,
and the garden scene where the light finally broke upon
him, be regarded as the first, second, and third turning-
points in his life, a fourth Wundt would date about the
beginning of 391, when Augustine first began to realize
the significance of Divine Grace. It is his increasing
understanding of Divine Grace which is the chief aid he
has furnished to the life of the human soul, and it is in
this little commentary on select passages of the Epistle to
the Romans that we get some of his earliest meditations
on this inexhaustible subject. Some passages will be
quoted in illustration later on.

His other work on the Epistle to the Romans is his
Epistulae ad Romanos inchoata Expositio. It is evident,
from the fact that his exposition of the salutation at the
beginning (i. 1–7) occupies eighteen columns in the Migne
edition, that the commentary on the Epistle was planned
on a large scale, worthy of its grandeur and importance,
but beyond the salutation he felt unable to proceed, and
turned, as he says, to easier tasks.[2] The book naturally
did not circulate widely, and in fact the Benedictines had
to resort to one Vatican MS., finding none in France. The
complete commentary on the Epistle to the Galatians
belongs to about the same date, and will fall to be considered
below.

[1] *Z. N. T. W.* xxi (1922), 53–64. [2] *Retr.* i. 25.

The Benedictines had nine manuscripts of Romans (*propositiones*) and Galatians together, and four of Galatians alone.[1] The following list, which I have compiled from the printed catalogues, comprises in all fifty-nine manuscripts, to set over against their fourteen. It will be surprising if some considerable improvement does not take place in the text, when these MSS. have been carefully examined, for among them are MSS. of the eighth, ninth, and tenth century, which were unknown to the Benedictines. The fact that the connexions of these MSS. are Insular, Rhenish, Swiss, and Bavarian makes it probable that they will furnish a valuable control of the French tradition.[2] It may be that some of the MSS. here indicated are MSS. of later compilations from Augustine. Neither in this respect, nor in distinguishing the two Augustinian works, can one in all cases rely on the knowledge of the cataloguers, and it has not been possible for me to examine the MSS. themselves.

Amiens 81 (saec. xiii) (Rom. Gal.).
Angers 159 (151) (saec. xi) (Gal.).
       292 (283) (saec. xii) (Gal.).
Assisi 90 (saec. xiii) (Rom. Gal.).
Avranches 72 (saec. xi–xii) (Gal.).
       79 (saec. xi) (Rom. Gal.) (?).
Berlin lat. 293 (theol. fol. 348) (Lisborn) (saec. xii) (Rom. expos. inch.).
       Görres 97 (ii) (S. Maximin, Trèves) (saec. x) (Rom. Gal.).
Brussels 1024 (5504–12) (Gembloux) (saec. xi) (Rom. Gal.).
       1058 (48) (Corsendonck ?) (saec. xv) (Rom. Gal.).
       1124 (312–20) (saec. xiv) (Rom. Gal.).
Cambridge, University Library Ll. ii. 3 (2151) (saec. xv) (Rom. Gal.).
       Trinity College, 76 (B. 2. 33: 146) (Canterbury) (saec. xii) (Rom. Gal.).

---

[1] Ed. Bened. tom. iii pars ii (Paris, 1680), pp. 983–4.
[2] The Vienna edition appears to be at the moment unassigned.

Cambridge, Trinity College, 164 (B. 5. 18 : 333) (Canterbury) (saec. xv) (Rom. Gal.).

Chartres 157 (107) (saec. xii) (Rom. Gal.).

Cologne lxxvii (Darmst. 2078) (saec. xii) (Rom. expos. inch.).

Douai 251 (Marchiennes) (saec. xii) (Rom.).

Einsiedeln 139 (saec. xii) (Rom. Gal.).

Erlangen 223 (Heisbrunn) (saec. xiv, A.D. 1310) (Rom.).

Geneva 15 (saec. xii–xiii) (Gal.).

Grenoble 201 (Chartreux) (saec. xii) (Gal.).

London, B.M. Harl. 3027 (saec. xii) (Rom.).

Oxford, Bodl., Laud. Misc. 134 [1] (Würzburg) (saec. ix) (Rom.).

  ,, ,, ,, 398 (S. Mariae Visicampi) (saec. xii–xiii) (Gal.).

Paris, B. N. 1639 (Colbertinus) (saec. xii) (Rom. Gal.).

  ,, 1974 (,,) (saec. xiv) (Rom. Gal.).

  ,, 1975 (Strasbourg) (saec. x) (Rom. Gal.).

  ,, 1976 (Béthune) (saec. xii) (Rom. Gal.).

  ,, 2033 (St. Amand) (saec. xiii) (Rom. Gal.).

  ,, 1957 (Colbertinus) (saec. xiii) (Rom.).

  ,, 1977 (,,) (saec. xiv) (Gal.).

  ,, 2700 (Thuaneus et Colbertinus) (saec. xi) (Gal.).

  ,, 10444 (saec. xii) (Rom. Gal.) (?).

  Arsenal 1032 (Grands Augustins) (saec. xiv) (Gal.).

  Mazarine 632 (274) (saec. xiii) (Rom. Gal.).

    ,, 636 (270) (saec. xiv) (Rom. Gal.).

    ,, 644 (880) (saec. xv) (Gal.).

Reims 82 (E. 246) (saec. xii) (Rom. Gal.).

Rome, Vat. lat. 445 (saec. xv) (Rom. expos. inch.[2] Rom. Gal.).

  ,, ,, 491 (saec. viii,[3] insular minuscule) (Rom. Gal.).

  ,, Urbin. lat. 69 (113) (53) (saec. xv) (Rom. expos. inch. Gal.).

St. Gall, Stiftsbibl., 137 (saec. x) (Rom. Gal.).

    ,,   151 (saec. x) (Rom. Gal.).

    ,,   789 (saec. xiii) (Rom.) (?).

---

[1] 132 wrongly in index.

[2] The only MS. known to the Benedictines.

[3] So Lindsay, *Notae Latinae* (Cambr. 1915), p. 478; Reifferscheid (*Wien. SB.* lxiii, p. 594) and Bannister (private note) saec. ix.

Strasbourg 309 (latin 257) (saec. xiii) (Gal.).

Tours 288 (Marmoutier) (saec. x) (Gal.).

Trèves 156 (saec. xvi in.) (Gal.).

Troyes 40 (ii) (Clairvaux) (saec. xii) (Rom. expos. inch. Rom.
    Gal.).

        412 (Clairvaux) (saec. xii) (Rom. Gal.).

Utrecht 68 (Eccl. 186, antea 296 r) (saec. xv, A. D. 1464) (Rom.
    Gal.).

Vendôme 192 (saec. xii) (Gal.).

Venice 42 membr. (saec. xv, A. D. 1471) (Rom. Gal.).

Vienna 735 (saec. xiii) (Rom.).

   ,,   795 (saec. x) (Rom.) (?).

Wisbech 27 (saec. xii) (Rom.) (?).

Wolfenbüttel 4112 (28 Weissenb.) (saec. x) (Rom.).

Zwettl 32 (saec. xii) (Rom. Gal.).

      296 (saec. xii–xiii) (Rom.).

The question of the particular Latin text or texts of the
Epistles of St. Paul employed by Augustine is one of very
special interest. It is quite certain, to begin with, that he
never used the Vulgate text. We are indebted to the
researches of Sabatier, Ziegler,[1] Rönsch,[2] Wölfflin,[3] Morin,[4]
and latterly of De Bruyne,[5] for a solution of the question.
The monastery of Freising in Bavaria at one time possessed
a manuscript written in the sixth century, containing *inter
alia* the Epistles of St. Paul in Latin. The mutilation of
this manuscript began not later than the thirteenth century,

---

[1] *Italafragmente der Paulinischen Briefe* u. s. w. (Marburg, 1876);
*Die lateinischen Bibelübersetzungen vor Hieronymus und die Itala des
Augustinus* (Munich, 1879).

[2] *Z. f. wiss. Theol.* xxii (1879) pp. 224–38. By the kindness of the
Prior, I had the pleasure of examining the Göttweig leaves in
August 1924.

[3] *SB. bay. Akad.* 1893 (ii), pp. 253–80.

[4] *Revue Bénédictine*, xxviii (1911), pp. 221–7.

[5] *Les Fragments de Freising* (Collectanea Biblica Latina cura et
studio monachorum S. Benedicti, vol. v), (Rome, 1921).

and of it only thirty-five leaves are now known to exist.
The manuscript represents the recension habitually used
by St. Augustine. It was written probably in Spain,
which in many respects was the child of Africa.

De Bruyne [1] shows, after Ziegler, that Augustine did not
at first use this form of text, but that it begins to appear in
his writings from 389 onwards. It was apparently about
this latter date that he encountered the type, in Africa
itself, and he remained thenceforth faithful to it throughout
his life. This does not mean that the Augustinian citations,
even if we had them as they left his hands, agree *ad
litteram* with the Freising MS. De Bruyne has shown good
reason for the view that Augustine retouched this text from
time to time, that in fact he was labouring towards an ideal,
and gradually corrected its defects. It is an interesting
discovery that, for this part of the Bible at least, Augustine
was a real textual critic.

The portions of the Freising MS. now extant, for Romans
and Galatians, and therefore available for comparison with
the text in the commentaries on these epistles, are *Rom.*
v. 16–vi. 4, vi. 6–19, xiv. 10–xv. 13; *Gal.* ii. 5–v. 2, vi. 5–18.
Our best plan will be to arrange in three parallel columns
the readings of the Freising MS., the Augustinian citations,
and the Vulgate.

[1] *Op. cit.*, p. xviii.

READINGS

	Fris.	*Aug.*	*Vulg.*
Rom. v. 16.	nam iudicium ex uno in *condemnatione* gratia autem ex multis delictis in *sanctificatione*	nam iudicium *quidem* ex uno in condemnationem gratia autem ex multis delictis *ad* iustificationem	nam iudicium ex uno in condemnationem gratia autem ex multis delictis in iustificationem
17.	si enim *ob* unius delicto mors regnauit per unum multo magis *habundantiam* gratiae et donationis et iustitiae accipientes in uita regnabunt per unum Iesum Christum	si enim *ob* unius *delictum* mors regnauit per unum multo magis *qui* abundantiam gratiae et iusti- ∧ tiae *accipiunt* in uita regnabunt per unum Iesum Christum	si enim in unius delicto mors regnauit per unum multo magis abundantiam gratiae et donationis et iustitiae accipientes in uita regnabunt per unum Iesum Christum
18.	igitur sicut per unius delictum ∧ omnes homines in condemnationem sic et per unius iustitiam ∧ omnes homines in iustificationem uitae	*itaque* sicut per unius delictum in omnes homines *ad* condemnationem *ita* et per unius *iustificationem in* omnes homines *ad* iustificationem uitae	igitur sicut per unius delictum in omnes homines in condemnationem sic et per unius iustitiam in omnes homines in iustificationem uitae
19.	sicut enim per in-	sicut enim per in-	sicut enim per in-

	Fris.	*Aug.*	*Vulg.*
Rom. v. 19.	oboedientiam unius hominis peccatores constituti sunt multi ita et per unius *oboedientiam* iusti. *constituuntur* multi	obedientiam unius hominis peccatores constituti sunt multi ita et per unius *obedientiam* iusti constituentur multi	oboedientiam unius hominis peccatores constituti sunt multi ita et per unius oboeditionem iusti constituentur multi
20.	lex autem subintrauit ut habundaret delictum ubi autem habundauit delictum superhabundauit gra-	lex ∧ subintrauit ut abundaret delictum	lex autem subintrauit ut abundaret delictum ubi autem abundauit delictum superabundauit gra-
21.	tia ut sicut regnauit peccatum in *mortem* ita ∧gratia regnet per iustitiam in uitam aeternam per Iesum Christum dominum nostrum.		tia ut sicut regnauit peccatum in morte ita et gratia regnet per iustitiam in uitam aeternam per Iesum Christum dominum nostrum.
vi. 1.	quid ergo dicemus permanebimus in peccato ut gratia	quid ergo dicemus permanebimus in peccato ut gratia abundet absit	quid ergo dicemus permanebimus in peccato ut gratia abundet absit
2.	abundet absit		

	Fris.	*Aug.*	*Vulg.*
Rom. vi. 2.	qui enim mortui	qui ⟨ mortui	qui enim mortui
	sumus peccato	sumus peccato	sumus peccato
	quo modo adhuc	quo modo ⟨	quo modo adhuc
	uibemus in illo	uiuemus in *eo*	uiuemus in illo
3.	an ignoratis *fra-*		an ignoratis ⟨
	tres quia quicumque		quia quicumque
	baptizati sumus in		baptizati sumus in
	Christo Iesu in morte		Christo Iesu in morte
	ipsius baptizati sumus		ipsius baptizati sumus
4.	consepulti enim sumus		consepulti enim sumus
	cum illo per baptis-		cum illo per baptis-
	mum in mortem ut		mum in mortem ut
	quem ad modum sur-		quo modo sur-
	rexit Christus a mor-		rexit Christus a mor-
	tuis per gloriam patris		tuis per gloriam patris
	ita et nos in *nouitatem*		ita et nos in nouitate
			uitae ambulemus
5.			si enim conplantati
			facti sumus simili-
			tudini mortis eius
			simul et resurrectionis
6.		hoc scientes	erimus hoc scientes

	Frs.	*Aug.*	*Vulg.*
Rom. vi. 6.	homo noster simul *confixus est cruci* ut destruatur corpus peccati ut ultra non seruiamus peccato	quia uetus homo noster simul crucifixus est ut *euacuaretur* corpus peccati ut ultra non seruiamus peccato	quia uetus homo noster simul crucifixus est ut destruatur corpus peccati ut ultra non seruiamus peccato
7.	qui enim mortuus est iustificatus est		qui enim mortuus est iustificatus est
8.	a peccato si autem mortui sumus cum Christo credimus quia simul *conuibemus*	si ∧ mortui sumus cum Christo	a peccato si autem mortui sumus cum Christo credimus quia simul etiam uiuemus
9.	cum *illo hoc* scientes quod Christus surgens a mortuis iam non moritur mors *ei* ul- tra non dominabitur		cum Christo scientes quod Christus surgens a mortuis iam non moritur mors illi ul- tra non dominabitur
10.	quod enim mortuus est peccato mortuus est semel quod au- tem uiuit uiuit deo		quod enim mortuus est peccato mortuus est semel quod au- tem uiuit uiuit deo
11.	*itaque* et uos exis-		ita et uos exis-

Fris.	*Aug.*	*Vulg.*
Rom. vi. 11. timate uos mortuos		timate uos mortuos
quidem esse peccato		quidem esse peccato
uiuere autem deo ∧		uiuentes autem deo in Christo Iesu
12. non ergo regnet pec-	non ergo regnet pec-	non ergo regnet pec-
catum in uestro mor-	catum in uestro mor-	catum in uestro mor-
tali corpore *ad*	tali corpore *ad*	tali corpore ut
oboediendum concu-	*obediendum deside-*	oboediatis concu-
13. piscentiis eius ∧ neque	*riis* eius	piscentiis eius sed neque
exhibeatis membra ues-	{exhibeatis	exhibeatis membra ues-
tra arma iniquitatis	*praebeatis* membra ues-	tra arma iniquitatis
peccato sed exibete uos ∧	tra arma iniquitatis	peccato sed exhibete uos deo
tamquam ex mortuis	peccato	tamquam ex mortuis
uiuentes et membra		uiuentes et membra
uestra arma iustitiae		uestra arma iustitiae
14. deo peccatum enim	peccatum enim	deo peccatum enim
in uobis non domina-	*in* uobis non domina-	uobis non domina-
bitur non enim *estis*	bitur non enim *estis*	bitur non enim sub
sub lege sed sub gra-	*sub lege* sed sub gra-	lege estis sed sub gra-
15. tia quid ergo peccaui-	tia	tia quid ergo peccaui-
mus *quia* non sumus		mus quoniam non sumus
sub lege sed sub gra-		sub lege sed sub gra-

X

Fris.

Aug.

Vulg.

Rom. vi. 16. tia absit nescitis *quia* cui *uos exhibetis* seruos ad oboediendum serui estis eius cui *oboedistis* siue peccati siue *iustitiae fidei*	tia absit nescitis quoniam cui exhibetis uos seruos ad oboediendum serui estis eius cui oboeditis siue peccati siue oboeditionis ad iustitiam
17. gratias autem deo quod fuistis serui peccati oboedistis autem ex corde in eam formam doctrinae in *quam* traditi estis	gratias autem deo quod fuistis serui peccati oboedistis autem ex corde in eam formam doctrinae in qua traditi estis
18. liberati autem a peccato serui facti estis iustitiae	liberati autem a peccato serui facti estis iustitiae humanum dico propter infirmitatem carnis.
19. infirmitatem carnis	
xiv. (10.) omnes enim *adstabimus* ante tribunal 11. *Christi* scribtum est	omnes enim stabimus ante tribunal dei scriptum est

Fris.

Rom. xiv. 11. enim uiuo ego dicit
dominus *quia* mihi
curuabit omne genu
et *confitebitur omnis*
12. *lingua* deo *igitur* unus
quisque nostrum pro se
13. rationem reddet∧ non ergo
amplius inuicem
iudicemus sed hoc
magis iudicate ne
ponatis offendiculum
aut scandalum frat-
14. *ribus* scio et *certus sum*
in domino Iesu quia
nihil commune per
illum nisi ei qui
putat aliquid esse
commune illi com-
15. mune est *nam si*
propter *esca* frater
tuus *tristatur* iam
non secundum cari-

Aug.

Vulg.

enim uiuo ego dicit
dominus quoniam mihi
flectet omne genu
et omnis lingua confi-
tebitur deo itaque unus
quisque nostrum pro se
rationem reddet deo non ergo
amplius inuicem
iudicemus sed hoc
iudicate magis ne
ponatis offendiculum
fratri uel scanda-
lum scio et confido
in domino Iesu quia
nihil commune per
ipsum nisi ei qui
existimat quid com-
mune esse illi com-
mune est si enim
propter cibum frater
tuus contristatur iam
non secundum cari-

Fris.	Aug.	Vulg.
Rom. xiv. 15. tatem ambulas noli		tatem ambulas noli
in esca tua illum		cibo tuo illum
perdere pro quo Christus		perdere pro quo Christus
16. mortuus est non ergo	non ergo	mortuus est non ergo
blasphemetur bonum	blasphemetur bonum	blasphemetur bonum
17. nostrum non est *enim*	nostrum	nostrum non est
regnum dei esca et		regnum dei esca et
potus sed iustitia et		potus sed iustitia et
pax et gaudium in		pax et gaudium in
18. spiritu sancto qui enim		spiritu sancto qui enim
in hoc seruit Christo		in hoc seruit Christo
placet deo et probatus		placet deo et probatus
19. est hominibus itaque		est hominibus itaque
quae pacis sunt sec-		quae pacis sunt sec-
temur et quae *ad*		temur et quae aedi-
aedificationem ∧ in		ficationis sunt in inui-
20. inuicem ∧ *noli* prop-		cem custodiamus noli prop-
ter esca destruere		ter escam destruere
opus dei omnia qui-		opus dei omnia qui-
dem munda ∧ sed ma-		dem munda sunt sed ma-
lum est homini qui		lum est homini qui
per *offensionem* man-		per offendiculum man-

Iris.	*Aug.*	*Vulg.*
Rom. xiv. 21. ducat bonum est non manducare carnem *neque* bibere uinum neque in quo frater tuus *offenditur* ∧		ducat bonum est non manducare carnem et non bibere uinum neque in quo frater tuus offendit aut scandalizatur aut infirmatur
22. tu fidem *quam* ha- bes penes te ∧ipsum habe coram deo be- atus qui non iudicat semet ipsum in *quo*	tu fidem *quam* ha- bes penes temet ipsum habe coram deo be- atus qui non iudicat semet ipsum in *quo* probat	tu fidem ha- bes penes temet ipsum habe coram deo be- atus qui non iudicat semet ipsum in eo quod
23. probat qui autem *di- iudicat* si manduca- uerit damnatus est quia non ex fide om- ne autem quod non est ex fide peccatum est		probat qui autem dis- cernit si manduca- uerit damnatus est quia non ex fide om- ne autem quod non est ex fide peccatum est
xv. 1. debemus autem nos ∧ *infirmitatem* infirmorum *portare* et non nobismet *ipsis* pla-		debemus autem nos firmiores inbecillitates infirmorum sustinere et non nobis pla-
2. cere unus quisque		cere unus quisque

Fris.	*Aug.*	*Vulg.*
Rom. xv. 2. *nostrum* proximo ∧ pla- ceat in bonum ad 3. aedificationem *nam* *et* Christus non sibi placuit sed sicut scrib- tum est *obprobria ex-* *probrantium* tibi cae- ciderunt super me 4. quaecumque enim *ante* scribta sunt *ut* *nos doceremur* scribta sunt ut per patientiam et consolationem scrib- turarum spem habea- 5. mus deus autem pati- entiae et *consolationis* det uobis id ipsum sapere in *inuicem* secundum Iesum Chris- 6. tum ut *unianimiter* *in* uno ore *glorificetis* deum et patrem *et*		uestrum proximo suo pla- ceat in bonum ad aedificationem et- enim Christus non sibi placuit sed sicut scrip- tum est inproperia inpro- perantium tibi ce- ciderunt super me quaecumque enim scripta sunt ad nos- tram doctrinam scripta sunt ut per patientiam et consolationem scrip- turarum spem habea- mus deus autem pati- entiae et solacii det uobis id ipsum sapere in alterutrum secundum Iesum Chris- tum ut unanimes uno ore honorificetis deum et patrem

Fris.

Rom. xv. 6. *dominum nostrum Ie-*
7. *sum Christum* propter
quod suscipite inui-
cem sicut et Christus
suscepit *nos* in *glori-*
8. *am* dei dico enim
Christum ∧ ministrum
fuisse circumcisionis
∧
ad confirmandas pro-
9. missiones patrum gen-
tes autem super mise-
ricordia *glorificare* deum
sicut scribtum est
propterea confitebor tibi
in gentibus et *psallam*
10. *nomini tuo* et iterum
dicit laetamini gentes
11. cum plebem eius et
iterum *dicit* laudate
dominum omnes gentes
et *laudate* eum omnes

Aug.

dico enim
Christum Iesum ministrum
fuisse circumcisionis
propter ueritatem dei
ad confirmandas pro-
missiones patrum gen-
tes autem super mise-
ricordia *glorificare* deum

Vulg.

domini nostri Ie-
su Christi propter
quod suscipite inui-
cem sicut et Christus
suscepit uos in hono-
rem dei dico enim
Christum Iesum ministrum
fuisse circumcisionis
propter ueritatem dei
ad confirmandas pro-
missiones patrum gen-
tes autem super mise-
ricordiam honorare deum
sicut scriptum est
propter hoc confitebor tibi
in gentibus et nomini
tuo cantabo et iterum
dicit laetamini gentes
cum plebe eius et
iterum laudate
omnes gentes dominum
et magnificate eum omnes

Fris.

Rom. xv. 12. populi *dicit autem et*
Eseias ∧ erit radix
Iesse et qui exsurget
regnare in gentibus
in *eum* gentes spera-
13. bunt deus autem spei
adimpleat uos omni
gaudio et pace in cre-
dendo ut abundetis
in spe

Gal. ii. 5. (quibus *nec* ad horam
cessimus *subiectione* ut
ueritas)¹ euangelii perma-
6. neat *ad* uos *de* his autem qui *uidentur* esse
aliquid quales aliquan-
do fuerint nihil mea
interest deus personam
hominis non accipit
mihi enim qui *uiden-*

Aug.

quibus *nec* ad horam
cessimus subiectioni ut
ueritas euangelii *perma-
neret ad gentes* ² *de* his ∧ autem qui *uidentur* esse
aliquid quales aliquan-
do fuerint nihil mea
interest deus *hominis
personam* non accipit
mihi enim qui *uiden-*

Vulg.

populi et rursus
Esaias ait erit radix
Iesse et qui exsurget
regere gentes
in eo gentes spera-
bunt deus autem spei
repleat uos omni
gaudio et pace in cre-
dendo ut abundetis
in spe

quibus neque ad horam
cessimus subiectioni ut
ueritas euangelii perma-
neat apud uos ab his au-
tem qui uidebantur esse
aliquid quales aliquan-
do fuerint nihil mea
interest deus personam
hominis non accipit
mihi enim qui uidebant-

¹ These words are supplied by conjecture.

² Gal. p. 2112, l. 10 paraphrastic.

Fris.

Gal. ii. 6. tur nihil *adposuerunt*
7. sed e *contrario* cum
uidissent *quia* cre-
ditum est mihi eu-
angelium praeputii
sicut Petro circum-
8. cisionis qui enim ope-
ratus est Petro in
apostolatum circum-
cisionis operatus est
et mihi *in gentibus*
9. et cum cognouissent
gratiam quae data
est mihi Iacobus et
Petrus et Iohannes
qui uidebantur colum-
nae esse dextras
dederunt mihi et

Barnabae societatis

ut nos *quidem* in

Aug.

tur nihil *apposuerunt*
sed e *contrario*

dexteras
societatis

et dederunt
dexteras

societatis
nobis dederunt

ut nos *quidem* in

Vulg.

tur nihil contulerunt
sed e contra cum
uidissent quod cre-
ditum est mihi eu-
angelium praeputii
sicut Petro circum-
cisionis qui enim ope-
ratus est Petro in
apostolatum circum-
cisionis operatus est
et mihi inter gentes
et cum cognouissent
gratiam quae data
est mihi Iacobus et
Cephas et Iohannes
qui uidebantur colum-
nae esse dextras
dederunt mihi et

Barnabae societatis

ut nos in

Fris.	*Aug.*	*Vulg.*
Gal. ii. 9. gentes ipsi autem in	gentes *iremus* ipsi autem in	gentes ipsi autem in
10. circumcisionem tan-	circumcisionem tan-	circumcisionem tan-
tum ut *pauperes* me-	tum ut pauperum me-	tum ut pauperum me-
mores essemus quod	mores essemus quod	mores essemus quod
et *studui* hoc *ip-*	et *studui* hoc ip-	etiam sollicitus fui hoc ip-
11. *sud* facere cum au-	sum facere	sum facere cum au-
tem *uenit Petrus* An-		tem uenisset Cephas An-
thiociam in faciem *il-*		tiochiam in faciem ei
li restiti quia *reprae-*		restiti quia repre-
12. *hensus* erat prius *au-*		hensibilis erat prius enim
tem cum uenirent		quam uenirent
quidam ab Iacobo		quidam ab Iacobo
cum gentibus *conbesce-*		cum gentibus ede-
batur cum autem ue-		bat cum autem ue-
nissent subtrahebat et		nissent subtrahebat et
segregabat *semet ipsum*		segregabat se
timens eos qui ex		timens eos qui ex
13. circumcisione *sunt* et		circumcisione erant et
simulatae consenserunt		simulationi eius consenserunt
illi et ceteri Iudaei		ceteri Iudaei
ita ut ⌃ Barnabas *ad-*		ita ut et Barnabas
duceretur illorum si-		duceretur ab eis in illa si-

	Fris.	*Aug.*	*Vulg.*
Gal. ii. 14.	*mutationem* sed cum		mutatione sed cum
	uidissem (*quia* non rec-		uidissem quod non rec-
	te *ingrediuntur* ad ue-		te ambularent ad ue-
	ritatem euangelii dixi		ritatem euangelii dixi
	Petro coram omnibus	coram omnibus	Cephae coram omnibus
	si tu cum *sis Iudaeus*		si tu cum Iudaeus sis
	gentiliter et non Iuda-		gentiliter et non Iuda-
	ice uiuis *quem ad modum*	*quem ad modum*	ice uiuis quo modo
	gentes cogis Iudaizare	gentes cogis Iudaizare	gentes cogis Iudaizare
15.	nos natura Iudaei et	nos natura Iudaei et	nos natura Iudaei et
	non ex gentibus)¹peccatores	non ex gentibus peccatores	non ex gentibus peccatores
16.	scientes autem *quia* non	*sed scientes quoniam* non	scientes autem quod non
	iustificatur homo ex ope-	iustificatur homo ex ope-	iustificatur homo ex ope-
	ribus legis nisi per fi-	ribus legis nisi per fi-	ribus legis nisi per fi-
	dem Iesu Christi et nos	dem *Christi Iesu* et nos	dem Iesu Christi et nos
		(*peccatores*)	
	in Christo Iesu credimus	in Christo Iesu *credidimus*	in Christo Iesu credimus
	ut iustificemur *per fidem*	ut iustificemur *per fidem*	ut iustificemur ex fide
	Christi et non ex operibus		Christi et non ex operibus
	legis *quoniam* ex operibus		legis propter quod ex operibus
	legis non *iustificatur* omnis		legis non iustificabitur omnis

¹ These words are supplied by conjecture.

	Fris.	*Aug.*	*Vulg.*
Gal. ii. 17.	caro *si autem* quaerentes		caro quod si quaerentes
	iustificari in Christo in-		iustificari in Christo in-
	uenti sumus et ipsi pec-		uenti sumus et ipsi pec-
	catores *ergo* Christus pec-	*ergo* Christus pec-	catores numquid Christus pec-
	cati minister est absit	cati minister est absit	cati minister est absit
18.	si enim quae de-	si enim quae de-	si enim quae de-
	struxi haec *eadem*	struxi haec *eadem*	struxi haec iterum
	reaedifico praeuari-	*rursus aedifico* praeuari-	aedifico praeuari-
	catorem me *ipsum*	catorem me *ipsum*	catorem me
19.	constituo ego enim	constituo	constituo ego enim
	per legem legi mortuus		per legem legi mortuus
	sum ut deo uibam	legi mortuus	sum ut deo uiuam
	Christus confixus sum	ut deo uiuam	Christo confixus sum
20.	cruci uiuo autem		cruci uiuo autem
	iam non ego uiuit	uiuo autem	iam non ego uiuit
	autem in me Christus	iam non ego uiuit	uero in me Christus
	quod autem nunc ui-	uero in me Christus	quod autem nunc ui-
	uo in *carnem* in fi-	quod autem nunc ui-	uo in carne in fi-
	dem uiuo filii dei	uo in carne in fi-	de uiuo filii dei
	qui *me dilexit* et	de uiuo filii dei	qui dilexit me et
	tradidit se ipsum	qui *me dilexit* et	tradidit se ipsum
	pro me non *inritam*	tradidit se ipsum	pro me non ab-
		pro me non *irritam*	

Frs.	Aug.	Vulg.
Gal. ii. 21. *facio* gratia dei *nam*	*facio* gratiam dei *nam*	icio gratiam dei si
si per legem iustitiam	si per legem} *ex lege* iustitia	enim per legem iustitia
ergo *Christus gratis*	ergo *Christus gratis*	ergo gratis Christus
iii. 1. mortuus est o *stul-*	mortuus est o *stul-*	mortuus est o insensa-
ti Galatae quis uos	*ti* Galatae quis uos	ti Galatae quis uos
fascinauit ante quo-	fascinauit ante quo-	fascinauit ante quo-
rum oculos *Chris-*	rum oculos *Chris-*	rum oculos Iesus
tus Iesus proscribtus	*tus Iesus proscriptus*	Christus praescriptus
2. est crucifixus hoc	est crucifixus hoc	est crucifixus hoc
solum uolo *discere*	solum uolo *discere*	solum uolo a uobis
a uobis ex operibus	*a uobis* ex operibus	discere ex operibus
legis spiritum acce-	legis spiritum acce-	legis spiritum acce-
pistis an ex auditu	pistis an ex auditu	pistis an ex auditu
3. fidei sic stulti estis	fidei sic stulti estis	fidei sic stulti estis
ut cum spiritu coe-	ut cum spiritu coe-	ut cum spiritu coe-
peritis nunc carne	peritis nunc carne	peritis nunc carne
4. *consumemini* tanta	*consummemini* tanta	consummamini tanta
passi estis sine causa	passi estis sine causa	passi estis sine causa
si tamen sine causa	si tamen sine causa	si tamen sine causa
5. qui ergo tribuit uobis	qui ergo tribuit uobis	qui ergo tribuit uobis
spiritum et *uirtutes*	spiritum et *uirtutes*	spiritum et operatur

Fris.

Gal. iii. 5. *operatur* in uobis ex
operibus legis an ex
6. auditu fidei sicut
Abraham credidit
deo et *deputatum*
est *illi* ad iustitiam
7. *intellegite ergo quon-*
iam qui ex fide ∧ hii
sunt filii *Abra-*
8. *ham* prouidens au-
tem scriptura quia
ex fide iustificat gen-
tes deus praenuntiauit
Abraham dicens quia
benedicentur in te omnes
9. gentes *ita ut* qui ex
fide sunt *benedican-*
tur cum fideli Ab-
10. raham *quaecumque*
enim ex operibus le-
gis sunt sub maledic-
to sunt legis scribtum

Aug.

operatur in uobis ex
operibus legis an ex
auditu fidei

quicumque
enim ex operibus le-
gis sunt sub maledic-
to sunt legis

Vulg.

uirtutes in uobis ex
operibus legis an ex
auditu fidei sicut
Abraham credidit
deo et reputatum
est ei ad iustitiam
cognoscite ergo quia
qui ex fide sunt hii
sunt filii Abra-
hae prouidens au-
tem scriptura quia
ex fide iustificat gen-
tes deus praenuntiauit
Abrahae quia
benedicentur in te omnes
gentes igitur qui ex
fide sunt benedicen-
tur cum fideli Ab-
raham quicumque
enim ex operibus le-
gis sunt sub maledic-
to sunt scriptum

Fris.	Aug.	Vulg.
Gal. iii. 10. est enim *quoniam*	qui	est enim
maledictus omnis qui		maledictus omnis qui
non *permanet* in om-	non *perman-* in om-	non permanserit in om-
nibus quae *his* scrib-	nibus quae scrip-	nibus quae scrip-
ta sunt in libro le-	ta sunt in libro le-	ta sunt in libro le-
gis ut faciat ea	gis ut fac- ea [1]	gis ut faciat ea
11. *quia* autem in lege	*quia* in lege	quoniam autem in lege
nemo iustificatur	nemo iustificatur	nemo iustificatur
aput deum mani-		apud deum mani-
festum est quia	quia	festum est quia
iustus ex fide ui-	iustus ex fide ui-	iustus ex fide ui-
12. uit lex autem non	uit lex autem non	uit lex autem non
est ex fide sed qui	est ex fide sed qui	est ex fide sed qui
fecerit ea uiuet in	fecerit ea uiuet in	fecerit ea uiuet in
13. illis Christus nos red-	illis Christus nos red-	illis Christus nos red-
emit de maledicto le-	emit de maledicto le-	emit de maledicto le-
gis factus pro nobis	gis factus pro nobis	gis factus pro nobis
maledictum quia	maledictum quia	maledictum quia
scribtum est male-	scriptum est male-	scriptum est male-
dictus omnis qui	dictus omnis qui	dictus omnis qui
14. pendet in ligno ut	pendet in ligno	pendet in ligno ut

[1] p. 2118, l. 13 from foot.

Fris.	*Aug.*	*Vulg.*
Gal. iii. 14. in gentibus benedictio		in gentibus benedictio
Abrahae fieret in		Abrahae fieret in
Christo Iesu ut *ad-*	ut *an-*	Christo Iesu ut pol-
nuntiationem spiri-	*nuntiationem* spiri-	licitationem spiri-
tus accipiamus per	tus *per fidem accipi-*	tus accipiamus per
15. fidem fratres secun-	*amus*	fidem fratres secun-
dum hominem di-		dum hominem di-
co tamen hominis	tamen hominis	co tamen hominis
confirmatum testa-	confirmatum testa-	confirmatum testa-
mentum nemo *in-*	mentum nemo *ir-*	mentum nemo
ritum facit aut	*ritum facit* aut	spernit aut
superordinat	superordinat	superordinat
16. Abrahae dictae	Abrahae dictae	Abrahae dictae
sunt promissiones	sunt promissiones	sunt promissiones
et semini eius non	non	et semini eius non
dicit et seminibus	dicit et seminibus	dicit et seminibus
tamquam in multis	*tamquam* in multis	quasi in multis
sed *tamquam* in uno	sed *tamquam* in uno	sed quasi in uno
et semini tuo *quod*	et semini tuo *quod*	et semini tuo qui
17. est Christus hoc au-	est Christus	est Christus au-
tem dico testamentum		tem dico testamentum
confirmatum a deo		confirmatum a deo

Fris.

Gal. iii. 17. ∧ post quadringentos et
triginta annos facta ∧
lex non *infirmata*
ad euacuandam pro-
18. missionem *si enim* ex
lege hereditas iam non
ex *promissionem* Abra-
hae autem per *promissi-*
19. *onem* donauit deus quid
ergo lex *transgressionis*
proposita est donec ue-
niret semen cui *promis-*
sum est disposi-
tum per angelos
in manu mediato-
20. ris mediator autem
unius non est deus
21. *uero* unus est lex
ergo aduersus pro-
missa dei absit si
enim data esset lex
quae posset uiuifi-

Aug.

quid
ergo lex *transgressionis*
gratia proposita est donec ue-
niret semen cui *promis-*
sum est disposi-
tum per angelos
in manu mediato-
ris mediator autem
unius non est deus
uero unus est lex
ergo aduersus pro-
missa dei absit si
enim data esset lex
quae posset uiuifi-

Vulg.

quae post quadringentos et
triginta annos facta est
lex non irritum facit
ad euacuandam pro-
missionem nam si ex
lege hereditas iam non
ex repromissione Abra-
hae autem per repromissi-
onem donauit deus quid
igitur lex propter transgressiones
posita est donec ue-
niret semen cui promi-
serat ordina-
ta per angelos
in manu mediato-
ris mediator autem
unius non est deus
autem unus est lex
ergo aduersus pro-
missa dei absit si
enim data esset lex
quae posset uiuifi-

	Fris.	*Aug.*	*Vulg.*
Gal. iii. 21.	care *omnino* ex	care *omnino* ex	care uere ex
	lege esset iustitia	lege esset iustitia	lege esset iustitia
22.	sed conclusit scrib-	sed conclusit scrip-	sed conclusit scrip-
	tura omnia sub	tura omnia sub	tura omnia sub
	peccato ut promissio	peccato ut promissio	peccato ut promissio
	ex fide Iesu Christi	ex fide Iesu Christi	ex fide Iesu Christi
	daretur credentibus	daretur credentibus	daretur credentibus
23.	prius autem quam	prius autem quam	prius autem quam
	ueniret fides sub	ueniret fides sub	ueniret fides sub
	lege custodiebamur	lege custodiebamur	lege custodiebamur
	conclusi in eam fi-	conclusi in eam fi-	conclusi in eam fi-
	dem quae *postea re-*	dem quae *postea re-*	dem quae re-
24.	*uelata est ita* lex	*uelata est* itaque lex	uelanda erat itaque lex
	pedagogus noster	pedagogus noster	pedagogus noster
	fuit in Christo ut	fuit in Christo	fuit in Christo ut
	ex fide iustificemur		ex fide iustificemur
25.	*postquam autem* uenit	*postea quam* uenit	at ubi uenit
	fides iam non sumus	fides iam non sumus	fides iam non sumus
26.	sub pedagogo omnes	sub paedagogo omnes	sub pedagogo omnes
	enim filii dei estis	filii dei estis	enim filii dei estis
	per fidem in Christo	per fidem	per fidem in Christo
27.	Iesu quicumque enim	quicumque	Iesu quicumque enim

	Fris.	*Aug.*	*Vulg.*
Gal. iii. 27.	in *Christum* baptizati	in Christo baptizati	in Christo baptizati
	estis Christum induistis	estis Christum induistis	estis Christum induistis
28.	non est Iudaeus neque	non est Iudaeus neque	non est Iudaeus neque
	Grecus non est serbus	Graecus non est seruus	Graecus non est seruus
	neque liber non est	neque liber non est	neque liber non est
	masculus *et* faemina	masculus *et* femina	masculus neque femina
	omnes enim uos unum	omnes *ergo* uos unum	omnes enim uos unum
29.	estis in Christo Iesu si	estis in Christo Iesu si	estis in Christo Iesu si
	autem uos Christi ergo	autem¹ ergo	autem uos Christi ergo
	Abrahae semen estis	*Abrahae semen* estis	semen Abrahae estis
	secundum promissionem	secundum promissionem	secundum promissionem
iv. 1.	heredes dico autem	heredes dico autem	heredes dico autem
		quamdiu	
	quanto tempore heres	quanto tempore heres	quanto tempore heres
	paruulus est nihil	paruulus est nihil	paruulus est nihil
	differt a seruo cum	differt a seruo cum	differt a seruo cum
	sit dominus omnium	sit dominus omnium	sit dominus omnium
2.	sed sub *procuratoribus*	sed sub *procuratoribus*	sed sub tutoribus
	est et actoribus usque	*et actoribus est* usque	est et actoribus usque
	ad praefinitum tempus	ad praefinitum tempus	ad praefinitum tempus
3.	a patre *sic* et nos	a patre *sic* et nos	a patre ita et nos

¹ *Aug.* (p. 2125) says we must punctuate here, and understand 'uos unum estis in Christo Iesu'.

Fris.	*Aug.*	*Vulg.*
Gal. iv. 3. cum essemus paruuli	cum essemus paruuli	cum essemus paruuli
sub elementis *huius*	sub elementis *huius*	sub elementis
(mundi eramus serui-	mundi eramus serui-	mundi eramus serui-
4. entes *cum autem* uenit	entes uenit	entes at ubi uenit
plenitudo temporis mi-	plenitudo temporis mi-	plenitudo temporis mi-
sit deus filium suum	sit deus filium suum	sit deus filium suum
factum ex muliere	factum ex muliere	factum ex muliere
5. factum sub lege ut	factum sub lege ut	factum sub lege ut
eos qui sub lege e-	eos qui sub lege e-	eos qui sub lege e-
rant redimeret ut ad-	rant redimeret ut ad-	rant redimeret ut ad-
optionem filiorum *re-*	optionem filiorum *re-*	optionem filiorum re-
6. *cipiamus*)[1] quoniam au-	*cipiamus* quoniam au-	ciperemus quoniam au-
	$(+\,dei\,\frac{1}{2})$	
tem *filii estis* misit	tem *filii* $\wedge$ *estis* misit	tem estis filii misit
deus spiritum fili sui	deus spiritum filii sui	deus spiritum filii sui
in corda nostra *clamantes*	in corda *uestra* clamantem	in corda nostra clamantem
7. abba pater *ita* iam	abba pater itaque iam	abba pater itaque iam
non est seruus sed	non est seruus sed	non est seruus sed
filius *si autem* filius	filius *si autem* filius	filius quod si filius
8. et heres per deum sed	et heres per deum sed	et heres per deum sed
nunc quidem ignoran-	tunc quidem ignoran-	tunc quidem ignoran-

[1] These words are supplied by conjecture.

Fris.	*Aug.*	*Vulg.*
Gal. iv. 8. tes deum *hii* qui natu-	natu- tes deum his qui *natu-* ra	tes deum his qui natu-
ram non sunt dii *ser-*	*raliter* non sunt dii *ser-*	ra non sunt dii ser-
9. *uiuatis* nunc autem	*uistis* nunc autem	uiebatis nunc autem
cognoscentes deum immo	*cognoscentes* deum immo	cum cognoueritis deum immo
cogniti ∧ a deo quo modo	cogniti ∧ a deo quo modo	cogniti sitis a deo quo modo
reuertimini iterum	*reuertimini* iterum [om. alt. loc.]	conuertimini iterum
ad infirma et egena	ad infirma et egena	ad infirma et egena
elementa quibus *rur-*	elementa quibus *rur-*	elementa quibus de-
sus ut antea seruire	*sus ut antea* seruire	nuo seruire
10. uultis dies obseruatis	uultis dies obseruatis	uultis dies obseruatis
et menses et *annos et*	et menses et *annos et*	et menses et tempora et
11. *tempora* timeo uos ne	*tempora* timeo uos ne	annos timeo uos ne
forte sine causa la-	forte sine causa la-	forte sine causa la-
boraberim in uobis	borauerim in *uos*	borauerim in uobis
12. estote sicut ∧ ego *quon-*	estote sicut et ego *quon-*	estote sicut et ego quia
iam ∧ ego sicut uos	*iam* et ego sicut uos	et ego sicut uos
fratres *praecor* uos	fratres *precor* uos	fratres obsecro uos
nihil me lesistis	nihil me laesistis	nihil me laesistis
13. scitis ∧ quia per in-	scitis ∧ quia per in-	scitis autem quia per in-

	Fris.	*Aug.*	*Vulg.*
Gal. iv. 13.	firmitatem carnis *iam*	firmitatem carnis *iam*	firmitatem carnis euange-
	pridem *euangelizaui*	*pridem euangelizaui*	lizaui uobis iam
	uobis et temptationem	*uobis* et temptationem	pridem et temtationem
		neque }	
	uestram in carne mea non	uestram in carne mea non	uestram in carne mea non
14.	spraeuistis neque respuis-	spreuistis neque respuis-	spreuistis neque respuis-
	tis sed sicut angelum	tis sed sicut angelum	tis sed sicut angelum
	dei excepistis me sicut	dei excepistis me sicut	dei excepistis me sicut
15.	Christum Iesum *quae*	Christum Iesum *quae*	Christum Iesum ubi
	ergo fuit beatitudo	*ergo fuit* beatitudo	est ergo beatitudo
	uestra testimonium	uestra testimonium	uestra testimonium
	∧ *uobis perhibeo quon-*	enim *uobis perhibeo quon-*	enim perhibeo uobis
	iam si fieri posset	*iam* si fieri posset	quia si fieri posset
	oculos uestros eruis-	oculos uestros eruis-	oculos uestros eruis-
	setis et dedissetis	setis et dedissetis	setis et dedissetis
16.	mihi ergo inimicus	mihi ergo inimicus	mihi ergo inimicus
	factus sum uobis ue-	*factus sum uobis* ue-	uobis factus sum ue-
17.	rum ∧ *praedicans* ae-	rum *uobis praedicans* ae-	rum dicens uobis ae-
	mulantur uos non be-	mulantur uos non be-	mulantur uos non be-
	ne sed excludere uos	ne sed excludere uos	ne sed excludere uos
	uolunt ut *eos* aemu-	uolunt ut illos aemu-	uolunt ut illos aemu-
18.	lemini bonum *est* au-	lemini bonum au-	lemini bonum au-

Frvs.	*Aug.*	*Vulg.*
Gal. iv. 18. tem *aemulari* in bono	tem *aemulari* in bono	tem aemulamini in bono
semper et non *solum*	semper et non *solum*	semper et non tantum
cum praesens sum	cum praesens sum	cum praesens sum
19. aput uos filioli	apud uos filioli	apud uos filioli
mei quos iterum	mei quos iterum	mei quos iterum
parturio (donec	parturio donec	parturio donec
Christus formetur in	*Christus formetur* in	formetur Christus in
20. uobis uellem autem	uobis uellem autem	uobis uellem autem
nunc adesse aput	*nunc adesse apud*	esse apud uos
uos et mutare uo-	*uos* et mutare uo-	modo et mutare uo-
cem meam *quia*	cem meam *quia*	cem meam quoniam
confundor in uobis	confundor in uobis	confundor in uobis
21. dicite mihi sub le-	dicite mihi sub le-	dicite mihi qui sub le-
ge *uolentes* esse le-	ge *uolentes* esse le-	ge uultis esse le-
	{ *audistis*	
gem non *audistis*	gem non { *legistis*	gem non legistis
22. scribtum est enim	scriptum est enim	scriptum est enim
quoniam Abraham)[1]	*quod* Abraham	quoniam Abraham
duos filios habuit	duos filios habuit	duos filios habuit
unum de ancilla	unum de ancilla	unum de ancilla
et unum de libera	et unum de libera	et unum de libera

[1] These words are supplied by conjecture.

Fris.	*Aug.*	*Vulg.*
Gal. iv. 23. sed *ille quidem* qui		sed qui
de ancilla secun-	de ancilla secun-	de ancilla secun-
dum carnem natus	dum carnem natus	dum carnem natus
est qui autem de	est de	est qui autem de
libera per *promissi-*	libera per repromissi-	libera per repromissi-
24. *onem* quae sunt *in*	onem	onem quae sunt per
allegoria ∧ haec enim		allegoriam dicta haec enim
sunt duo testamenta		sunt duo testamenta
unum quidem a mon-		unum quidem a mon-
te Syna in seruitutem		te Sina in seruitutem
gerens *quod* est Agar		generans quae est Agar
25. Syna enim mons est		Sina enim mons est
in Arabia *quae coniunc-*		in Arabia qui coniunc-
ta est *huic* quae nunc		tus est ei quae nunc
est Hierusalem *seruit*		est Hierusalem et seruit
enim cum filiis *suis*	est Agar	cum filiis eius
26. *quae autem* sursum		*illa autem quae* sursum
est Hierusalem libera		est Hierusalem libera
est quae est mater no-		est quae est mater no-
stra scribtum est enim		stra scriptum est enim
27. laetare sterilis quae	sterilis	laetare sterilis quae
non paris erumpe et		non paris erumpe et

Fris.	*Aug.*	*Vulg.*
Gal. iv. 27. *exclama* quae non		clama quae non
parturis *quoniam*	*quoniam*	parturis quia
multi filii desertae	multi filii desertae	multi filii desertae
magis quam eius	magis quam eius	magis quam eius
quae habet uirum	quae habet uirum	quae habet uirum
28. nos autem fratres	nos	nos autem fratres
secundum Isaac pro-	secundum Isaac pro-	secundum Isaac pro-
missionis filii sumus	missionis filii sumus	missionis filii sumus
29. sed *sicut* tunc qui		sed quo modo tunc qui
secundum carnem		secundum carnem
natus fuerat perse-		natus fuerat perse-
quebatur eum qui		quebatur eum qui
secundum spiritum		secundum spiritum
30. ita et nunc sed quid		ita et nunc sed quid
dicit scribtura eice	eice	dicit scriptura eice
ancillam et filium	ancillam et filium	ancillam et filium
eius non enim heres	eius non heres	eius non enim heres
erit filius ancillae		erit filius ancillae
cum filio liberae	cum filio liberae	cum filio liberae
31. *nos autem* fratres	*nos autem* fratres	itaque fratres
non sumus ancillae	non sumus ancillae	non sumus ancillae
filii sed liberae	filii sed liberae	filii sed liberae
quali libertate		qua libertate

A a

	Fris.	*Aug.*	*Vulg.*
Gal. iv. 31.	Christus nos liue-		Christus nos libe-
v. 1.	rabit state *ergo*	state *ergo*	rauit state
	et *ne* iterum ser-	et *ne* iterum ser-	et nolite iterum iu-
	uitutis iugo ad-	*uitutis iugo at-*	go seruitutis con-
Gal. vi. (5).	*tineamini* ecce ego	*tineamini* ecce ego	tineri ecce ego
	onus portabit¹	*proprium onus* portabit	onus suum portabit
6.	communicet autem ∧		communicet autem is
	qui catecizatur uerbum		qui cathecizatur uerbum
	ei qui se catecizat		ei qui se cathecizat
	in omnibus bonis		in omnibus bonis
7.	nolite errare deus	nolite errare deus	nolite errare deus
	non *subsannatur*	non *subsannatur*	non inridetur
8.	*quod* enim semina-	*quod* enim semina-	quae enim semina-
	uerit homo *hoc* et	uerit homo *hoc* et	uerit homo haec et
	metet *quia* qui se-	metet *quia* qui se-	metet quoniam qui se-
	minauerit in carne	*minauerit* in carne	minat in carne
	sua *ex* carne ∧ metet	sua *ex* carne ∧ metet	sua de carne et metet
	corruptionem qui au-	corruptionem qui au-	corruptionem qui au-
	tem *seminauerit* in	tem *seminauerit* in	tem seminat in
	spiritu de spiritu	spiritu de spiritu	spiritu de spiritu
	metet uitam aeternam	metet uitam aeternam	metet uitam aeternam
9.	bonum autem facientes	bonum autem facientes	bonum autem facientes

¹ It seems safe to conclude that Fris. had *proprium*.

	Frs.	*Aug.*	*Vulg.*
Gal. vi. 9.	non *infirmemur tem-*	non *infirmemur proprio*	non deficiamus tem-
	pore enim *proprio* me-	enim *tempore* me-	pore enim suo me-
	temus *infatigabiles*	temus *infatigabiles*	temus non deficientes
10.	*itaque* dum tempus	*itaque* dum tempus	ergo dum tempus
	habemus operemur	habemus operemur	habemus operemur
	quod bonum ad om-	bonum ad om-	bonum ad om-
	nes maxime autem	nes maxime autem	nes maxime autem
	ad domesticos fi-	ad domesticos fi-	ad domesticos fi-
11.	dei *uidistis* qualibus	dei *uidistis* qualibus	dei uidete qualibus
	litteris *uobis scribsi*	litteris *uobis scripsi*	litteris scripsi uobis
12.	mea manu quicum-	manu mea qui ⌄	mea manu quicum-
	que uolunt placere in	uolunt placere in	que uolunt placere in
	carne hii cogunt uos	carne hi cogunt uos	carne hi cogunt uos
	circumcidi tantum ut	circumcidi tantum ut	circumcidi tantum ut
	in crucem Christi per-	*in cruce* Christi per-	crucis Christi per-
	secutionem non patian-	secutionem non patian-	secutionem non patian-
13.	tur neque enim qui	tur neque enim qui	tur neque enim qui
	circumcisi sunt hii	*circumcisi sunt hi*	circumciduntur
	legem custodiunt sed	legem custodiunt sed	legem custodiunt sed
	uolunt uos circumcidi	uolunt uos circumcidi	uolunt uos circumcidi
	ut in *uestra carne*	ut in *uestra glorien-*	ut in carne uestra
14.	*glorientur* mihi autem	*tur carne* mihi autem	glorientur mihi autem
	absit gloriari nisi in	absit gloriari nisi in	absit gloriari nisi in

Fris.	*Aug.*	*Vulg.*
Gal. vi. 14. *crucem* domini nostri	cruce domini nostri	cruce domini nostri
Iesu Christi per quem	Iesu Christi per quem	Iesu Christi per quem
	{ *mundus mihi*	
mihi mundus cruci	mihi mundus cruci	mihi mundus cruci
fixus est et ego mun-	fixus est et ego mun-	fixus est et ego mun-
15. do ∧ neque enim cir-	do ∧ neque enim cir-	do in Christo enim Iesu neque cir-
cumcisio aliquid *est*	cumcisio aliquid *est*	cumcisio aliquid ualet
neque praeputium	neque praeputium	neque praeputium
sed noua crea-	sed noua crea-	sed noua crea-
tura et quicumque	tura et quicumque	tura et quicumque
hanc regulam *sec-*	hanc regulam *sec-*	hanc regulam secuti
16. *tantur* pax super	*tantur* pax super	fuerint pax super
illos et misericordiam	illos et misericordia	illos et misericordia
et super Israhel dei	et super Israhel dei	et super Israhel dei
de cetero *laborem*	de cetero *laborem*	de cetero nemo
nemo mihi praestet	*nemo mihi praestet*	mihi molestus sit
17. ego enim stigmata	ego enim stigmata	ego enim stigmata
domini Iesu *Christi*	*domini* Iesu *Christi*	Iesu
in corpore meo porto	in corpore meo porto	in corpore meo porto
18. gratia domini nos-	gratia domini nos-	gratia domini nos-
tri Iesu Christi	tri Iesu Christi	tri Iesu Christi
cum spiritu uestro	cum spiritu uestro	cum spiritu uestro
fratres amen	fratres amen	fratres amen

All readings in the above tables that differ from the Vulgate are distinguished by special type. It will be seen that the two texts 'Fris.' and 'Aug.' are not absolutely identical. Nor could they be expected to be. 'Fris.' is a solitary sixth-century codex. Augustine employed a fourth-century codex, and we have only the Benedictine recension of his works, good as it is, to rely on for the form of the quotations as they left his hands. It is all the more significant that in the passages where both 'Fris.' and 'Aug.' are extant, there are, if my numeration is correct, 106 agreements of 'Fris.' and 'Aug.' against the Vulgate, and that in other passages 'Fris.' goes its own way 31 times, and 'Aug.' 34 times.

Nor are we confined to numbers, significant as they are, for a proof of relationship. The quality of certain of the readings where they agree, is at least as striking. I should lay great stress for instance on such as these:

(A). Agreements in underlying Greek text shared by 'Fris.' and 'Aug.' Rom. xiv. 22 *quam habes* with אABC.

vg. *habes* with inferior Greek MSS.

(B). Agreements in striking renderings against the Vulgate:

Rom. xv. 9 *glorificare* versus *honorare*.

Dr. H. J. White shows in his large edition of the Vulgate that this is Augustine's invariable rendering in this passage, and that it occurs also in the Auctor *De Promissionibus* (an African work, written perhaps by Quodvultdeus, a pupil of Augustine) and in t (the Toledan Liber Comicus from Spain, which we have called 'the child of Africa').

Gal. ii. 6. *adposuerunt* versus *contulerunt* (Ambst. vg. Pelag.).
 iii. 1. *stulti* versus *insensati* (Ambst. vg. Pelag.).
 ,, 14. *adnuntiationem* versus *pollicitationem* (vg. Pelag.) and *benedictionem* (Ambst.).
 ,, 21. *omnino* versus *uere* (Ambst. vg. Pelag.).
 iv. 2. *procuratoribus* versus *tutoribus* (vg. Pelag.) and *curatoribus* (Ambst.).

Gal. iv. 12. *precor* versus *obsecro* (Ambst. vg. Pelag.).

    vi. 7. *subsannatur* versus *inridetur* (vg.) and *deridetur* (Ambst. Pelag.).

   „ 9. *infatigabiles* (Ambst.) versus *non deficientes* (vg. Pelag.).

There are also the agreement in the rendering of certain Greek particles against the Vulgate rendering, and the almost perfect agreement between 'Fris.' and 'Aug.' in long stretches like Gal. iii. 19-iv. 21, and Gal. vi. 7-18, to prove beyond any doubt that 'Fris.' represents the Augustinian text.

There is much more that might be said on the Augustinian text of the Epistles of St. Paul, but it would more properly be reserved for a comprehensive work in which the Augustinian text of these Epistles would be as nearly as possible reconstructed from the multitudinous quotations made in the other works of Augustine, with which we are not here concerned.

Augustine's three works on the Epistles of St. Paul differ somewhat in character from one another. The *Expositio quarundam Propositionum* is, as its title indicates, a treatment of particular passages on which his opinion had been asked by his clerical friends. There are in all eighty-four sections, each dealing with one particular clause, verse, or group of verses. For instance, in our chapter i, which is divided into thirty-two verses, 8 fall under review, and the treatment is very brief, almost glossarial in fact. When we come to chapter iii, verse 20, where the topics discussed by the Apostle begin to be of greater moment for the life of the Church, he begins to allow himself more space, and the lion's share is naturally assigned to chapters v to ix inclusive. Some of the notes will be quoted later.

The *Inchoata Expositio* is, as I have said, planned on a large scale. If the treatment devoted to the first seven verses had been proportionately carried out for the whole Epistle, with its 433 verses, the commentary would have required over 1,113 columns in Migne's edition. In other words, it would have been nearly double the length of his great work on St. John's Gospel, and about seven times as long as Ambrosiaster's commentary on the same Epistle. This great length would have been due to two causes, one that Augustine was, in contrast to the other commentators with whom we have to deal, a thinker of the highest rank, who required space to explain what he found latent in the Pauline thought, second that Augustine was above all things a preacher, as we see from the fact that his commentaries on the Psalms and on St. John's Gospel are really, like his master Ambrose's corresponding works, a series of sermons, where the topics which most appealed to him are treated with abundant fullness.

The complete commentary on the Epistle to the Galatians is on a scale intermediate between that of the *Propositiones* and the *Inchoata Expositio*. It covers the whole Epistle in forty-two columns of Migne as against rather more than thirty-six occupied by Ambrosiaster. Some passages from this also will be quoted below, to illustrate its character. From the earlier part of this chapter it will have become evident that a very considerable proportion of the text of the Epistle is cited *diserte*. For the most part the text of a passage is quoted first, and the comment then follows, in the usual fashion of the ancient commentators, who followed in this, as Dr. Alfred J. Smith will, I hope, make clear, the practice of the commentators on pagan writings. Indeed, his researches will show that Christian commentators use many of the same phrases as their predecessors, I mean such men as Servius, the commentator on Virgil. The comments, unlike those of Pelagius, are always, or almost always, longer than the passages with which they deal. A fair number of passages is quoted from other parts of Scripture, especially from the other Epistles, in illustration, as had been the practice from

Origen's time at least.[1] But it is fairly evident that in this, one of Augustine's earlier works, he has not yet acquired that exhaustive knowledge of Scripture which is so apparent in his later writings. Here again, when topics strike him as specially important, he allows himself a certain latitude of treatment. I will now proceed to translate some of the more important of his comments, taking them from the three works in the order in which we have been considering them.

On Rom. iii. 20, "because by the works of the law shall no flesh be justified in his sight: for through the law cometh the knowledge of sin."

'Some think that these words are intended to bring reproach on the law, but they must be read with great care, so that neither shall the law appear to be blamed by the Apostle, nor free-will be taken away from man. So let us distinguish these four stages of man: "before the law", "under the law", "under grace", "in peace". Before the law, we follow the desire of the flesh; under the law, we are pulled by it; under grace, we neither follow it nor are pulled by it; in peace, there is no desire of the flesh.' These four stages are further explained by Augustine in the course of the work,[2] as he keeps them in mind with the progress of the exposition. Here he proceeds: 'Therefore before the law, we do not struggle, because we not only desire and sin, but also approve of sins: under the law we fight, but we are beaten; for we admit that our actions are evil, and by admitting that they are evil, we are of course unwilling to perform them; but because grace is not yet, we are overcome. In this stage it is shown to us how low we lie, and while we will to rise and yet fall, we are the more grievously struck down. Thus it is that the words occur

[1] It is interesting to note that even at this date he is conversant with the *Book of Wisdom* and with *Ecclesiasticus*, both of them favourites also with Pelagius (*Sap.* quoted pp. 2063, 2064, 2065; *Eccli.* p. 2064).

[2] Cf. cc. xxx, xlvi, li.

here: "the law came in secretly that the trespass might abound" (*Rom.* v. 20). Thus it is also that we get what is now written: "through the law cometh the knowledge of sin" (*Rom.* iii. 20). For it is not the taking away of sin; because it is by grace alone that sin is taken away. The law is therefore good, because it forbids those things that ought to be forbidden, and commands those things that ought to be commanded. But when any man thinks that he can fulfil it in his own strength, not through the grace of his Saviour, this conceit does him no good: nay rather it does him so much harm that he is both carried away by a stronger desire for sin, and in sins is found to be a transgressor also.'

A little farther down in this section occur these important words: 'Therefore free-will existed in perfection in the first man, but in us, before grace, there is no free-will enabling us to refrain from sin, but only free-will enabling us to be unwilling to sin. Grace therefore brings it about that we should not only will to do rightly, but also be able so to do; not by our strength, but by the help of the Saviour, who will grant us also perfect peace in the resurrection, which perfect peace attains the good will. For "Glory to God in the Highest, and on earth peace to men of good will" (*Luke* ii. 14).'

On Rom. v. 14, he observes that this verse is punctuated in two ways: 'But death reigned from Adam until Moses, even over them that did not sin after the likeness of Adam's transgression': first, 'death reigned after the likeness of Adam's transgression' (because even those who did not sin died because of their origin in Adam's mortality); second, 'death reigned even over them who did not sin after the likeness of Adam's transgression' (but sinned before the law, that they should be understood to have sinned after the likeness of Adam's transgression, who received the law, because Adam also sinned, after receiving a law containing a command).

The allegorical interpretation of Rom. vii. 2, &c.: 'for the woman that hath a husband is bound by law to the husband while he liveth; but if the husband die, she is discharged from the law of the husband,' &c. 'The woman is the soul, the husband is the sinful passions (verse 5), the law of the husband is the (Mosaic) law.'

An opinion expressed by him in § XLI is modified in the *Retractations* (i. 23, 1). On Rom. vii. 14 the original words are: 'As to his words, "We know that the law is spiritual; but I am carnal", he sufficiently shows that the law cannot be fulfilled unless by spiritual persons, such as the grace of God makes.' In the *Retractations* he says: 'This I did not wish to be taken as referring to the Apostle himself, who was already spiritual, but to the man who is under the law, not yet under grace. For thus did I first understand these words, which after reading certain expositors of scripture, whose authority might influence me, I considered more carefully, and saw that they could be understood even of the Apostle himself. I have carefully shown this, as far as I could, in the books I have recently written against the Pelagians.' What follows enlarges upon his new view.

Take again § LV, on c. viii. 28-30: 'Not all that were called, were called *secundum propositum* (according to his purpose): for this purpose is closely bound up with the foreknowledge and pre-determination of God: and he did not pre-determine any one, unless he foreknew that he would believe and would follow his own call: there are those he calls also "chosen". For many do not come when they are called; but no one comes that has not been called.'

§ LX is important, on ch. ix, vv. 11-13: 'For the children being not yet born, neither having done anything good or bad, that the purpose of God according to election might stand, not of works, but of him that calleth, it was said unto her, "The elder shall serve the younger". Even

as it is written, " Jacob I loved, but Esau I hated ".' ' By
these some are moved to think that the Apostle Paul has
done away with free-will, by which we gain God's favour
by the good of piety, or alienate him by the evil of impiety.'
Augustine points out, however, that God knew even before
they were born, what each was to be like. In § LXI
(ch. ix, 11-13) he says : ' It is ours to believe and to will,
but His to give to believers and "willers" the power to
work well through the Holy Spirit, through whom the love
of God is spread abroad in our hearts to make us merciful.'

Finally in § LXII, on the crucial verses, chap. ix. 15-21 :
" So then it is not of him that willeth, nor of him that run-
neth, but of God that hath mercy," he says : ' These words
do not do away with free-will, but they say that ours is not
sufficient, unless God help, making us merciful, to work
well through the gift of the Holy Spirit, referring to that
which he said above, " I will have mercy on whom I have
mercy, and I will have compassion on whom I have compassion ". Because we cannot even will unless we be
called ; and when after the call we will, our will and our
running is not enough, unless God both grant strength to
runners and lead them to the place whither He calls them.
It is clear therefore that it is not of him that wills nor of
him that runs, but of God that has mercy, that we work
good, even if our own will also be there, which by itself
could do nothing. Thus there follows also the evidence
about Pharaoh's punishment, when Scripture says about
Pharaoh, " For this very purpose did I raise thee up, that
I might shew in thee my power, and that my name might
be published abroad in all the earth." For as we read in
Exodus, Pharaoh's heart was hardened (*Exod.* x. 1), that
he should not be moved by so clear signs. Therefore
Pharaoh's former disobedience to God's teachings now
resulted in punishment. No one can say that that hardening
of the heart came upon Pharaoh undeservedly, but rather

by God's judgement repaying to his unbelief the punishment it deserved. It is not therefore this that is laid to his charge, that he did not then obey—since with his hardened heart he could not obey—but because he showed himself worthy to have his heart hardened by his earlier unbelief. For just as in those whom God has chosen, it is not works, but faith, that starts the merit that by God's gift they work well, so in those whom he condemns, unbelief and impiety start the merit of punishment, that through punishment itself they should work even ill; even as above (*Rom.* i. 28) also the same apostle says : "And even as they refused to have God in their knowledge, God gave them up unto a reprobate mind, to do those things which are not fitting." Wherefore the Apostle thus sums up : "So then he hath mercy on whom he will, and whom he will he hardeneth." He makes him on whom he hath mercy, to work well; and him whom he hardeneth he leaves to work ill. But both that mercy is granted to the preceding merit of faith, and this hardening to the preceding impiety, that we should work both good through God's gift, and evil through punishment : and yet man is not robbed of his free-will, either to believe God so that mercy should reach us, or to impiety that punishment should come upon us.'[1] After stating this conclusion, he introduces a question as if from a disputant. For he says : "Thou dost say then unto me, Why doth he still find fault? For who withstandeth his will?"[1] This inquiry he thus answers, that we should understand that to spiritual men and to those not now living according to the earthly man, there can lie open the first merits of faith and impiety, how God foreknowing chooses those that will believe, and condemns the unbelieving, neither choosing the former from their works, nor condemning the latter from their works; but granting good working to the

---

[1] The expressions of opinion in this section were afterwards modified in *Retr.* i. 23, §§ 3, 4.

former's faith, and hardening the latter's impiety by deserting them, that they work evilly. Since this understanding, as I said, is revealed to the spiritual, but is far removed from the carnal understanding, he thus refutes the questioner, so that he understands he ought first to lay aside the earthly man, that he may deserve to search out these questions by the spirit. Therefore he says: "O man, who art thou that repliest against God? Does the thing formed say to him that formed it, Why didst thou make me thus? Or hath not the potter a right over the clay, from the same lump to make one part a vessel unto honour, and another unto dishonour?" "Since you are a thing formed," he says, "and belong to the lump of earth, having not yet been conveyed to spiritual things, so as to be a spiritual man judging everything, and to be judged by nobody (cf. 1 Cor. ii. 15),[1] you must restrain yourself from an inquiry of this kind, and not answer God. He that would know His plan, must first be received into His friendship: this can happen only to the spiritual, who already bear the image of the heavenly man" (cf. 1 Cor. xv. 49).[1] For "Now", he says, "I will not call you slaves, but friends: for all that I have heard from my Father, I have made known unto you" (John xv. 15). As long therefore as you are a moulded vessel, this itself must first be shattered in you by that iron rod, about which it is said: "Thou shalt rule them with a rod of iron, and as a potter's vessel shalt thou shatter them" (Ps. ii. 9): that when the outer man has been wasted away, and the inner man has been renewed (cf. 2 Cor. iv. 16), you may "rooted and founded in love, be able to understand the breadth, length, height, and depth, to learn also the love of God that surpasseth knowledge" (Eph. iii. 16-19). Now therefore since God from the same mass makes some vessels for honour, others for dishonour

[1] The Benedictines have overlooked this reference.

(2 Tim. ii. 20), it is not yours to dispute this, you who are still living like this mass, that is, are wise with earthly sense, and carnally.'

Not much need be quoted from the *Inchoata Expositio*. Augustine's statement of the purpose of the Epistle is admirable. It is the consideration of the question, 'Whether the Gospel of our Lord Jesus Christ came to the Jews alone, on account of their merits shown in works of the law, or without any merits shown in works preceding, justification of faith which is in Christ Jesus, came to all nations ; so that men did not believe because they were righteous, but being justified by believing, they then began to live righteously'. One of the most interesting passages is a reference to Virgil as 'a certain one of the poets, the best known in the *Roman*[1] tongue' (p. 2089): there also he makes a reference to the Sibyl, and, quoting the fourth Eclogue, 'ultima Cumaei uenit iam carminis aetas', he says that it suits very well the kingdom of Christ. His reference to the Epistle to the Hebrews is very interesting. 'With the exception of the Epistle to the Hebrews, where he is said to have purposely omitted the greeting at the beginning, lest the Jews, who were showing their teeth and yapping at him, might be offended at his name, and either read in a hostile spirit, or not bother at all about reading what he had written for their salvation : whence some have been afraid to receive it into the canon of the Scriptures : but whatever be the truth about that question, with the exception of that Epistle', &c. (p. 2095).

He tells a story of his predecessor Valerius which is not without interest: 'At this point I do not think I should omit mention of a feature which father Valerius observed with surprise in the conversation of certain rustics. When

---

[1] *Romana* for the more usual *Latina*, see Lewis and Short (Harper), s. v. *Romanus*. Add this ex. and also § 13 (p. 2096) below.

one said to another, "Salus", he asked him who knew both Latin and Punic, what "Salus" meant: the answer was given "three". Then he, recognizing with joy that our salvation was the Trinity, judged that this coincidence in sound between the two languages was not accidental, but was due to the secret dispensation of Divine Providence, so that when the word "salus" was used in Latin, the Punic people should understand it to mean "three", and that when the Punic people name "three" in their language, it should be understood in Latin as "salus".' He then brings the Syro-Phoenician woman of the Gospels into connexion with these words' (p. 2096).

In this same fragment he deals with the sin against the Holy Spirit. He defines it thus: '*He* sins against the Holy Spirit who despairing of, or mocking at and despising the preaching of the Grace by which sins are washed away, and of the peace by which we are reconciled to God, refuses to repent of his sins, and decides that he must persist in the sort of impious and deadly sweetness they bring, and continues thus to the very end.' Later Augustine very pertinently points out that it is not the mere name ' Holy Spirit', but all that is implied by it, that is intended, and defines this sin as sinning after one has learned God's will. The discussion of this question occupies a large part of the work, some five columns, in fact (pp. 2097-101), and deserves every attention. There the phrase 'pagani qui appellantur' (p. 2098) seems to show that at that time the word had not yet become firmly fixed in Christian usage, at least in Africa. He tells us that the pagans even then attacked the whole Christian religion with curses and insults, because they were already forbidden to use sword and slaughter against it. He mentions particularly the contempt they had for the doctrine of the Trinity. Altogether this is, for its size, one of the most interesting of Augustine's works, and we can only deeply regret that his hopes that he would one day finish it (pp. 2103, ll. 18–19, 2106 at the end) were not destined to be realized.[1]

The exposition of the Epistle to the Galatians is the only complete work of the three, and we can conclude this part of our investigation by selecting passages of special interest from it.

'James, the Lord's brother (§ 8 i. 15–19, p. 2110) is defined as either one of the sons of Joseph by another wife, or as one of the relatives of His mother Mary.'

On the question whether the words in i. 20, 'Now touching the things which I write unto you, behold, before God, I lie not', are an oath or not, he maintains that they are, and quotes in support 1 Cor. xv. 31, 'I protest by that glorying in you, brethren, which I have in Christ Jesus our Lord', stating that the Greek copies prove clearly that this is an oath. What he means is the use of the word νή. Pelagius, who certainly did not know much Greek when he wrote his commentary, argues from the Latin *per* and denies that there is an oath.

Augustine leaves it uncertain whether Titus was actually circumcised or not. 'Although Titus was a Greek, and no custom or parental relationship compelled him to be circumcised, as in Timothy's case, yet the Apostle would easily have permitted him also to be circumcised. For he did not teach that salvation was taken away by such circumcision, but he showed that if the hope of salvation were fixed in it, this was contrary to salvation. He would therefore put up with it, as with something superfluous, with an easy mind, according to the opinion which he expressed elsewhere: "circumcision is nothing, and uncircumcision is nothing; but the keeping of the command-

---

[1] Sanday and Headlam's commentary on *Romans*, p. 149 f., contains a short *résumé* of some of Augustine's more important opinions, derived from other works of his.

ments of God" (1 Cor. vii. 19). "But because of the false brethren privily brought in, Titus was not compelled to be circumcised": that is, circumcision could not be wrested from him, because those who came in privily, he says, to spy out our liberty, were keenly on the watch, and desired that Titus should be circumcised, that they might then preach circumcision, as declared by the support and agreement even of Paul himself to be necessary to salvation, and thus, as he says, bring them into bondage, that is, call them back again under the slavish burdens of the law. To these persons he says he did not yield subjection even for an hour, that is even for a time, that the truth of the Gospel might continue with the Gentiles.' Note that he has the negative reading in ii. 5, contrary to many of the western authorities.

The Paul-Peter episode is, of course, the subject of a well-known correspondence between Augustine and Jerome, belonging to a later date.[1] But even here Augustine's remarks are well worth attention. Peter is not blamed for returning to Judaism, but for forcing Gentiles to live as Jews. 'The public reproval was really for the benefit of others: an error that was inflicting public injury could not be secretly corrected.' He points out also how well Peter bore this reproof from a junior, as it was for the good of the flock. 'He showed an excellent example of humility. Humility is the greatest part of Christian training, and it is by humility that love is preserved : nothing outrages it more readily than a haughty spirit' (p. 2114).

The interpretation of *proscriptus* (ch. iii, v. 1) (§ 18, p. 2116) is curious: 'Before whose eyes Jesus Christ was *proscriptus* crucified': that is, before whose eyes Christ lost his inheritance and his possession.[2]

Augustine is perfectly conscious of the division of works

[1] Hier. *epist.* 112; 116 (= Aug. *epist.* 82).   [2] Cf. Victorin., p. 24 above.

of the Law into those concerned with 'sacramenta' and
those concerned with 'mores'. Under the 'sacramenta'
come circumcision of the flesh, the temporal sabbath, new
moons, sacrifices, and all the innumerable practices of this
kind. Under the 'mores' come the avoidance of murder,
adultery, falsehood, and such-like (§ 19, p. 2117).

A strange interpretation of the words, 'Cursed is everyone that hangeth on a tree' is mentioned by Augustine.
'Some Christians less learned in the Scriptures, fearing
this thought too much and with due piety approving the
ancient Scriptures, do not think that this refers to the
Lord, but to Judas his betrayer. For they said that
the reason why the words are not "Cursed is everyone
that is fixed on a tree" (crucified), but "that hangs on
a tree", is because it is not the Lord that is meant here,
but he who hung himself by a noose. But they are very
wrong, and overlook the fact that their view contradicts
the Apostle, who says: "Christ redeemed us from the
curse of the Law, being made a curse for us, because it is
written: Cursed is everyone that hangeth on a tree,"'&c.
(§ 22, pp. 2119–20).

The *procuratores et actores* of ch. iv. 2, are identified with
the *elementa huius mundi*, and these *elementa* are connected
with the Gentiles (§§ 29, 30, p. 2126: cf. also § 32, pp. 2128–9).
In a later passage these 'elementa' are looked upon as
sun, moon, stars, sky, earth, &c., OR evil spirits dissociated
from the Jews.

The treatment of the passage iv. 4, 'born of a woman',
is strange to our modern ideas. He tells us that 'mulier'
is here put for 'femina', after the Hebrew way of speech.
What he means is practically this, that *mulier*, like its
Italian derivative 'moglie', in his day meant 'wife', but
that here it is used in the sense 'woman' simply.[1]

[1] Cf. Aug. *c. Faust.* xi. 3 (p. 317 Zycha), which is practically in the
same terms.

Vict. and Pel. make similar remarks in commenting on this passage, and as Pel. quotes in illustration the same passage of Genesis (ii. 23), with reference to Eve, he may very well be borrowing from Augustine (Aug. § 30, p. 2126).

The note on 'Abba, Father' (iv. 6), is interesting: 'The words he uses are two, that the first may be interpreted by the second: for "Abba" is the same as "Pater". But it is proper to understand that it was not to no purpose that he used words of two languages with the same meaning, on account of the whole people which was called into the unity of Faith from Jews and Greeks: that the Hebrew word should be associated with the Jews, the Greek with the Gentiles, but that the identical meaning of both words should be connected with the unity of the same faith and spirit.' Then he illustrates from the parallel passage in Romans (viii. 15) (§ 31, p. 2127).

There is an ambiguous passage later (§ 32, p. 2129): 'Quem locum latius et uberius in libris aliis [1] tractauimus.' The question is whether 'locum' there means the topic of free-will, or the passage of Galatians (iv. 7–8) to which this section is dedicated, or the just quoted 1 Cor. v. 3–5. The Benedictines refer the passage to Augustine's earlier work *De libero arbitrio*. The *De libero arbitrio* is assigned by De Labriolle to 388–395, and the Exposition of Galatians to 393–4. If the Benedictines are right, and the latter work is correctly dated, it would seem that the *De libero arbitrio* should be put earlier than 395.

The note on the observation of days, months, &c. (§ 34, ch. iv, 10–11, pp. 2129–30) is of particular interest as it makes mention of pagan customs in these matters. 'It is a prevalent error of the Gentiles to observe the days, months, years, and seasons, marked by the astrologers and Chaldaeans, whether it be in the conduct of their affairs or in waiting for occurrences in their life and

---

[1] Some authorities wrongly add 'saepe' here.

business.' He goes on to say that it is perhaps not necessary to refer these remarks to the Gentiles, seeing that the Jews also observe days, and so on. But both Ambrosiaster and Pelagius prefer the Gentiles. Augustine proceeds (§ 35): 'Let the reader therefore choose whichever of the two opinions he likes, so long as he understands that the superstitious observances of seasons are so closely bound up with danger to the soul that the Apostle added here the words: "I fear lest I have laboured in vain among you." Although this passage is read in churches throughout the world amid such crowds and with such authority, our congregations are full of people who get the seasons for conducting their affairs from the astrologers. Again, they often do not hesitate even to warn us that nothing should be begun, no building or any work of this kind, on the days that they call Egyptian.[1] "They don't know where they are," as the saying is. But if this passage is to be understood about Jewish superstitious observance, what hope have they, though they wish themselves to be called Christians, steering a wrecked life by diaries, since if, like the Jews, they were to observe seasons out of the divine books, which God gave to that people when it was still carnal, the Apostle would say to them: "I am afraid lest perchance I have laboured in vain among you?" And yet if any one, even only a catechumen, were caught observing the sabbath in the Jewish fashion, the church is in an uproar. But now a countless number of the faithful tell us to our faces with great assurance: "I don't start on a journey on the second day of the month." And this we hardly seek to prevent even quietly, since we smile upon them lest they get angry, and we are afraid

---

[1] These were Jan. 2, 6, 16; Feb. 7, 25; Mar. 3, 24; May 21; June 7, 20; July 6, 18; Aug. 6, 21; Sept. 2; Oct. 20; Nov. 2, 24; Dec. 4, 14. (See *Thes. Ling. Lat.* i, 963, where also a shorter, different list is given.)

lest they fall in love with some novelty. Alas for men's
sins! it is only the unusual that fill us with horror; the
usual, for the washing away of which the Son of God's
blood was shed, however great they may be, and cause the
Kingdom of God to be altogether shut in their faces,
by often seeing them we are forced to put up with them
all, by often putting up with them, we are forced even
to commit some of them! and, O Lord, may we not
commit all that we have not been able to check!'

On the great verse v. 17, " For the flesh lusteth against
the spirit, and the spirit against the flesh; for these are
contrary the one to the other; that ye may not do the
things that ye would", he says: 'Men think that the Apostle
here denies that we have free-will, and do not understand
that this is said to them, if they refuse to retain the free
gift of faith they have accepted, by which alone they can
walk by the spirit, and not accomplish the desires of
the flesh; if therefore they refuse to retain it, they will not
be able to do what they wish. For they want to work the
works of righteousness which are in the law, but they are
overcome by the desire of the flesh, which following, they
abandon the free gift of faith.' There is a good deal more,
but the passage is too long to quote.

Definitions of words are not so characteristic of Augustine as of Jerome, but there are a few. 'Even in colloquial language', he says, 'we have *aenea* (adj.="bronze")
used of things whose number remains' (§ 22, p. 2121).[1]
The fine distinction between *inuidia* and *aemulatio* in
§ 52, p. 2142, should be quoted. He says they sometimes
mean the same, but as they both occur in the list in
Gal. v. 20, 21, there must be a distinction intended between
them here. '*Aemulatio* is pain felt when someone attains
an object on which two or more had set their hearts, and
which cannot be owned by more than one. This failing

---

[1] The *Thesaurus* shamefully ignores this passage.

is healed by "peace" (v. 22) by which we seek that which makes all seekers after it one in it, if they are successful. But *inuidia* is pain felt when someone seems unworthy to attain even that on which you did not set your heart. This failing is healed by "meekness" (v. 22), when anyone, appealing to God's judgment, refrains from resisting his will, and rather believes him that it was rightly done, than himself that he thought it unworthy.'

The last note which I shall quote is that on the *stigmata* (§ 64, vi. 17, p. 2148). '"For I bear the marks of the Lord Jesus Christ in my body": that is, I have other conflicts and struggles with my flesh, which fight with me in the persecutions which I suffer. For *stigmata* means certain marks of slaves' punishments: as if a slave, for instance, were in fetters because of a *noxa*, that is because of an offence, or had suffered something of that kind, he might be said to have *stigmata*; and therefore in the right to manumission he is of a lower rank than another without the marks, that is. Now therefore the Apostle wished to apply the term *stigmata* to the marks of punishment as it were coming from the persecutions which he suffered.' Augustine goes on to say that he was thus paid back for the persecution he had inflicted on the churches of Christ, and connects the result with the prophecy made to Ananias of Damascus in Acts ix. 16.

The question of the sources used by Augustine in the compilation of his commentaries is not easy to answer. Augustine of course possessed a library, and if Professor Baxter is right, there was in that library Ambrosiaster on Galatians, as well as Ambrosiaster on Romans. But we have no certain evidence that he possessed Ambrosiaster on Romans at the time when he wrote his commentaries on that Epistle, and we are left to internal evidence to help us to a decision. Dr. Alfred J. Smith finds that the *Expositio quarundam Propositionum* 'shews traces of

dependence on Ambrosiaster '.[1] He also points out that
'Augustine's view of Foreknowledge was exactly that
of Ambrosiaster ',[2] and that there is ' a close resemblance
between the remarks of Ambst., Aug., and Pelag. on
Rom. v. 20 '.[3] He further discloses a parallel between the
Inchoata Expositio and Ambrosiaster, in the note on
Rom. i. 7.[4]

So far as I have observed, there does not appear in the
commentary on Galatians any clear evidence that Augustine
had made use of Ambrosiaster's commentary on the same
Epistle. It would perhaps be hazardous to argue from
the frequent use of *liberator* in the sense ' saviour ' that
Augustine had used Victorinus Afer for the commentary
on Galatians, yet nothing is more antecedently probable
than that Augustine, who knew and esteemed the works
of his fellow-countryman, consulted his commentaries on
the Pauline Epistles in the course of his own work.[5]

The truth, however, is that Augustine was less a slave
to his books than perhaps any other Latin Father. Above
all, perhaps, where St. Paul was concerned, he may have
felt that he could best do service to his generation by
personal thinking out of the problems involved. Augustine
was a robust and wonderfully independent thinker, always
growing in power and grasp, and never afraid to retract
an earlier opinion of his own, if further study, either of the
biblical text or of other commentators, led him to change
his opinion.

We now turn to our last section, that of style and
language. We have here no such guide as Goelzer has
supplied for St. Jerome. The poverty of works of
reference on Augustine's style is most evident from the
amount of attention that has been paid to the very

---

[1] *J. T. S.* xix (1917–18), p. 202.   [2] Ibid. xx (1918–19), pp. 55, 59.
[3] Ibid., p. 58, cf. also p. 61.   [4] Ibid., p. 64.
[5] Cf. p. 193, n. 2.

mediocre work of Regnier on the Sermons of St. Augustine.
If it had not stood alone, little or no attention would have
been paid to it. In more recent years the admirable
indexes in volumes 53 (by Petschenig) and 60 (by Vrba
and Zycha) of the Vienna *Corpus* have added substantially
to our knowledge of Augustine's language. Without
attempting to exhaust the linguistic interest of Augustine's
commentaries on the Pauline Epistles, I have endeavoured
to collect the most interesting words and expressions, and
to arrange them in lexical order. Where the *Thesaurus*
has already got the passage referred to, it will not be
given here.

accommodate: *comp.* ⁓ius in Gal. 41.

accumulo: in Rom. 37; in Gal. 59.

acrimonia: aliquam medicamenti ⁓am uerbo correptionis asper-
gimus in Gal. 56.

adiunctio: primogenitus dicitur cum ⁓one fratrum in Rom. 56.

adnuntiator: in Gal. 4.

adsertor: spiritum sanctum, ⁓em ac ducem libertatis suae in
Gal. 54.

adtero: erat ⁓enda superbia in Gal. 25.

adtestatio: in Gal. 11 *bis*.

adtestor: *c. dat.* in Rom. imperf. 13; 15; in Gal. 22.

adulescentula: de matre ⁓a in Gal. 40.

aeneus: etiam uulgo quippe dicuntur ⁓ea quorum numerus manet
in Gal. 22.

allegorice: in Gal. 40.

alterno: fluctu dilectionis et timoris ⁓ante quassati in Gal. 54.

angelicus: in Rom. imperf. 4.

blande: *comp.* ⁓ius: siue acrius siue ⁓ius proferatur in Gal. 56.

carnaliter: in Gal. 32.

catechumenus: in Gal. 35.

christianitas: in Rom. imperf. 22.

clarificatio: in Gal. 2; 31.

conmaculo: in Rom. 78.

conflagro: illa carnaliter non obseruando, carnalium ⁓auit inuidiam (*read probably* inuidia) in Gal. 22.

congelasco: in Rom. 49.

consonantia : in Rom. imperf. 13.

contribulatio : in Rom. 71.

contribulo : in Rom. imperf. 19.

conturbatio : in Gal. 20 ; 42 ; 43.

conuenticulum : plena sunt ⌐a nostra hominibus qui . . . in Gal. 35.

conuersio : haec est evangelii ⌐io retrorsus in Gal. 20.

coopto : quae uocatio illum ⌐auit ecclesiae in Rom. imperf. 2.

copulatio : corporali ⌐one in Gal. 40.

corruptibilis : ut eam (substantiam) commutabilem et ⌐em putent in Rom. imperf. 15.

crucifixio : in Rom. 34.

crudesco : tanto errore ⌐at in Rom. imperf. 21.

custoditio : illam ⌐onem legis in Gal. 62.

decenter : in Gal. 37.

deceptor : in Rom. imperf. 14.

deitas : in Gal. 24.

deprecatio : ipsius Chananaeae ⌐em in Gal. 31.

deputo : *c. acc. et dat.* in Rom. imperf. 16.

diiudicatio : in Rom. imperf. 20 *bis* ; in Gal. 37.

do : quod autem deum dicit . . . ait . . . *datur intellegi* ad nocendum pertinere ista quae nunc dicit, id est facinora in Rom. 6.

dominicus : hac prudentia in homine ⌐o destructa et ablata in Rom. 48 ; ⌐ae illi sententiae in Rom. imperf. 18 ; holocausto ⌐ae passionis *ibid.* 19.

dominor c. dat. : in Rom. 35.

edomo : in Gal. 50.

ephemerida (*nom. sing.*) : ex ⌐idis uitam naufragam gubernantes in Gal. 35.

euacuatio (*metaph.*) : in Rom. 72.

euidentia : in Rom. imperf. 15.

examinatus : *compar.* in Gal. 50.

exsufflo : sacramenta eius ⌐ent in Rom. imperf. 15.

exsuscito : in Gal. 15 ; 54.

exustio : in Rom. 71.

finis : alio ⌐e, quo liberos ea facere decet in Gal. 43.

fixe : *compar.* in Gal. 51.

fortuitu : in Rom. imperf. 13.

fraterne : in Rom. imperf. 18.

furiosus : *superl.* bellum ⌐issimum in Gal. 51.

D d

gentilitas: in Rom. 68 *bis*.

immolaticius: in Rom. 78.

imperfectio: in Gal. 12.

inardesco: tantis ⌇scunt facibus odiorum in Rom. imperf. 18.

incarno: in Gal. 24.

incircumcisus: in Gal. 31.

incitamentum: in Rom. 36.

incommutabilitas: in Gal. 23.

incommutabiliter: in Rom. imperf. 10.

inconcusse: in Rom. imperf. 10.

increpito: *c. acc. et dat.* in Rom. imperf. 15.

inde: cum inde loqueretur: in Rom. imperf. 16.

indifferentia: in Gal. 63.

indubitanter: in Rom. imperf. 17.

infero: deinde intulit: *sic stulti estis*, &c. in Gal. 20; infert: *lex nondum data erat* in Gal. 23; *cf.* 24 *bis*.

infestatio: in Rom. imperf. 22.

innouatio: in Rom. imperf. 3.

inremissibilis: in Rom. imperf. 17.

inrisor: in Rom. imperf. 14.

instanter: in Rom. imperf. 18.

intellector: in Gal. 5.

intentio: ne intentionem causae . . . subito in aliud temere detorquere uelle uideamur in Gal. 34.

intereo: *fut. particip.* in Rom. 53.

intuitus: terrenae mercedis ⌇ u in Gal. 56.

iuratio: in Gal. 9 (six times).

liberator (= 'Saviour', *saluator* being perhaps absent from these works[1]): in Rom. 13–18 *ter*; 44; 45–6; 48; 52; in Gal. 57.

manumissio: in Gal. 64.

misericorditer: in Rom. 61; in Rom. imperf. 9; 23.

moror: *c. infin.* in Rom. imperf. 18.

mortaliter: in Gal. 17; 48.

neglegenter: in Rom. imperf. 15.

numquidnam: in Gal. 19.

obduratio: in Rom. 62 *bis*; 63. The Pelagians preferred *induratio*.

---

[1] As it is from Tertullian; it is found once only in Cyprian (Watson, *Style and Language of St. Cyprian*, p. 248 f.). As we have seen (ch. i), Victorinus Afer uses *liberator* often.

obduro: (from *Rom.* ix. 18): in Rom. 62, five times.

oblatro: of persons, in Rom. imperf. 11 ; 15.

obsequenter: in Gal. 46.

oppressio: in Rom. imperf. 18.

ordinate: *superl.* in Gal. 47.

orior: orirentur, in Rom. imperf. 4.

paganus: ‿i qui appellantur in Rom. imperf. 15; 22 ; in Gal. 22.

parturitio: (*metaph.*) in Gal. 38 *bis*.

perniciose: *compar.* in Gal. 25.

phantasma: in Rom. imperf. 4.

poenalis: in Rom. 53 ; in Rom. imperf. 9.

praecessor: in Gal. 13 *bis*.

praedestinatio: in Gal. 40.

praedicator: in Rom. imperf. 15.

praenuntiator: in Rom. imperf. 4.

praepollens: *compar.* in Gal. 49.

praepotentia: in Gal. 27.

praeputio: in Gal. 19.

praerogo: ut uocatio peccatori ‿etur in Rom. 60.

praescientia: in Rom. 60.

praesens: *superl.* in Gal. 21.

pressura: in Rom. imperf. 10.

propheticus: in Gal. 24.

**prosculto: *Gal.* ii. 4, *qui subintroierunt* proscultare ˙*libertatem eorum* (*ap.* in Gal. 11), where the Vulgate has *explorare*. This word, which has escaped the compilers of lexicons, is obviously connected with *auscultare*, and, if it be not an artificial coinage, would seem to shed some new light on the origin of the latter.

pugnaciter: in Rom. imperf. 11 ; 13.

pulsator: bonus intellector, pius ‿or in Gal. 5.

quatriduanus: ‿a cadauera in Gal. 15.

recaleo: bellum . . . cuius reliquiae, quamuis tritae diu, adhuc tamen ‿ent in Gal. 51.

recuro: manente fundamento ‿ari aedificium potest in Rom. imperf. 19.

reflecto: tribulationes et molestiae . . . bonos et iustos . . . non ‿unt ad peccandum, sed ab omni labe penitus purgant in Rom. imperf. 10.

reformatio: cum ‿io corporis in resurrectione facta fuerit in Rom. 36.

refrico : ⁓ans ipsam quaestionem in Gal. 25.

refundo : in me causam ⁓ite, si timetis in Gal. 42.

regulariter : r. ait in Rom. imperf. 16.

renouatio : ⁓io in baptismo est in Rom. imperf. 19.

reparatio: damnatio non sine spe ⁓onis inrogata est naturae nostrae in Rom. 53.

repugnantia : nulla inter se ⁓ia in Gal. 5.

salubriter : *compar.* in Gal. 57.

salutatorius: principium (epistulae) ⁓um in Rom. imperf. 11.

scribo: huc usque dixit ipse quis esset qui scribit epistulam : est enim qui scribit epistulam *Paulus seruus,* &c. in Rom. imperf. 7.

seductio: in Gal. 38.

seminatio : *metaph.* in Gal. 61.

sensibilis : ⁓ibilibus miraculis in Gal. 20.

sequestro : ⁓ata interim meliore consideratione in Rom. 80.

seruiliter : in Gal. 30 ; 34 ; 41.

simulate : in Rom. 74 ; in Gal. 15 ; 28 ; 63.

simulator : in Rom. imperf. 20.

singularitas : in Gal. 23 ; 27.

sanctus spiritus : in Gal. 20 *bis.*

subaudio : in Gal. 28 ; 49.

subdistinguo : in Gal. 28.

susceptio : in Rom. 48 ; 56 ; 59 *bis* ; in Gal. 27 ; 30.

testator : in Gal. 23 *ter.*

torcular : in Rom. 78.

transitorius : (*opp.* stabilis) in Gal. 17.

transitorie : in Rom. imperf. 15.

**translate* : in Gal. 36. This word, which is wanting to the dictionaries, is found also in Aug. *c. Adim.* 11 (p. 137, l. 4 Z.).

uendo : ⁓ebatur in Rom. 78.

uenenosus : malitiosi et ⁓i animi signa in Rom. imperf. 20.

uerbi gratia (cf. Span. *verbigracia*) : in Rom. imperf. 17 ; in Gal. 49 ; 64.

ueridicus : in Gal. 24.

uestibulum : ipso epistulae ⁓o in Gal. 1.

uictoriosus : hoc maxime in eo ⁓um est in Gal. 20.

uulgatus : *superl.* in Gal. 34.

V

PELAGIUS[1]

THE last of our early commentators is Pelagius. Of his life very little is known. He was a native either of the Roman province Britain or of Ireland, it is uncertain which, as his contemporaries call him now *British*, now *Irish*. He wrote expositions of thirteen Epistles of St. Paul in Rome in the period A.D. 406-9: in these he denied original sin. He is afterwards found in Africa with his follower Caelestius, and later defended himself before a synod at Diospolis in Palestine. Ultimately excommunicated in A.D. 417, he disappears entirely from history. He was a lay solitary, distinguished for the purity of his life, and may have retired to his native land, then abandoned by the Romans to barbarian attacks. It is evident that he had received a good education, though he is not quite on the same plane as a writer with Jerome or Augustine, his contemporaries.

The original form of Pelagius' Expositions was only recently discovered, in two copies, one a ninth-century (about A.D. 800) anonymous manuscript at Karlsruhe (Aug. cxix), the other a fifteenth-century manuscript (under the name of Jerome) at Balliol College, Oxford, No. 157. At the time of writing, the work is in type, but not yet published. The writer's heresy and excommunication explain the extraordinary vicissitudes through which his commentary passed. There is apparently no copy in

---

[1] For most of the facts in this chapter consult A. Souter, *Pelagius's Expositions of Thirteen Epistles of St. Paul. I, Introduction* (Cambridge, 1922), but there are here additions and corrections.

existence with his name upon it. But in addition to the two copies of the original form just referred to, there are many copies of various adaptations of it, which must be briefly described.

The form in the Karlsruhe MS., formerly at Reichenau on Lake Constance, and apparently copied from an Italian MS. in half-uncials of the fifth or sixth century, contains almost the whole of the Pauline text in a form which is nearly identical with the Vulgate. It is significant that the only portions of the text omitted are certain salutations near the end of the Epistles, which Pelagius apparently left out because they did not minister to edification.

The Balliol MS., apparently copied from a MS. in pointed Irish writing of about the year 800, gives an Old-Latin Biblical text, and omits none of the salutations. It differs also from the Karlsruhe MS. in furnishing occasional pieces of comment that are lacking in its rival. These comments are few in number, and almost confined to the Epistle to the Romans. Though not found in the Karlsruhe MS., they appear in certain interpolated manuscripts. But this MS., on the contrary, omits a number of notes, especially on the Epistle to the Philippians.

How do we know that these manuscripts represent the original form? By a comparison with the contemporary quotations made from the commentary by Augustine and Marius Mercator. These are the only two authorities whose form of the text agrees with these quotations. They have also the advantage of being shorter than the rival forms, and are therefore much more likely to be original. Their very character also explains how the expanded forms were constructed.

If we postulate one original form of the commentary, then it would be represented by the type, biblical text as in the Balliol MS. (minus the salutations) *plus* the expositional text in the Karlsruhe MS. But some will naturally prefer to speak of two original forms, one containing omitted biblical passages and a few notes added to the other. I mean that Pelagius himself may have added a few pieces of text and notes to one copy that were not in the other, or his companion Caelestius may be the author of these additions. The question of biblical text will be considered later in this chapter.

It should here be mentioned that a comprehensive Merton College, Oxford, MS., No. 26, has proved to be a copy of the Balliol MS., as far as the Pelagian part is concerned, and it has therefore no place in the restoration of the archetype.

Certain seventh-century fragments found at Rome, and other early ninth-century fragments found at Freiburg, appear to belong to the same short form, and the Roman fragments, while they support the Balliol MS. in biblical text, support the Karlsruhe MS. in omitting certain short notes that are present in the Balliol MS. The same type of text is also supported by an interpolation made in one family of Ambrosiaster MSS. not later than the sixth century. For a long passage missing at the end of First and the beginning of Second Corinthians, a scribe had substituted the corresponding passage from the original form of the Pelagius commentary. The biblical text of this interpolation amply confirms the Balliol tradition. But we must now turn to the longer manuscripts.

There is a large number of interpolated manuscripts. Most of these attribute the commentary to Jerome, and it is one of these forms that is represented in print, from the ninth volume of Erasmus' edition of Jerome (Basle, 1516) down to the edition in Migne's Patrology, vol. xxx. There are in all ten manuscripts bearing the name of Jerome,[1] and they divide themselves into three classes. First, there

---

[1] Leaving out of account the Balliol and Merton MSS.

is the shorter form, represented by the Echternach MS. (now Paris MS. 9525), which was written before the end of the eighth century, and has a Welsh ancestor; the Salisbury Cathedral MS. 5 (saec. xii); and the Munich Staatsbibliothek MS. 13038 (written at Ratisbon early in the ninth century), as uncorrected. There is also a late copy of this MS. in Munich University Library. The Echternach MS. was that used by Erasmus as the basis of his text. As the manuscript swarms with corruptions, it was a most unfortunate choice, and has vitiated the whole study of the question ever since. The biblical text in this class of MSS. is on the whole Vulgate, but here and there preserves old British readings. It contains a number of notes, by a Pelagian, which are probably not much later in date than the Pelagian original itself. There is no commentary on Hebrews, and the Epistles are in the order 1, 2 Thess. Col., the true Pelagian order.

The second type of pseudo-Jerome MSS. is longer than the first, and appears to have been constructed by the addition of the Pelagian notes to an early copy of the Vulgate; for this form is even more Vulgate than the shorter form is. And we not only find the Vulgate text, but we find the prefatory matter and the lists of chapter headings characteristic of Vulgate MSS. duly incorporated. The representatives of this form are Paris, 1853 (saec. viii–ix), Epinal, 6 (saec. ix in.), the corrector of the above-named Munich MS. 13038, Troyes 486 (saec. xii), Florence, R. Bibl. Mediceo-Laur. Plut. xv dext 1 (saec. xii ex.), a descendant of the Troyes MS., and Cambridge University Library Ff. 4, 31 (saec. xv). In this family there is a commentary on Hebrews, and the Epistles are in the usual order Col. 1, 2 Thess.

The third form is represented by one MS. only, 23 (36 (saec. xii) of the collection at Göttweig Abbey, near Krems. Lower Austria. The existence of this manuscript was first made known by Dom de Bruyne in October 1922,[1] and assigned by him to the second class. An examination of it made in August 1924, by the kind permission of the Abbot and the Prior of Göttweig, has enabled me to say that it belongs neither to the first nor to the second class, but forms a class by itself. It has the same commentary on Hebrews as the second class has, but it has the Epistles in the order 1, 2 Thess. Col. It is also without many of the special readings of the second class, and often agrees with MSS. of the first class against the second class. It has some special agreements with the Munich MS. 13038, but very often it goes its own way. Whether it preserves a single true reading of Pelagius that has been lost by all our other authorities it is premature to say, but it is at least clear that it constitutes a class by itself, and will shed a real light on the history of the Pseudo-Jerome form, if it does nothing else.

The St. Gall anonymous MS. 73, of the first half of the ninth century, was made known by Heinrich Zimmer in his *Pelagius in Irland* (Berlin, 1901). Subsequent study has helped to place it nearer its proper position among the authorities. It is like the copies of pure Pelagius in that it preserves the passages quoted by Augustine and Marius Mercator, which have been deliberately excised from the pseudo-Jerome form. It is also like pure Pelagius in First Corinthians, for there, and there alone, it has no interpolations, and it at the same time gives us the same biblical text as is found in the Balliol MS. But elsewhere the biblical text is very close to the Vulgate on the whole, and besides containing the vast majority of pseudo-Jerome interpolations, even those of the longer form, this manuscript, along with passages of genuine Jerome, &c., has the Epistles in the usual order, Col. 1, 2 Thess., and has

---

[1] *Bulletin d'Ancienne Littérature chrétienne latine*, p. 59, n. 3.

substantially the same commentary on Hebrews as is found in the second family of pseudo-Jerome MSS.

Towards the end of his long life, in the middle of the sixth century, Cassiodorus took the Pelagius commentary, which he had in an anonymous form, without knowing that it was Pelagius, and purged the commentary on Romans from its Pelagian poison, while he left the other twelve to be similarly treated by his pupils. This revision has now been successfully identified with a commentary wrongly published in 1537 by Jean de Gaigny under the name of 'Primasius', and surviving also in an anonymous twelfth-century manuscript (numbered 270) at Grenoble. This is a definitely anti-Pelagian edition of Pelagius, from which much Pelagian teaching is absent, and in which passages of Augustine and other writers have been substituted on occasion for the original expositions. This form of the Pelagian commentary was much appreciated in certain quarters in the Middle Ages, and was used by Claudius of Turin, Haymo of Auxerre, and other medieval compilers. The commentary on Hebrews in the printed edition and the manuscript has been proved by Riggenbach to be the work of this Haymo, and to be therefore a ninth-century production, which was attached to the anonymous revision of Pelagius in the same way as Alcuin was attached to Ambrosiaster, and a commentary on Hebrews was added to the second and third forms of the pseudo-Jerome, to complete the set of Pauline commentaries in a day when Hebrews was definitely canonical. Even Pelagius regarded this Epistle as Pauline, though not apparently as canonical.

A very strange manuscript of Veronese origin has survived in Paris B.N. lat. 653, of the end of the eighth or the beginning of the ninth century. It represents an anonymous compilation which, from internal evidence, must have been made in Spain some time between the middle of the sixth century and the middle of the eighth. This period covers the life of St. Isidore, Archbishop of Seville, and it may very well be that he himself put the work together. The biblical text agrees mainly with the Vulgate, but where it disagrees, goes most frequently with the Old-Latin manuscript d., the Latin side of Codex Claromontanus. The Epistles are arranged in the Pelagian order, 1, 2 Thess. Col. The exposition comprises practically the whole of the original Pelagius, including the passages quoted by Augustine and Marius Mercator, as also part of a short commentary on Hebrews,[1] which bears some relationship to that already referred to as present in two classes of pseudo-Jerome MSS. and the St. Gall MS. 73. The expositions of First and Second Timothy, Titus, and Philemon are practically unaltered Pelagius, but in all the other Epistles the exposition has been enlarged by the use of pseudo-Jerome and of Cassiodorus' revision of Pelagius. The use of the latter is perfectly clear, not only from cases where a note exists in both forms, the Pelagian and the Cassiodorian,[2] but also from cases where the Cassiodorian phraseology is definitely preferred to the Pelagian; for example, in the notes on Rom. xv. 31; 2 Cor. xi. 12, xiii. 10; Eph. ii. 14, v. 32; Col. ii. 20, iv. 5-6 *bis*. A study of the passages proves that it is the manuscript and not Cassiodorus that is the borrower.

But the compiler drew upon still other sources. Jerome *Against Jovinian* is used without acknowledgement on 1 Cor. vii, and there are eight very long insertions, three of them controversial passages, where genuine Jerome is followed by passages from Pelagius' work *De libero arbitrio*, which is otherwise for the most part lost; and of the other five, three would seem to belong to some African writer of the same school as Fulgentius of Ruspe, and to his

---

[1] Now published in *Miscellanea Fr. Ehrle*, vol. iv (Roma, 1924), pp. 39 ff.

[2] The suggestion in Souter, vol. i, pp. 255, 259, must be discarded.

date, the first half of the sixth century; they are expositions of Trinitarian doctrine. The two remaining fragments occur at the beginning of the MS. and have not been assigned.

Of all authorities for the text of Pelagius none would exceed in value the copy in the possession of Sedulius Scottus, an Irishman who lived and taught in the Rhine country in the middle of the ninth century. For he adopted Pelagius, biblical text and all, as the basis of his collections on St. Paul's Epistles, first printed by Johannes Sichardus at Basle in 1528. The printed text can be considerably improved by reference to the surviving MSS. of Sedulius' work. A study of Sedulius' text proves the accuracy with which he copied Pelagius' comments, and the author frankly acknowledged his obligations to Pelagius and other early writers by adding symbols in the margin to indicate the authors used, each symbol occurring opposite the beginning of the extract made.

A still earlier writer, Zmaragdus of St. Mihiel, used Pelagius for his *Expositio Libri Comitis*, compiled about 825. He also acknowledged obligations in the same way as Sedulius. But the symbol $\overline{P}$ in him seems to indicate, not a pure Pelagius, but a pseudo-Jerome of the second class, unless we contradict the medieval maxim and suppose that he had both. Certain sections [1] prove use of a pseudo-Jerome of the second class, and Zmaragdus was a man of learning who could quite well see that the pseudo-Jerome was not Jerome, but rather a form of Pelagius, even if his copy did not have the name Pelagius on it. The cases here given of writers who used Pelagian material might be added to, but it is of more importance now to name the references to Pelagius' work by his own name, as hitherto the material of the commentary rather than the name has claimed our attention.

---

[1] e.g. Migne, *P. L.* cii, pp. 63 D, 64 A, 92 C, 113 C, 200 A, 222 A, 434 B, 443 B–C, 503 A, 506 B, &c. Correct thus Souter, op. cit., vol. i, p. 336.

Augustine and Marius Mercator are followed by Arnobius Junior, who wrote, perhaps in Rome, about 450. It
is not till after the lapse of two hundred years that we
come across the next reference, in an Irish-Latin commentary on the 'canonical' epistles preserved in a Karlsruhe MS. (cod. Aug. ccxxxiii, saec. ix). Soon after this
Pelagius is quoted once or twice by name, with every
respect, in the Irish Canons. The bulk of the references
occur in the ninth century. There are four catalogues
belonging to that century, showing that the libraries to
which they belonged claimed to possess Pelagius' commentary. The libraries were at St. Riquier in Picardy, at
Murbach in Alsace, at Lorsch[1] near Darmstadt, and at
St. Gall in north-east Switzerland. After the ninth century
there are sporadic references down to and including the
thirteenth century. Perhaps the most interesting of these
are in a group of manuscripts connected with St. Albans,
England, and the close of the twelfth century, where the
general preface to the Epistles is rightly given under
Pelagius' name.

The Text. The printed text of the pseudo-Jerome expositions swarms with corruptions, of which there can
hardly be fewer than six thousand. But the text that can
be restored from the recently found authorities, contains
very few corrupt passages indeed. It is not too much to say
that the reader will find the expositions practically in the
state in which they left Pelagius. As regards the biblical
texts, they are also in a wonderful state of purity. The
bulk of the MSS. furnish a text of great importance for
the textual criticism of the Vulgate, and the remainder
present us with an Old-Latin text of much interest.

The Biblical Text. As has just been said, the majority
of the MSS. furnish us with a very pure Vulgate text.
But that this is not the text habitually used by Pelagius, is

---

[1] The Lorsch catalogue should be dated about A.D. 850 (P. Lehamnn).

proved by the character of the Pauline quotations which occur in the body of the notes. In that part of the work, where alteration was less likely to be made by scribes, the quotations show a tendency to agree with the text of the *Book of Armagh*, where it diverges from the Vulgate. This same type of text is that which is given by the Balliol MS. in all the *lemmata*; throughout in the portion 1 Cor. xv to 2 Cor. i, used by the early scribe to fill up the gap in Ambrosiaster; from beginning to end of First Corinthians in the St. Gall MS. 73; often in the Veronese MS.; and throughout in Sedulius Scottus. Even MS. A itself sometimes shows a striking agreement with the *Book of Armagh* against the Vulgate: e. g. 1 Cor. xii. 2 (where the Balliol MS. is wanting) *gentes eratis simulacrorum formae similes* (with GV.) against *cum gentes essetis ad simulacra muta* of the Vulgate and most MSS. containing adaptations of Pelagius' work.[1]

As a piece of Latin this text is not as good as the Vulgate. It shows more contact with the text used by St. Ambrose than with that of any other of the Latin Fathers. But in view of the fact that it appears with certain modifications in Gildas, and occasionally in some of the pseudo-Jerome MSS. of the shorter family (the Welsh or Anglo-Saxon family), as well as in the *Book of Armagh* and the other authorities mentioned above, it would seem that it is really a British text, and if that be so, it is a find of considerable interest. The divergences from this text found in our Pelagian authorities are due to conscious harmonization with the Vulgate. It was only natural that scribes, finding an exposition of the Epistles of St. Paul attributed to St. Jerome, should seek to alter the biblical *lemmata* to the Vulgate form. They would reason that, if St. Jerome were the author of the expositions, he must have used his own text, the Vulgate, as their basis.

---

[1] Other instructive passages are Rom. ix. 11, xv. 24.

Quotations made in the notes from other parts of the Bible than the Pauline Epistles are uniformly Old-Latin, not Vulgate. These facts suggest that Pelagius took no interest in the Vulgate at all. We pass now to the Expositions themselves.

The shortness of the notes is probably the first characteristic that strikes the reader. They are often shorter than the passage commented on, but they never lack point. Yet, short as they are, they often provide alternative explanations. One explanation will be given, and then another, the latter generally introduced by the word 'Siue', but sometimes by 'Aliter'.

Very often the note points out what the Apostle is *not* referring to, as a means of making clearer what the reference really is. For example, on Titus i. 1, 'Paul bondslave of God', the comment is simply: 'Not of sin.'

No previous commentators are referred to by name, unless the names of heretics should happen to include such. The vague word *quidam* (certain persons) is the author's favourite method of referring to other commentators, whose views he generally rejects. It is one of the interesting and pathetic features of Pelagius' commentary that he condemns by name practically all the leading heretics of the time, Marcionites, Manichaeans, Arians, Photinians, Novatians, Jovinianists, Apollinarians, and Macedonians, and yet was himself destined to become an heresiarch, simply because his teaching contradicted what was not yet a settled part of Christian dogma at all.

In spite of the fact that the exposition is arranged clause by clause, the writer is fully alive to the succession of topics in the Epistles, and not infrequently indicates where the discussion of a particular topic begins or ends.

A curious characteristic is the way in which the notes are often made part of the structure of the Pauline text. For instance, a note will consist on occasion of a relative clause, dependent on some word in the biblical *lemma*, the note itself therefore not forming even a sentence.

The same underlying ideas reveal themselves throughout the whole commentary. The writer is constantly alluding to the influence of example on conduct, particularly the example of the Apostle on the lives of his converts, and he speaks of the joy the teacher finds in the progress of his pupils. Again, he repeats that we are saved gratuitously, by God's grace, not by our own merits. He very often states the Pauline doctrine that we are justified by faith alone. He also identifies foreknowledge and predestination.

His favourite biblical quotation is from Acts v. 41: ' The apostles departed, rejoicing that they were counted worthy to suffer dishonour for the Name ': we find it ten times quoted or alluded to. Another verse, 1 John iii. 2, 'it is not yet made manifest what we shall be: we know that if he shall be manifested, we shall be like him ', is a great favourite of his, as it was of his predecessor, Ambrosiaster. It is also observable that he is fond of quoting the Wisdom literature of the Old Testament (including the Apocrypha).

Pelagius' short notes, though they are the most characteristic, hardly do justice to his real power. I will therefore quote in English a number of his longer notes in addition to certain of the shorter notes:

Rom. i. 16, " I am not ashamed of the Gospel ". ' This is a skilful attack on the pagans, who, although they are not ashamed to believe that their own God Jupiter changed himself into animals devoid of reason, and lifeless gold, for the gratification of his outrageous lust, yet think that we ought to be ashamed to believe that our Lord for the sake of the salvation of His own image (man) was crucified, in the flesh he had assumed, although in the one there is shocking disgrace, and in the other a pattern of goodness and virtue. At the same time also he attacks those heretics

who shun these beliefs as unworthy of God, not understanding that nothing is more worthy of the Creator than
to care for the salvation of His own creation, especially as
He, being incapable of suffering, cannot feel in this any
loss to his own nature.'

Rom. i. 19, " Because that which may be known of God ".
' What can be naturally known of God, that He is and that
He is righteous.' " Is manifest in them." ' In their
consciences : for every creature testifies that it knows (or
is not) God, and shows that it is made by another, whose
will it must obey.   For if God is the highest good, invisible,
incomprehensible, inestimable, and is above all things, that
is, one to whom nothing can either be preferred or equalled,
either in greatness, or glory, or power, it is clear that this
can apply to no creation, which is both seen by the eyes
and grasped by the reason and judged by the judging
faculty.   No creation is greater than all others in every
respect, because all surpass one another in turn, some in
size, as the heaven and the earth, others in brightness, as
the sun and the moon or the stars, others in depth, as the
sea.   So therefore it is clearly seen that God is no element.
Further, that they were made, is shown by their changing
quality, which can be no property of eternity.   That they
did not make themselves is, however, clear, because, if
they made themselves, they already existed before they
came into being, in order to be able to make themselves,
which is a very ridiculous statement.   In varying and
changing their ranks and yielding to one another, they
show that, on the one hand, they were made by one author,
and, on the other, that they carry out not their own will,
but that of their Lord, whose rule they cannot transgress.'

Rom. ii. 3-4, " And reckonest thou this, O man, who
judgest them that practise such things, and doest the same,
that thou shalt escape the judgment of God ?   Or despisest
thou the richness of His goodness and forbearance and

long-suffering, not knowing that the goodness of God leadeth thee to repentance?" 'Or do you flatter yourself that you will get off unpunished for the reason that God does not repay in the present, and considering the length of the time and His overflowing goodness, do you think that there is no judgement now? Hear then the opinion of scripture: "The Lord is not slack concerning his promise, but is long-suffering to you-ward, not wishing that any should perish, but that all should come to repentance" (2 Peter iii. 9). He shows His goodness in waiting, His righteousness in punishing, where the prophet warns us: "Do not be slow to turn to the Lord, nor postpone it from day to day: for His wrath comes suddenly, and in time of vengeance will He destroy thee" (Eccli. v. 8-9). And again: "Say not: I have sinned, and what distressful thing happeneth unto me? For the Most High is a patient rewarder" (Eccli. v. 4). Men lead themselves far astray because of God's patience, [and] because He will not punish sinners at once: He is thought either to care very little about human affairs, or to forgive faults, because He postpones. Very many even, contrary to their own interests, ask falsely why He does not repay in the present, not understanding that, if that were done, hardly a human being would have remained, and never would unrighteous men become righteous. The reason why God seems to men to wait long for sinners is that we, living as we do but a short time, think a hundred years an eternity. But He, "with whom a thousand years are as one day" (Ps. xc. 4), does not regard a hundred years as equal to the space of one hour. Thus this is a little matter with God, since even men are in the habit of waiting a long time for the reform of sinners.'

Rom. v. 15, "For if by the trespass of the one the many died, much more did the grace of God, and the gift by the grace of the one man, Jesus Christ, abound unto the many", the passage to which Augustine objected, and which brought trouble upon Pelagius :

‘ Righteousness had more power in making alive than sin had in putting to death, because Adam put to death only himself and those that were to follow, but Christ freed not only those that were then in the body, but also those that were to follow.   Those who are against the view that sin is inherited, endeavour thus to attack it : “ If ”, they say, “ the sin of Adam injured even those that do not sin, therefore also the righteousness of Christ benefits even those that do not believe, because Paul says that salvation is brought about similarly, or rather to a greater degree, by *one*, than destruction was previously brought about by *one*.”   Then they say : “ If baptism cleanses away that old sin, the children of two baptized persons must lack present sin : for they could not transmit to posterity that which they themselves did not at all possess.   Further, if the soul is not inherited, but only the flesh, the latter alone has the inherited sin, and it alone deserves punishment.”   They declare it to be unjust, that a soul born to-day, not from the mass of Adam, should carry so ancient a sin which was another’s.   They say also that it is inadmissible that God, who forgives one’s own sins, should charge us with another’s.’   Note how what would appear to be Pelagius’ own opinions are so curiously put into the mouths of people indicated by the third person.   Such a vague, tentative way of putting forward opinions is not common in ancient times.

Rom. xv. 24, “ Whensoever I go unto Spain ”.   ‘ It is regarded as uncertain whether he was in Spain.’

Rom. xvi. 1, “ [Phoebe our sister], who is a servant of the church that is at Cenchreae ”.   ‘ Even as now in oriental places deaconesses,[1] (married ?) women, are seen to serve in connexion with their own sex.   Either : In Baptism, Or :

[1] Cf. 1 Tim. iii. 11 (note).

In the ministry of the word, because we find that women taught privately, like Priscilla, whose husband's name was Aquila.'

Rom. xvi. 14-15, "Salute Asyncritus, Phlegon, Hermes, Patrobas, Hermas and the brethren that are with them: salute Philologus and Julia, Nereus and his sister Olympias,[1] and all the saints that are with them". 'By his own example he teaches us what sort of friends we ought to send greetings to in our letters, not those that are rich in worldly possessions, or in high official positions, but those that are rich in grace and faith.'

1 Cor. i. 19, "And the prudence of the prudent will I reject". 'By choosing fishermen he condemned the art of rhetoric and philosophy. The question is certainly put from time to time whence comes the wisdom that God condemns: for it is written (Ecclesiasticus i. 1) that all wisdom is from the Lord God, that is, gets its beginning from a nature that is good. This is a characteristic of human understanding, that to whatsoever point you stretch it, it follows, and by gradual practice makes progress. This is how many illiterate persons compose poems so choice that men of learning admire them. This understanding, therefore, which God had given for the learning of Himself from the study of His creatures, and for the search into His will, *they* have turned to the study of the superfluous and the curious. Similarly we can form an estimate of riches and strength and all those things of which we make a bad use.'

1. Cor. x. 6, "Now these things were our examples, to the intent we should not lust after evil things, as they also lusted". 'In their case these things really happened, which were in a figure for us, that we might fear to do such things, lest we might incur such punishment. All those things that happened in the case of the people Israel at that time *in a figure*, are now celebrated in us *in reality*.

[1] Such seems to be the Pelagian text.

For as they were freed by Moses from Egypt, so we by some bishop or teacher are freed from the present world. Then, when we have become Christians, we are led through deserts, that by practising contempt of the world and abstinence, we may forget the pleasures of Egypt, in such a way that we shall not know how to return to this world. When we cross the sea of baptism, then indeed for us is the devil, with his host, drowned like Pharaoh. Then are we fed with manna, and we do receive of the drink that trickles forth from Christ's side. The brightness also of knowledge is shown, like unto a pillar of fire in the night of this world, and amidst the scorching heat of tribulation we are covered by the cloud of divine consolation. If after all those experiences we sin, they alone will not be able to help us, even as the Hebrews also are told: "A man that hath set at nought Moses' law dieth without compassion on the word of two or three witnesses: of how much sorer punishment, think you, shall he be judged worthy, who hath trodden under foot the Son of God,"' &c. (Hebr. x. 28 f.).

1 Cor. x. 15–16, "Judge ye what I say. The cup of blessing which we bless". 'The reason why he named the cup first, is that he might discuss the bread at greater length.'

1 Cor. xiii. 3, "And if I bestow all my goods to feed the poor, and if I give my body to be burned, but have not love, it profiteth me nothing". 'It must be noted that contempt of the world is coupled with martyrdom, which contradicts the views of those that strive by various arguments to shut the latter out of the Gospel, where a rich man is thus addressed: "Go, sell all your possessions," &c. For the Apostle, treating of the highest blessing, love, must undoubtedly be believed to have preferred it to great things; for small things could not be compared with the greatest thing. This is recognized from the examples themselves; for who would not know that to speak with

the tongues of men and of angels, and to have prophecy, and to know all mysteries, and to possess all knowledge, and to have all faith, and to resign one's self to fires to be burnt, are great things? To those therefore contempt of the world is also joined, which if it were not great, would neither be compared with the highest thing, which is love, nor placed among the great things at all. This overthrows the opinion of those who make out that we are taught to renounce the affairs of the world at a definite time, under stress of persecution, that they may both rob the apostles of their glory, since they did that not willingly, but unwillingly, and make out the perfect of our day to be fools, since they have sought in vain to put into force now what belongs to another period. The question is certainly put how anyone can bear martyrdom without love, if it be experienced not for God's sake, but for that of human glory, or, at least, if one in the act of martyrdom maintain anger against his brother, thinking lightly of Him who ordered us to forget our neighbour's ill nature, showing himself a transgressor even in the moment of death itself.'

1 Cor. xiv. 19, "Howbeit in the church I had rather speak five words with my understanding, that I might instruct others also, than ten thousand words in a tongue". 'But I prefer to speak a very few words according to my own understanding and in a simple way, in order to do good, rather than many words to do good to no one. Certain people actually ask what are the five words: I must ask them in retaliation what are the ten thousand.'

1 Cor. xv. 28, "And when all things have been subjected unto him, then shall the Son also himself be subjected to him that did subject all things unto him". 'Here also the Arians misrepresent the truth, and say that after the resurrection of all and the end, the Son will be subjected to the Father, as the less of course to the greater. They must be told in reply that they are impious, because they

deny that He is now subjected to the Father. But "subjection" does not always involve a decrease of honour,
but is also related to the duty of love, especially as the
spirit of the prophets also is said to have been subject to
the prophets, that God may be a god not of disagreement,
but of peace, seeing that the Lord Himself is recorded to
have been subject to Joseph and Mary. Many, it is true,
have had various opinions about this section. For certain
writers say: "Even as He starves or is fed in the person of
His own, when they starve, so also He Himself is subjected
in His Church, which is His body." Others say that the
human nature itself which He assumed, can in the giving
of thanks always be subject to the divinity, because by
making it one with Himself He subjected everything to it.
Many also express other different opinions, which it would
take too long to insert and to enumerate.'

2 Cor. iii. 6, " For the letter killeth, but the spirit giveth
life ". Part of the note on this reads : ' Certain writers say
that the literal understanding kills, not knowing that
neither the literal nor the allegorical interpretation can be
everywhere maintained : for although certain statements
are figurative, yet, if you try to interpret commands alle-
gorically, emptying them of all their force, you have
opened a door of sin to all.' This note very well illustrates
Pelagius' attitude to allegory. His position is midway
between the Antiochian literal interpretation and the
Alexandrian allegorical, with perhaps somewhat of a bias
in the Antiochian direction.[1]

2 Cor. xii. 7, "To buffet me, [that I should not be
exalted overmuch]". ' By raising up tribulations or pains :
for certain commentators say that he suffered from frequent
headaches.'

Gal. ii. 3, " But not even Titus, who was with me ".

---

[1] Cf. *in Gal.* iv. 24.

'Ran in vain.' " Being a Greek, was compelled to be circumcised, but it was because of the false brethren privily brought in." ' He gives reasons why he circumcised Titus, not because circumcision benefited him, but that a threatening stumbling-block might be avoided.'

Gal. iii. 11, " For the righteous lives by faith ". ' Perfect faith consists not only in believing that Christ is, but also in believing Christ,' the distinction between *Christum* and *Christo.* It is notable that he says nothing of *in Christum.*

Eph. i. 10, " To restore all things in Christ, the things in the heavens, and the things upon the earth, in him ". ' Many have expressed different opinions on this subject. For some say that *heavens* is to be taken as meaning souls, *earth* bodies. Others affirm that *heavens* means the Jews, who had had heavenly precepts, and that *earth* ·means the Gentiles. But others claim that *in the heavens* the angels were not *restored*, but that their knowledge had progressed at the time of Christ : for they asked, being ignorant, who was this king of glory, and they are taught that he is the Lord of powers (cf. Ps. xxiv. 10). But since the word *restored* can only be used of what has fallen, it would be better to say that their joy was *restored* in the salvation of mankind, that joy which they had had before men fell away entirely from righteousness : that on earth the race of men was restored by Christ, is known to all.'

Phil. iv. 3, " Clement ". ' Clement, an ex-philosopher, a man of great learning, who was bishop at Rome.'

1 Tim. ii. 4, " Who willeth that all men should be saved ". ' From this it is proved that God does not force anyone to believe, nor does He take away the freedom of the will : this passage also solves the question of the hardening of Pharaoh, and all other such questions as are flung at us.'

1 Tim. ii. 9, " Or costly raiment ". ' Which from its excessive fineness will not keep out cold, and with whose

price besides very many human beings of the same nature could have been clothed.'

1 Tim. iv. 8, "For bodily exercise is profitable for a little ". 'Dietings, baths, hunting and such like, which for a short time are helpful to bodily health.'

1 Tim. v. 6, "For she that giveth herself to pleasure is dead while she liveth ". 'Whatever exceeds nature's measure is reckoned as luxury. Here he specially strikes at widows of our time, who though they will not clothe a human being of their own nature even with a rag, yet adorn their walls with valuable marble slabs.'

These notes will perhaps give some idea of the nature of Pelagius' Expositions. They are the work of a man who did not neglect other writers, though he thought for himself, and made up his mind on many questions in the Epistles.

The question of the sources from which the material of the Expositions was derived will perhaps never be fully answered, because so much of the Greek exegetical literature has been lost. Richard Simon and Alfred J. Smith alone have systematically studied Pelagius' indebtedness to literature still surviving, and much yet remains to be done. As Dom Chapman has justly cast suspicion on Pelagius' knowledge of Greek[1] at the time he wrote his expositions, it is a wise procedure to begin with Latin authorities. Dr. Smith has made a thorough comparison of Pelagius on Romans with Ambrosiaster, Origen-Rufinus, and Augustine on the same epistle, and his results may here be summarized, along with such other information as has become available.

Tertullian may have been known to Pelagius. The passage about Rumour in Pelagius on 1 Thess. i. 8 may have been influenced by the parallel passage in Tertullian's *Apology*, c. 7 (Oehler, vol. i, p. 138, 10). The reference on

---

[1] *Revue d'Histoire Ecclésiastique*, xviii (1922), pp. 472 ff.

2 Cor. xii. 7 to St. Paul's headaches may have been derived from Tertullian, *De Pudicitia*, c. 13 (*C. S. E. L.* xx, p. 245). One or two passages seem to show reading of Tertullian's *De Carnis Resurrectione*; e. g. c. 57 of Tertullian's treatise refers to the same problem as Pelagius considers on 1 Cor. xv. 35, the condition of maimed bodies at the resurrection, and in similar terms; c. 30 on the dry bones of Ezekiel seems reflected on 2 Tim. ii. 8. The passage quoted above (on Rom. i. 19) describes God in terms very like those in the *Apology*, c. 17, and other later writings like Novatian's *De Trinitate*. The sentiment that 'the truth is always hated' (*in Gal.* iv. 16) may be taken from *Apology*, c. 7. The explanation of the term 'pater familias' (*in Col.* iv. 1) may come from *Apology*, c. 34.

Cyprian is among those that interpret the 'great house' of 2 Tim. ii. 20 as 'the Church': Pelagius quotes this opinion of 'quidam', but rejects it.

There is very clear evidence of the use of Ambrosiaster, for example:

Ambst.	Rom. iv. 4.	Pelag.
'It is a debtor's duty to carry out the law, because the necessity has been imposed by the law, that willy nilly he should carry it out, lest he be condemned.'		'It is a debtor's duty to carry out what is commanded, and unless he obey, he is condemned.'

Rom. vii. 24, 25.

'Man is double, composed of flesh and spirit.'   'Man of flesh is in a sense double and divided in himself.'

Ambst. in Gal. iii. 13.   Pelag. in Rom. viii. 3.

'Even as in the Law (i.e. the Old Testament) the victim offered for sins was named "the sin".'   'Even as the victims which in the Law they offered for sin, were called by the name of sin.'

Other clear cases of borrowing from Ambrosiaster are at 1 Cor. ix. 9 (pointed out by Mundle, diss. Ambst.,

p. 9, n. 1); 1 Cor. xv. 3-4; 2 Cor. ii. 15, v. 22, xi. 18; Col.
ii. 5. There can be no doubt that Ambrosiaster lay open
on Pelagius' desk.[1]

Nor is there any less certainty about the use of the
Origen commentary as translated by Rufinus:[2] we cannot
doubt, after Smith's investigation, that it was the translation, not the original, of Origen[3] that lay before him. It
would in fact need a very good Greek scholar to-day to
read Origen with ease. One or two examples will suffice
to prove borrowing by Pelagius:

Orig.-Ruf.	Rom. iv. 8.	Pelag.
'But the question is asked whether God seems really to preserve judgment towards those whose iniquities are remitted through the grace of baptism, or whose sins are covered through penitence, or those to whom sin must not be imputed, through the glory of martyrdom.		'Certain writers say that sin is remitted through baptism, covered by the labours of peni-tence, not imputed through martyrdom.'

Rom. v. 8, 9.

'*commendat* vel confirmat in-tellegitur vel amabilem facit pro beneficiis praestitis.'	'*commendat*: amabilem facit.'

Use of Augustine's small commentaries on Romans by
Pelagius has also been pointed out by Dr. Smith, e. g.

Aug.	Rom. v. 14.	Pelag.
'forma . . . a contrario, ut quo modo per illum mors, sic per dominum nostrum uita.'		'forma a contrario; hoc est; sicut ille (Adam) peccati caput, ita et iste (Christus) iustitiae.'

---

[1] These are additional to those given in Souter, vol. i, pp. 181 ff.

[2] On Rufinus' methods of 'translation' see J. A. Robinson, *The Philocalia of Origen* (Cambridge, 1893), pp. xxxiii ff; G. Bardy, *Recherches sur l'Histoire du Texte et des Versions latines du* De Princi-piis *d'Origène* (Paris, 1923), &c.

[3] Cf. Smith *J. T. S.*, xx. (1918–19) p. 156.

Rom. vii. 2.

| 'The "mulier" corresponds to the "anima".' | 'The "mulier" means the "plebs" or the "anima".' |

It can also be shown that Augustine's *De diuersis Quaestionibus ad Simplicianum* (date 397) was used by Pelagius. The identification of the '*mulieres*' of 1 Cor. ix. 5 may not come from Augustine *De opere monachorum* iv. 5, as the same opinion was also expressed by Ambrosiaster and by Jerome, *Adversus Iouinianum* i. 26. It is possible that Augustine's commentary on Galatians was used by Pelagius; cf. both *in Gal.* iv. 4.[1] There are also parallels between Pelagius and Augustine *Contra Faustum* (date 400): *in 2 Cor.* iv. 4 and *c. Faust.* xxi. 2 ; *in Rom.* ii. 26 and Faust. ap. *c. Faust.* xxv. 1 (see also the note below): compare, too, *in 1 Thess.* ii. 7 and *Catech. Rud.* x. 15.

I have noticed one parallel with Ambrose (*in Ps.* 37, 38), namely *in Col.* iii. 4.

Parallels with Jerome abound. There can be little doubt, I think, that Pelagius used Jerome's commentaries on Galatians, Ephesians, and Titus. Take the following passages of Jerome with their parallels :

Hier. in Gal. iii. 1.	Pelag. ad loc.
„ iv. 20 (t. vii. 468 E).	„
„ iv. 27 (474 A).	„
„ iv. 29 (475 B).	„
in Eph. 1, 14 (561 C).	„
„ 1, 22–3 (568 c ff.).	in Rom. iii. 4.
„ prol. iii. (635–6).	1 Cor. xv. 32.
„ iii. 18.	ad loc.
„ v. 22–3 (654 E).	„
„ vi. 3 (664 D).	„
in Tit. i. 1 (688 D).	in 1 Tim. i. 1.
„ i. 5.	„ iii. 8.

But Pelagius was acquainted also with other works of

[1] Quoted in chapter iv above, p. 194. See also *c. Faust.* xi. 3.

Jerome than his commentaries: *De Uiris Inlustribus* 5
is used in the general argument to the Epistles, and
knowledge of certain of his Epistles, as well as of the
Aduersus Heluidium and the *Prologus Galeatus*, has been
pointed out.

Of other Latin Christian writings, Pelagius shows knowledge of the Apostles' Creed, the Baptismal Formula, and
the Canon of the Mass.

Long ago Simon[1] stated that Pelagius ordinarily follows
the opinions of the Greeks, principally those of Chrysostom.
One parallel may be given:

Chrys. in Phil. iv. 15.	Pelag.
(ἐκοινώνησαν) εἰς λόγον δόσεως τῶν σαρκικῶν καὶ λήψεως τῶν πνευμα-τικῶν.	dantes carnalia et spiritalia accipientes (2nd explanation).

It has been noted that Pelagius' interpretation of the
Kenosis passage (Phil. ii. 6) is Greek and not Latin.

There are many parallels between Pelagius and the
Latin translation of Theodore of Mopsuestia's commentary
on the shorter Epistles. On Gal. ii. 2 both remark that
the phrase 'lest by any means' does not indicate doubt.
On 1 Tim. iii. 1 both refer to the 'good work', pointing
out that it is to this, and not to the high position, that he is
urging him, and so on. The question of the relationship
between the two is complicated by the loss of the work of
Diodorus of Tarsus.

Pelagius seems also to have some school recollections
of Lucretius, Virgil, Horace, and Juvenal, possibly also of
Seneca.

On the style and language of Pelagius it is not necessary
to dwell at length. Though both are adequate, and much
superior to that of the pseudo-Jerome as published, they
lack distinction, such distinction as we find in Jerome,

---

[1] *Hist. crit. des Comm.*, p. 242.

or even in Augustine. On the whole he is rather common-place in style, and one of the ways which this shows itself is in the extent of the vocabulary.

As regards word-forms, he prefers the classical *uetere* to the (originally) poetical *ueteri*; the genitive plural of present participles ends in *-um* rather than *-ium*; and he has throughout a preference for syncopated forms like *praescii*, *potarunt*, *iudicarint*, over the fuller forms (cf. Rom. xiv. 5; 2 Cor. xii. 13; Gal. i. 13, 18; Eph. v. 21, &c.).

He makes much use of the ablative of the gerund, and of the ablative absolute (particularly abstract noun and present participle). He often separates a noun, usually the object, from its adjunct, by interposing the governing verb. A sentence frequently ends with four long syllables.[1]

Calumnia and *calumniari*, of the statements of heretics, are characteristic; *habeo* sometimes occurs, followed by a relative word and an infinitive; *tollo* is found with the acc. of the thing taken away, and the dative of the person from whom it is taken.

There are very few rare words.[2]

[1] In Col. ii. 13, *estis consortes effecti*, we have an eight-long-syllable clausula.

[2] See Pelagius' *Expositions*, vol. ii, p. 553, and add *uenialiter* (p. 162, 4.)

INDEXES

A. GENERAL

B. SCRIPTURE REFERENCES

C. LATIN WORDS

ISBN 0–19–	Author	Title
8143567	ALFÖLDI A.	The Conversion of Constantine and Pagan Rome
6286409	ANDERSON George K.	The Literature of the Anglo-Saxons
8219601	ARNOLD Benjamin	German Knighthood
8228813	BARTLETT & MacKAY	Medieval Frontier Societies
8111010	BETHURUM Dorothy	Homilies of Wulfstan
8142765	BOLLING G. M.	External Evidence for Interpolation in Homer
814332X	BOLTON J.D.P.	Aristeas of Proconnesus
9240132	BOYLAN Patrick	Thoth, the Hermes of Egypt
8114222	BROOKS Kenneth R.	Andreas and the Fates of the Apostles
8203543	BULL Marcus	Knightly Piety & Lay Response to the First Crusade
8216785	BUTLER Alfred J.	Arab Conquest of Egypt
8148046	CAMERON Alan	Circus Factions
8148054	CAMERON Alan	Porphyrius the Charioteer
8148348	CAMPBELL J.B.	The Emperor and the Roman Army 31 BC to 235 AD
826643X	CHADWICK Henry	Priscillian of Avila
826447X	CHADWICK Henry	Boethius
8219393	COWDREY H.E.J.	The Age of Abbot Desiderius
8148992	DAVIES M.	Sophocles: Trachiniae
825301X	DOWNER L.	Leges Henrici Primi
814346X	DRONKE Peter	Medieval Latin and the Rise of European Love-Lyric
8142749	DUNBABIN T.J.	The Western Greeks
8154372	FAULKNER R.O.	The Ancient Egyptian Pyramid Texts
8221541	FLANAGAN Marie Therese	Irish Society, Anglo-Norman Settlers, Angevin Kingship
8143109	FRAENKEL Edward	Horace
8201540	GOLDBERG P.J.P.	Women, Work and Life Cycle in a Medieval Economy
8140215	GOTTSCHALK H.B.	Heraclides of Pontus
8266162	HANSON R.P.C.	Saint Patrick
8224354	HARRISS G.L.	King, Parliament and Public Finance in Medieval England to 1369
8581114	HEATH Sir Thomas	Aristarchus of Samos
2115480	HENRY Blanche	British Botanical and Horticultural Literature before 1800
8140444	HOLLIS A.S.	Callimachus: Hecale
8212968	HOLLISTER C. Warren	Anglo-Saxon Military Institutions
8219523	HOUSLEY Norman	The Italian Crusades
8223129	HURNARD Naomi	The King's Pardon for Homicide – before AD 1307
8140401	HUTCHINSON G.O.	Hellenistic Poetry
9240140	JOACHIM H.H.	Aristotle: On Coming-to-be and Passing-away
9240094	JONES A.H.M	Cities of the Eastern Roman Provinces
8142560	JONES A.H.M.	The Greek City
8218354	JONES Michael	Ducal Brittany 1364–1399
8271484	KNOX & PELCZYNSKI	Hegel's Political Writings
8225253	LE PATOUREL John	The Norman Empire
8212720	LENNARD Reginald	Rural England 1086–1135
8212321	LEVISON W.	England and the Continent in the 8th century
8148224	LIEBESCHUETZ J.H.W.G.	Continuity and Change in Roman Religion
8141378	LOBEL Edgar & PAGE Sir Denys	Poetarum Lesbiorum Fragmenta
9240159	LOEW E.A.	The Beneventan Script
8241445	LUKASIEWICZ, Jan	Aristotle's Syllogistic
8152442	MAAS P. & TRYPANIS C.A .	Sancti Romani Melodi Cantica
8142684	MARSDEN E.W.	Greek and Roman Artillery—Historical
8142692	MARSDEN E.W.	Greek and Roman Artillery—Technical
8148178	MATTHEWS John	Western Aristocracies and Imperial Court AD 364–425
9240205	MAVROGORDATO John	Digenes Akrites
8223447	McFARLANE K.B.	Lancastrian Kings and Lollard Knights
8226578	McFARLANE K.B.	The Nobility of Later Medieval England
9240205	MAVROGADO John	Digenes Akrites
8148100	MEIGGS Russell	Roman Ostia
8148402	MEIGGS Russell	Trees and Timber in the Ancient Mediterranean World
8142641	MILLER J. Innes	The Spice Trade of the Roman Empire
8147813	MOORHEAD John	Theoderic in Italy
8264259	MOORMAN John	A History of the Franciscan Order
9240213	MYRES J.L.	Herodotus The Father of History
8219512	OBOLENSKY Dimitri	Six Byzantine Portraits
8116020	OWEN A.L.	The Famous Druids
8131445	PALMER, L.R.	The Interpretation of Mycenaean Greek Texts
8143427	PFEIFFER R.	History of Classical Scholarship (vol 1)
8143648	PFEIFFER Rudolf	History of Classical Scholarship 1300–1850

8111649	PHEIFER J.D.	Old English Glosses in the Epinal-Erfurt Glossary
8142277	PICKARD–CAMBRIDGE A.W.	Dithyramb Tragedy and Comedy
8269765	PLATER & WHITE	Grammar of the Vulgate
8213891	PLUMMER Charles	Lives of Irish Saints (2 vols)
820695X	POWICKE Michael	Military Obligation in Medieval England
8269684	POWICKE Sir Maurice	Stephen Langton
821460X	POWICKE Sir Maurice	The Christian Life in the Middle Ages
8225369	PRAWER Joshua	Crusader Institutions
8225571	PRAWER Joshua	The History of The Jews in the Latin Kingdom of Jerusalem
8143249	RABY F.J.E.	A History of Christian Latin Poetry
8143257	RABY F.J.E.	A History of Secular Latin Poetry in the Middle Ages (2 vols)
8214316	RASHDALL & POWICKE	The Universities of Europe in the Middle Ages (3 vols)
8154488	REYMOND E.A.E & BARNS J.W.B.	Four Martyrdoms from the Pierpont Morgan Coptic Codices
8148380	RICKMAN Geoffrey	The Corn Supply of Ancient Rome
8141076	ROSS Sir David	Aristotle: Metaphysics (2 vols)
8141092	ROSS Sir David	Aristotle: Physics
8142307	ROSTOVTZEFF M.	Social and Economic History of the Hellenistic World, 3 vols.
8142315	ROSTOVTZEFF M.	Social and Economic History of the Roman Empire, 2 vols.
8264178	RUNCIMAN Sir Steven	The Eastern Schism
814833X	SALMON J.B.	Wealthy Corinth
8171587	SALZMAN L.F.	Building in England Down to 1540
8218362	SAYERS Jane E.	Papal Judges Delegate in the Province of Canterbury 1198–1254
8221657	SCHEIN Sylvia	Fideles Crucis
8148135	SHERWIN WHITE A.N.	The Roman Citizenship
9240167	SINGER Charles	Galen: On Anatomical Procedures
8113927	SISAM, Kenneth	Studies in the History of Old English Literature
8642040	SOUTER Alexander	A Glossary of Later Latin to 600 AD
8270011	SOUTER Alexander	Earliest Latin Commentaries on the Epistles of St Paul
8222254	SOUTHERN R.W.	Eadmer: Life of St. Anselm
8251408	SQUIBB G.	The High Court of Chivalry
8212011	STEVENSON & WHITELOCK	Asser's Life of King Alfred
8212011	SWEET Henry	A Second Anglo-Saxon Reader—Archaic and Dialectical
8148259	SYME Sir Ronald	History in Ovid
8143273	SYME Sir Ronald	Tacitus (2 vols)
8200951	THOMPSON Sally	Women Religious
8201745	WALKER Simon	The Lancastrian Affinity 1361–1399
8161115	WELLESZ Egon	A History of Byzantine Music and Hymnography
8140185	WEST M.L.	Greek Metre
8141696	WEST M.L.	Hesiod: Theogony
8148542	WEST M.L.	The Orphic Poems
8140053	WEST M.L.	Hesiod: Works & Days
8152663	WEST M.L.	Iambi et Elegi Graeci
9240221	WHEELWRIGHT Philip	Heraclitus
822799X	WHITBY M. & M.	The History of Theophylact Simocatta
8206186	WILLIAMSON, E.W.	Letters of Osbert of Clare
8208103	WILSON F.P.	Plague in Shakespeare's London
8114877	WOOLF Rosemary	The English Religious Lyric in the Middle Ages
8119224	WRIGHT Joseph	Grammar of the Gothic Language